Administration and Supervision of the Reading/Writing Program

Related Titles of Interest

Administration and Supervision of the Reading/Writing Program

Marguerite C. Radencich
Dade County Public Schools
Miami, Florida

Allyn and Bacon
Boston • London • Toronto • Sydney • Tokyo • Singapore

Copyright © 1995 by Allyn & Bacon
A Simon & Schuster Company
Needham Heights, Massachusetts 02194

Portions of this book first appeared in Marguerite C. Radencich, Penny G. Beers,
and Jeanne Shay Schumm, *A Handbook for the K–12 Reading Resource Specialist* (Boston: Allyn & Bacon, 1993).

Library of Congress Cataloging-in-Publication Data

Radencich, Marguerite C.
    Administration and supervision of the reading/writing program /
Marguerite C. Radenich.
       p.   cm.
    Includes bibliographical references and index.
    ISBN 0-205-15217-1
    1. Language arts—United States—Administration.   2. School
management and organization—United States.   3. School supervision—
United States.   4. Reading—United States.   5. English language—
Composition and exercises—Study and teaching—United States.
I. Title.
LB1576.R25   1995
372.6—dc20   94-26365
                                                 CIP

Printed in the United States of America
10 9 8 7 6 5 4 3   98 97

To Anne, who has taught me the meaning of friendship

Contents

Foreword

In a job category that is often undervalued, administrators, supervisors, curriculum specialists and reading resource specialists (like others who do not have students assigned directly to them) sometimes feel like members of an endangered species. When school boards look for places to cut district budgets, these jobs are often first to be offered up.

We feel lonely because there is rarely another person with the same job assignment in a school or office. We lack opportunities for daily dialogue with our counterparts and would cherish opportunities for networking. Whether at state reading conferences or at the annual conventions of the International Reading Association or the National Council of Teachers of English, you can always find a group of us exchanging ideas. Professional groups like the IRA special interest groups for supervisors in reading and for administrators give us an opportunity to discuss current theory and research in reading/language arts and to compare notes on leadership strategies, instructional materials, and assessment.

However unappreciated our role, our contributions are crucial in ensuring the implementation of a strong reading program at the classroom, school, and district levels. For all of us who are concerned with improving reading instruction in our elementary and secondary schools, Marguerite Radencich has written a book that provides us with concrete ideas and examples of ways to do our jobs better.

I doubt that any reading supervisor has taken his or her responsibility more seriously than Marguerite Radencich or, in turn, been taken more seriously by her colleagues. A continuing learner, Margie always studies the literature and shares her applications with other educators. Many of us willingly share our ideas, but Margie has gone the extra step to document her ideas for posterity. I only wish she had done this sooner—I've needed a book like this in my job for a long time. Imagine a list of tips on "Working within District Constraints" or "Making Presentations," with appendixes that include "Tools of the Trade" ("Audiovisual Tips," "Handout Tips," etc.). Now, in one volume, we have a resource that discusses daily concerns such as committee craft, conducting effective meetings, long-range planning, and grant writing. The continuing challenges and new ideas—they are all there.

The next time I teach a graduate course on the Organization and Supervision of Reading Programs, I'll have a text that I wish I'd written.

Administrators, supervisors, and resource specialists will especially value Marguerite Radencich's application of ideas borrowed from the business world.

Ann McCallum
Fairfax, Virginia, Public Schools

Preface

This book is unique in that it addresses administrators and supervisors of reading/writing programs from the perspective of someone whose professional life has been largely dedicated to fulfilling these roles. Previous texts on the topic have all, to our knowledge, been written by persons outside of these roles. Previous books have also focused only on reading rather than on the reading/writing connection.

Administrators, supervisors, professors and students will all find this book easy to use because it is packed with lists of practical guidelines, ready-to-use checklists and other resources, and both *elementary* and *secondary* examples—all with a solid research base. Detailed guidelines are provided for processes such as selecting textbooks and technology, implementing change, conducting classroom demonstrations, conducting staff development, and dealing with district constraints. Tools provided include Tips Sheets for using handouts and audiovisual (AV) materials, Tips Sheets for test taking and for grant writing, a list of common questions and answers, a needs assessment form, program review forms, reading and writing contracts, a text friendliness checklist, portions of a sample curriculum, an action plan, a glossary of key curriculum terms, a detailed index, and a list of publisher addresses, as well as resource lists for students, parents, and administrators.

The book's appendix includes some of these resources, as well as suggestions that will help the growing number of administrators whose responsibilities now include preschool or adult education.

The book has a section specifically addressed to school-based administrators, another to supervisors (coordinators, directors), and a third with issues that pertain to both. The book addresses cutting-edge issues such as flexible grouping, assessment, technology, whole language, teacher as researcher, and special needs students. Present-day challenges addressed include ways of managing the information load, dealing with censorship and controversial materials, working with budgetary and other district constraints, being effective with school-based management, working with publishers, and dealing with changing roles of supervisors.

University students who used a preliminary version of this book found its conversational style to be user-friendly.

Acknowledgments

Appreciation for their advice on portions of this manuscript is extended to Betty Key, Christine Master, Susan Oestreicher, Debbie Weiler, and my Fall 1993 Administration and Supervision of Reading class at Florida International University. A special thank-you goes to Gerry Bohning and Anne McKinney, whose suggestions for the book as a whole were most helpful. Thank you to the following reviewers for their thoughtful comments and suggestions: Priscilla Nelson, Jan LaBonty, and Thomas Gunning. Finally, a note of thanks goes to all the administrators cited in this book whose ideas and experience provided the backbone of this product.

About the Author

Marguerite C. Radencich has been both an assistant principal and a reading supervisor for Dade County, Florida, the fourth largest district in the nation. She has served as president of the Reading Supervisors of Florida, chair of the International Reading Association (IRA) Supervisors and Reading Committee, and initiator and chair of the IRA Special Interest Group for Supervisors and Reading. Dr. Radencich has published numerous articles, two pieces of software, and several books, including Allyn and Bacon's *Handbook for the K–12 Reading Resource Specialist* and Free Spirit's *How to Help Your Child with Homework* and *School Power—Strategies for School Success*. She has served on the editorial review boards of *Reading Teacher, Journal of Reading,* and *Yearbook of the National Reading Conference.*

Administration and Supervision of the Reading/Writing Program

Issues for Both District Supervisors and School-Based Administrators

The first four chapters of this book deal with issues for both district supervisors and school-based administrators. Included are chapters on setting the stage, analyzing and improving the curriculum, analyzing and improving instruction, and using effective leadership skills. Later sections detail issues that are more specific to either district or school-based personnel.

C h a p t e r 1

Setting the Stage

> *It's interesting that if the principal/administrator is growing and*
> *learning, it seems that it's easier for him or her to support*
> *appropriately a teacher who is growing and learning, and a*
> *teacher who is a learner understands and can support*
> *appropriately his or her students in the same process.*
> —Linda Cameron (Weaver, 1990, p. 273)

Before making any plans or undertaking any action, supervisors and administrators need to examine their overall roles. It helps to see these roles in a historical context. Then there is a need to look inward in terms of philosophy and knowledge, to see oneself in the whole picture. This chapter addresses the overall roles of the administrator and supervisor with regard to the reading/writing program.

A History of the Administration and Supervision of Reading/Writing Programs

Messerli (1977) decries the arrogance of presentism—our tendency to ignore, mindlessly, lessons from the past. Knowing where we've been in educational supervision not only keeps us from reinventing the wheel but also helps us defend and maintain positions that all too often disappear when their value is not understood.

  The histories of district and school-level supervision are intertwined and characterized by differences of opinion about schooling, differences that have surfaced as both internal struggles over mission and a more external struggle for identity as a distinct field of practice. Despite differences, there is some consensus that the function of supervision is an important one whether it is carried out by a superintendent, a supervisor, a curriculum worker, or a peer (Bolin & Panaritis, 1992).

Burg, Kaufman, Korngold, and Kovner (1978) describe four periods of supervisory function, which parallel historical and societal changes in the United States: administrative inspection, efficiency orientation, democratic supervision, and research orientation. These stages will be explored, followed by an analysis of current and future roles of supervision. For a series of quotes that provide a brief the history of supervision, see Chapter 5.

1642–1875: Administrative Inspection

During this period, local or religious officers and special committees of laymen inspected schools (Lucio & McNeil, 1969). These efforts marked the beginnings of public responsibility for education (Burton & Brueckner, 1955). These officers and committees hired teachers, decided on pupil admissions, developed courses of study, and conducted examinations. The incident that follows (Brown, 1911) illustrates how deeply ingrained in American thought is the belief that laypersons can render accurate judgments about good teaching (Tanner & Tanner, 1987, p. 8):

> [The visitors], "observing most of the scholars pronounce badly . . . order the master to be particularly attentive to make them express their words and syllables as distinct and clear as possible" [and they] "advise and admonish the scholars to use their utmost endeavors to break themselves of the bad habit which they have heretofore contracted in uttering their words in a thick confused manner."

Inspection was not always an attempt to help teachers improve instruction but, rather, to determine whether or not teachers were doing what they were supposed to do and, if not, to replace them with teachers who would (Burg et al., 1978, p. 4). The quality of supervision would not improve appreciably after 1776 until the end of the next century (Tanner & Tanner, 1987).

1876–1936: Efficiency Orientation

This period was marked by the establishment of state control, with pressure placed on teaching procedures by efficiency-oriented experts. Although some understood that "a teacher, to be in the best way successful must not be subjected to dictation in details" (Gove, 1891, p. 260), supervision was still seen generally as inspection and coercion. Teachers were compelled to follow detailed prescribed courses of study and classroom methods. The assumptions behind this authoritarian concept were that there exists a well-defined body of knowledge desirable for all pupils to learn, and that an annual timetable for acquiring this knowledge, applicable to all students, should be established.

Between 1915 and 1925 there was considerable discussion concerning supervision of the basic subjects in the elementary curriculum (Nila Banton Smith, 1965). A number of cities organized special supervisory departments in arithmetic, language, spelling, reading, social studies, and science (Burg et al., 1978; Smith, 1965).

In 1927, two books specifically on the supervision of reading appeared. Smith (1965, p. 262) cites one as being directed largely toward principals. In the early days of the principalship, when it was impossible to obtain trained teachers, the principal's role was teacher training (Tanner & Tanner, 1987). "The principal was looked upon as a kind of foreman who through close supervision helped to compensate for ignorance and lack of skills of his subordinates." Until the 1920s, it was the principal's responsibility "to take over classes on occasion, and to demonstrate to the teacher exactly how the job should be done" (Elsbree & Reutter, 1954, p. 23).

Tanner and Tanner (1987) describe teacher intervisitations under the guidance of the superintendent. General meetings were devoted to lectures or to a discussion of professional literature from professional libraries developed in many cities by the superintendent. But the responsibility for supervision was starting to move from the superintendent to the principal, especially in large cities. Principals were often in charge of meetings, and they might administer a group of schools in addition to their own building.

Lucio and McNeil (1969) state that the "scientific management" theories of the business world were applied to school supervision during the time between the two world wars, with an emphasis on careful empirical research and administrative efficiency. These values represented faith in the possibility of objectively measuring effective teaching behavior, with the implied assumption that teaching behavior could be carefully controlled for optimal operation (Mosher & Purpel, 1972). The essence of the approach was as follows:

> *Scientific management proposed to alter the personal relations between supervisors and teachers. Instead of the supervisors directing the methods . . . in a personal and arbitrary manner . . . the primary task of the scientific supervisor was to discover educational "laws" and apply them through the labors of the teacher. The teacher would be expected to find the controlling law through cooperation with the supervisor. Neither was to be personally over the other, for both were under the law of science. . . . (Lucio & McNeil, 1969, p. 8)*

Pajak (1993) debates the extent to which scientific management really took hold. Courtis (1926) noted that teachers were actually allowed considerable latitude in practice. Even if scientific management never achieved full acceptance, however, elements of the philosophy are still visible today.

1937–1959: Cooperative Group Effort or Democratic Supervision

Thomas Jefferson's proposals for education had forecast the democratic supervision that would later emerge (Tanner & Tanner, 1987). After the great Depression and World War II, the nation's attention became refocused on democracy (Bolin & Panaritis, 1992). With roots in Dewey's ideas of progressive education, democratic supervision emphasized the dignity and talent of the individual teacher (Mosher & Purpel, 1972). During this period, cooperative group effort constituted both a means and an end in the change process. Leadership was shared, and authority was derived from and conferred by the group. Unified effort was achieved through careful group planning, built-in flexibility, and constant experimentation in pedagogical principles derived from new scientific research in psychology and the social sciences.

During the 1930s, the field of supervision distinguished itself from administration, and the Association for Supervision and Curriculum Development (ASCD) was born (Callahan & Button, 1964, p. 90). Another milestone of this period was the firm establishment of the supervision of reading. *The Thirty-sixth Yearbook of the National Society of the Study of Education* called for adequate supervision of reading from kindergarten through college (Smith, 1965, p. 305). Smith cites Betts's findings in 1949 (p. 306) regarding the status of reading supervision:

> *In most states, general supervisors help teachers to discover individual needs and to provide the necessary differentiated instruction in reading. . . . Departments of public instruction for three states provide special supervisors or consultants in reading. . . . A number of county, district, and local school systems have supervisors of reading instruction. Occasionally, however, the supervisor is given the responsibility for all the language arts. . . . Supervisory service is rendered through consultations, demonstrations, workshops, child study groups, institutes, and course-of-study committees. This service is most effective when attention is given to reading needs in all curriculum areas.*

Principals and supervisors at this time were engaging in more self-education in the supervision of reading through summer sessions, reading conferences and workshops, and professional literature on reading. A broad program of study was suggested for reading supervisors, with coursework to be followed by a year of internship in the field (Smith, 1965).

1960–Present: Research Orientation

During this period, two themes dominate: "research orientation" (Burg et al., 1978) and "the organizational change agent" (Pajak, 1993). Burg and colleagues saw the phase of research orientation—current research that takes into account changing norms and prescriptions—as lasting until "the present." They saw supervisors as influenced not only by demands for greater account-ability and effectiveness, but also by constraints stemming from growing teacher professionalism and independence. They saw the future of the super-visor as being significantly affected by issues such as "collective bargaining, inequities in school financing, public attitudes toward education, changing career patterns, and the provision of services to students with special needs" (p. 11). Indeed, we have seen the truth of these predictions.

As noted, Pajak (1993) views supervisors in this period as true change agents, with different thinking than had gone into previous visions of super-visors as agents of change (Benne, 1949). In the earlier vision (Cunningham, 1963), supervisors identified problems; established priorities; and decided to whom, where, and how an intervention would be introduced. Teachers were seen as a problem of resistance to be overcome (Mosher & Purpel, 1972; Toepfer, 1973). Franseth in 1955 wrote of action research as applicable to teachers' concerns, but it served primarily as a means to shatter complacency resulting from long experience (Heffernan & Bishop, 1965).

During this period, supervision textbooks (e.g., Sergiovanni & Starratt, 1979) studied theories of leadership styles from business management and industrial psychology (Pajak, 1993). Pajak cites authors (e.g., Ogletree, 1972; Sommerville, 1971) who felt that, during this period, responding to the needs of our rapidly changing society seemed to replace a concern for the needs of students, teachers, and administrators.

McKoy in 1961 proposed that school leaders be less concerned about whether their behavior was democratic and more concerned with whether it was effective in bringing about change. The lack of democracy during this period may be partly an unfortunate outcome of Lucio's (1967) previously mentioned writing on scientific management. Pajak (1993) cites a 1968 report sponsored by the U.S. Department of Health, Education and Welfare as delivering the coup de grace to democratic leadership. The author of the report concluded that educational supervisors should rely more on formal power and technical competence than on democratic strategies and informal influ-ence (Helwig, 1968).

The 1960s and 1970s were also a period of social innovations. The new programs of that era were another force in effectively removing the initiative for change from local schools and dislodging the tradition of leadership that had been based on democratic principles (Pajak, 1993).

Pajak (1993) explains that supervisors had been in the forefront of efforts to empower teachers and involve them in decision making during the 1940s and 1950s. But collective bargaining usurped the supervisor's tools of coop-erative planning and problem solving, and reinterpreted instructional and curricular decisions as conditions of employment (Kinsella, Klopf, Shafer, & Young, 1969). An ASCD Commission on Problems of Supervisors and Cur-riculum Workers struggled with the fact that unionization suddenly placed supervisors in an untenable no-man's land between management and labor (Kinsella et al., 1969; Young, 1969).

Have we moved beyond this period of the 1960s and 1970s? Yes and no. The following section will show how we have evolved toward further teacher empowerment. We have actually courted a "research orientation" since perhaps 1925, "the first period of intensive research and application" (Smith, 1965). What has changed is more a matter of how research is conducted and applied—no longer through authoritarian control by an outside expert, but through increasing teacher ownership and even leadership in the process.

Current and Future Roles of School-Based Administrators and Supervisors in the Reading/Writing Program

Having examined four historical stages of supervision, we now have a basis for looking at the present and future roles. Pajak (1993) sees a remarkable consistency in supervision among the stages of the last fifty years since we first tried to "give cooperative planning a *real* chance" (Department of Supervisors and Directors of Instruction, 1943). Indeed, voices for cooperation were heard even at the turn of the century (Elliott, 1914, p. 2), with a distinction between "administrative efficiency"—centralization of administrative power—and "supervisory efficiency" or decentralized, cooperative effort.

Following are a number of current perspectives on the role of supervision.

Pajak's Vision. Pajak (1993) calls the 1980s a period of the corporate visionary, with a vision of economic competition as the prime educational goal, and legislated bureaucratic policy as the road to reach it. "Effective schools" research from the 1970s had pointed to the principal as the corporate visionary who was key to school success (e.g., Edmonds, 1979).

Fortune magazine (Dumaine, 1989) predicted that the most successful corporation of the 1990s will be a learning organization that can adapt quickly in a rapidly changing environment. Many school districts have adapted and moved toward less bureaucratic, decentralized structures (Hill & Bonan, 1991), but others have not. Pajak points out that schools, although they are *teaching* institutions, are not necessarily *learning* organizations. Most schools are designed to transmit information rather than to generate or invent it. If the 1980s, with their educational reforms, were aimed at helping schools to *teach* better, then the 1990s, he feels, must help schools *learn* better. Toward this end, leadership will not be able to emanate solely from a formal position in the organization, but will have to come from short-term, problem-focused groups, as needed.

Senge's Vision. Senge (1990a, 1990b) echoes Pajak's (1993) call for educational leaders to be teachers when he proposes that our images of leaders become those of designer, steward, and teacher. The role of designer requires a systemic sense of vision and core values, and a nurturance of effective learning processes. The role of steward implies a commitment of service to the mission of the organization and to its people. But it is the leadership role of teacher, Senge notes, that is most central to the fundamental process of learning as an organization:

> *Leaders as teachers help people restructure their views of reality to see beyond the superficial conditions and events into the underlying causes of problems— and therefore to see new possibilities for shaping the future. (1990b, p. 12; emphasis in the original)*

Glickman's Vision. Glickman (1992) suggests that the term *instructional supervision* may be outliving its usefulness. He reminds us that, with the reordering and redefining of societies, governments, and economies in "the very air" (p. 1), similar changes are being asked of public schools. Glickman feels that when schools become decentralized, engage in shared governance, and see themselves as the center of action research, the term *supervision* has little meaning to staff members. Instead, they think of improving education through shared leadership and collegiality; through their plans for staff development and curriculum development; and through their own goal setting, actions, and research. The notion of a supervisor with hierarchical control is antithetical to them, as is the concept of supervision, a term derived from its industrial roots of closely inspecting the work of employees. Glickman asserts that a real voice must be given to administrators, teachers, students, and parents. He states that today's risk-taking practitioners have replaced the term *supervisory* with terms such as *coaching, collegiality, reflective practitioners, professional development, critical inquiry,* and *study* or *research groups.* He feels that replacing *supervisor* with *instructional leader* would help us see every talented educator as an instructional leader and supervisor.

Whether it is necessary to change the term *supervision* is open to debate. As noted, the roles of supervisors historically have often included many of the positive elements Glickman describes. Yet, if the connotation of *supervision* is negative, then a change in term as well as in practice might be in order.

Darling-Hammond and Sclan's Vision. Darling-Hammond and Sclan (1992) see supervision in the future as being affected by certification standards from the National Board of Professional Teaching Standards. Darling-Hammond and Sclan see career ladders as having wide-ranging influences on supervision, including various forms of self-evaluation, peer review, and portfolio development. Career ladders also often include roles for senior teachers as supervisors or mentors of beginning teachers, and as consultants to other veteran teachers.

Harris's Vision. Other predictions come from Harris (1986), who hypothesizes that job requirements will expand to include (1) more leadership demonstrated through technical competence, (2) more leadership with clarity of purpose and commitment to ideals for a better society, and (3) more leadership with deep attachments to the traditional values of public education. Harris sees educational leadership as nothing less than social reconstruction. Taking issue with popular comparisons of educational leadership with industrial management, he urges that leaders resist the growing clamor of reactionaries who would centralize, homogenize, and take control of public education, parents, and students alike.

The International Reading Association's Perspective. Roles of reading supervisors differ widely from locale to locale, but one picture that is helpful comes from the International Reading Association's 1986 definition of a coordinator/supervisor:

> *[A person who] supervises a district-wide reading and language arts program as central office staff person, or directs public, private, or corporate educational, vocational, penal, or social agency serving learners at any level. Responsible for student progress toward reading maturity through: (a) improvement of curriculum, methodology, and management of district-wide reading/language arts programs and policies; (b) application of current research/theory in the refinement of reading and language arts instruction; (c) coordination and implementation of collaborative reading research; (d) attainment of resources through budget processes and grant applications; (e) development of community support for the reading/language arts program; (f) supervision and evaluation of classroom teachers, diagnostic-remedial specialists, and reading consultants; and (g) support of professional development through provision for attendance at workshops, conferences, and conventions.*

Roles as Defined by Supervisors Themselves. A clear perspective of current roles can be obtained from surveys of supervisors themselves. Cook et al. (1983) surveyed English language arts supervisors at district, state, and regional levels and in U.S. territories. Responses revealed a wide diversity in title and scope of the position. The most common titles suggested a role oriented more to people and human resources than to administration, particularly for district-level supervisors. Other findings were that supervisors saw lack of time and money as real constraints; they saw state mandates as impediments when considered in concert with union regulations and competency testing; and the majority of district and state supervisors have experienced an expansion of their responsibilities in the past five years. In my experience, these trends are true for reading supervisors as well and have probably intensified in the years since this survey.

Another survey of supervisors was conducted by Mack (1991). In this research, the 11 most common roles of reading supervisors in Pennsylvania, from a list of 63, were as follows:

1. Encourage and support classroom teachers and reading staff in their efforts to provide appropriate reading instruction.

2. Maintain a high level of knowledge of research, practical application, materials, and the like related to reading and the instructional process.

3. Participate in curriculum development related to developmental and remedial reading programs.

4. Coordinate federal reading programs (e.g., Chapter 1) with regard to staff, instruction, and record keeping.

5. Supervise reading personnel.

6. Serve the staff as instructional leader in the reading program.

7. Maintain a flexible schedule to accommodate the needs of school personnel, students, and community.

8. Supervise implementation of reading programs by classroom teachers.

9. Work with reading staff to evaluate and recommend textbooks, basals, and supplementary reading materials.

10. Maintain high visibility and accessibility to staff, students, parents, and community.

11. Coordinate developmental reading programs in schools and among schools in the district.

When supervisors were asked what they saw as their desired roles, there was a close correlation with actual roles. However, the most desired role, "Coordinate developmental reading programs in schools and among schools in the district," was #11 in the list of actual roles. Other roles that were highly desired but not common as actual roles were "Contribute to policies related to methods of reading instruction" and "Assist in selection of instructional staff for reading."

It is of interest also to note the 11 least frequent actual roles. As with the most frequent roles, there was a high correlation between actual and desired least frequent roles.

The least frequent actual roles were as follows:

1. Involve the community (including businesses and senior citizens) in recreational reading programs.

2. Meet with other subject area coordinators to develop a balanced curriculum.

3. Develop school recreational reading programs involving storytellers, authors, and illustrators.

4. Plan, along with reading staff, the integration of reading instruction with other curriculum areas.

5. Develop abilities of content area teachers to integrate reading/study skills with content instruction.

6. Solicit input from the community and parents relative to reading instruction and programs in the district.

7. Assist in formal evaluations of classroom teachers as requested by principals.

8. Conduct research, share, and implement research findings in the reading curriculum.

9. Assist in planning facilities—such as computer labs, resource rooms, or storage areas—used for reading instruction or storage of materials.

10. Interpret standardized or criterion-referenced test results in reading to school board, parents, and community.

11. Assist in writing criteria for evaluating reading instruction.

A Synthesis. Wepner (1989) provides a depressing climax to the history of supervision in reading when she explains that, for whatever reasons—the tightening of school budgets, the decrease in federal funding, or the establishment of new priorities (Wilson & Becker, 1984)—reading personnel have been suffering from a great deal of role conflict and role ambiguity (Pierson-Hubeny & Archambault, 1985). Wepner is referring to school-level specialists as well as to supervisory personnel, but the issue of role definition has been raised specifically for instructional supervisors as well (Alfonso & Firth, 1990). And this is in a period when principals are not readily able to "take up the slack" from decreased specialized support because "today, the principalship is more complex and demanding than at any time in the past" (Barnard & Hetzel, 1986, p. 1).

Perhaps some of the role uncertainty is due to the lack of attention to supervision even within the field. Between 1944 and 1981, the ASCD had published more than forty yearbooks, but only four were devoted to supervision (Bolin & Panaritis, 1992). Darling-Hammond and Sclan (1992) blame some of the role confusion on national reforms and legislative activity, which have, on the one hand, resulted in policies launched under the banner of professionalism, with teachers seen as an important part of the educational equation. On the other hand, the reforms have often adopted a bureaucratic view of teaching. These authors point out that competing visions of teaching and learning, as well as supervision and evaluation, are embodied in this raft of new teacher policies.

Reports from the field point also to changing roles. I will cite just one example to highlight what I expect most readers see in their areas as well. Language arts/reading supervisor Lyn McKay in Pinellas County, Florida, saw her responsibilities changing as a result of downsizing and district adoption of quality management. McKay found herself, together with a principal, starting a specialized new school. Simultaneously, along with the rest of the district administrative staff, she was learning to implement quality management. All this came soon after the district had been forced to reduce the language arts staff from three to two, and to eliminate the primary specialists in the elementary schools. State support had similarly been reduced, with the state language arts consultant taking on the role of reading as well, and with each state consultant being directed to become more of a generalist and less of a specialist.

It is perhaps more important than ever—with changing expectations, with pressures to put all available school dollars in the classroom, with often-difficult social conditions, with our increasingly diverse populations, with a technologically advanced society that requires students to be producers as well as consumers (Pajak, 1993), and with vast amounts of research to digest each year—that administrators and supervisors in charge of reading/writing programs be thoroughly knowledgeable, work hard and smart, and make their efforts known. The first of these competencies, professional knowledge, is discussed in the next section. Armed with this professional knowledge, instructional leaders are then prepared to tackle the final issue of this chapter, that of building a philosophy of reading/writing instruction.

Keeping on the Cutting Edge

Administrators who are on the cutting edge serve as powerful tools for change. By contrast, those who depend on others rather than take the responsibility to stay informed themselves can unwittingly serve as roadblocks.

Managing the Information Load

Keeping on the cutting edge is difficult with the volume of information in the literature, particularly for school-based administrators, who must deal with any number of subject areas. School-based administrators may wish to use the following tips in managing this volume of information:

- Spend time networking. Visit other schools and talk to other administrators and teachers.

- Read general publications such as *Educational Leadership* and *Phi Delta Kappan*, as well as reading/language arts publications. Dombart (1992) recommends that other school-based administrators follow his strategy of catching up on this reading during summer months.

- In addition to your own reading, assign specific staff members to monitor publications from each subject area and share key articles. When appropriate, portions of articles can be highlighted for quick reference before they are disseminated.

- Keep in your office a library of professional books, journals, and videotapes for easy reference and for lending out. This might duplicate the collection in the school library/media center.

- Attend conferences whenever possible. Interactions with other professionals at conferences broaden your horizons, heighten your awareness of what's new, and provide a forum for you to share your good work. When you are not able to go to a conference, ask colleagues who do attend to share with you what they learned. National conferences you may wish to attend include those of the International Reading Association (IRA) in the spring, the National Council of Teachers of English (NCTE) in November and in the spring, the Association for Supervision and Curriculum Development (ASCD) in April, and the Whole Language Umbrella in the summer. IRA and NCTE also have excellent regional and state annual meetings.

In the words of Jane Bartow (Weaver, 1990, p. 269):

We teachers helped to educate our already child-centered administrator by telling her about workshops we had attended, by sharing good books with her, by helping her to know which were the "big names" in our movement. We encouraged her to set up a library of books for the teachers to use, but we have also made certain that there is money in the budget for any teacher to choose and purchase his/her OWN copy of any book on the resource shelf.

Appendix D contains a list of professional resources—materials you will want to own, use, and share as you work continually toward keeping yourself and your colleagues on the cutting edge. See also the "Glossary of Curriculum Terms," "Using Research," and "Common Questions and Answers" in Appendix C, and "Keeping Educators Informed" in Chapter 3.

Curriculum and Instruction: A Historical Overview

It has been said that historical ignorance is the mother of "educational innovation" (Messerli, 1977). Indeed, our ignorance has resulted in many a pendulum swing. Yet each new era has incorporated the use of new research so that we can also see a spiraling movement around a larger research base. Instructional leaders who know curriculum history will be prepared to evaluate future instructional innovations soundly.

Your curriculum is probably set by state and district rules, by past practice, and by a stated or unstated philosophy for literacy education. It is beyond the scope of this book to cover curriculum and instruction in any depth, but I will provide a historical overview of the most prominent instructional approaches used in the United States. Knowledge of this history can be invaluable as new trends come along.

Smith's (1965) history of reading instruction in the United States is summarized here. In the colonial period, an alphabet spelling system was used to teach reading. Instruction was given in single-letter recognition, then combined letter–sound pairs such as *ab* and *ac*; then parts of words, such as *tab*; and finally the whole word, *table*. Reading was almost totally an oral process.

In U.S. schools in the mid-1800s, Horace Mann introduced the whole-word method, which involved memorizing entire words before analyzing letters and letter patterns. Mann emphasized silent reading and reading for comprehension. About this time, the *McGuffey Eclectic Reader* was introduced with its controlled repetition of words and with texts being leveled to match students' developmental levels.

In the latter half of the nineteenth century, a synthetic phonics system was introduced. This method was temporarily abandoned when teachers became dissatisfied because too much attention was placed on word analysis and too little on comprehension. It was replaced around 1910 with the new "look-and-say" method, which also lost favor because every word had to be learned as a sight word, with children making little progress in learning to read.

Around 1920, the silent reading method, similar to Horace Mann's program, emerged. In the 1930s, the basal reading method was launched with its controlled vocabulary and syntactic complexity. With variations, it became the core of most reading instruction for decades. In the 1950s and 1960s, dissatisfaction with the basal as the only form of reading instruction prompted a return to phonics.

In the 1960s, the beginning of the period of humanistic influences, efforts focused on meeting individual needs. Techniques were encouraged for individualizing reading instruction, and programmed materials were developed. During this era, the language experience method, an updating of an earlier practice, was promoted. From the late 1960s until the early 1980s, linguistic (*man-can-fan*) points of view influenced the structure of many basal readers (Lapp & Flood, 1983).

Beginning in the 1980s, the United States started taking note of the holistic approaches that had historically been used in other English-speaking countries, and grassroots movements began using this "whole language" instruction. Whole language is generally seen not as a method but as a philosophy and a movement of empowering teachers and students. Yet whole language has taken on the role of a method. Many whole language schools have decreased or abandoned their use of basal readers in favor of trade books.

Skills management systems have begun to be replaced by checklists, anecdotal records, student interviews, portfolios, and other forms of informal assessment, with instruction and assessment becoming more interwoven. Traditional ability grouping has begun to be replaced by more flexible groupings (Radencich & McKay, in press).

By the early 1990s, many people found themselves avoiding the term *whole language* because it meant so many different things to different people. Bergeron (1990) surveyed 64 articles in an attempt to define *whole language* and found different definitions in each. The focus descriptors associated with whole language in over 25 percent of the sources were: "construct meaning," "functional," "pupil-centered," "empowerment," "communication," "integrate language arts," and "risks." Techniques identified in over 25 percent of the sources were: literature, writing process, sharing, invented spelling, independent reading, functional writing, art, journals, reading aloud, functional print, dramatics, big books, and choral reading. With such variety in definition, myths (Newman & Church, 1991) have begun to proliferate, among them the following:

- You don't teach phonics, spelling, or grammar in whole language.

- In a whole language classroom, you don't have to teach.

- A whole language classroom is unstructured.

- There's no evaluation in whole language.

- Whole language teachers deal just with the process; the product doesn't matter.

- Whole language philosophy applies only to teaching children in the early grades.

- Whole language won't work for kids with special needs.

- All you need for whole language is a commercial "whole language" program.

- Giving teachers a few whole language tips makes them whole language teachers.

- Whole language simply involves a change in classroom practice; it's business as usual for administrators.

- There is one right way to do whole language.

In fact, it is the opposite of each of these statements that more truly represents what whole language can be.

Educators who are aware of the pendulum swings in our history are likely to be cautious and to avoid extremes. As Faulkner (1975) wrote in *Requiem for a Nun*, "The past is never dead. It's not even past."

Chapter 3 will discuss making transitions from traditional approaches to holistic instruction. Other sources you can turn to for updated coverage of whole language issues are Christopher-Gordon, Heinemann, Scholastic, and Owen publishers, the National Council of Teachers of English; and the International Reading Association. See also Appendix C, which includes a list of publishers, glossary of terms, list of professional resources, and list of common questions and answers.

Building and Using a Philosophy of Reading/Writing Instruction

Once you have a strong reservoir of knowledge about the field, you are ready to develop a philosophy of reading/writing instruction—that is, a belief about how literacy instruction should proceed. A philosophy or a mission statement has little value if it is simply written and then forgotten. But there is often great success when businesses or school staffs pull together and then march in the same direction. Bird (1989, p. 22) puts it well when she states that "trying to teach without a philosophy . . . is like trying to sail without a compass. You will inevitably sail somewhere but you may not reach your destination."

Coral Gables Senior High in Dade County (Miami, Florida) won the meritorious high school award for the county three years in a row. Although they did not specifically start with a mission statement, they did spend an entire planning day each year developing a schoolwide focus. The resulting sense of ownership was quite powerful. In the case of an elementary school, schoolwide decisions on whether to use a basal reading series or on which series to use can be traumatic when everyone is going his or her own way. Having a literacy philosophy drafted by a committee and then modified by the staff can pave the way for a less traumatic decision-making process.

A philosophy guides decisions about goals and objectives, materials, and the organizing and ordering of instructional tasks. If teachers have different philosophies, students will be faced with different approaches that can result in learning gaps as they progress through the grades (Barnard & Hetzel, 1986).

The Parkway District Summer Essentials Program in Creve Coeur, Missouri (Sandweiss, 1990) based its philosophy on three assumptions: (1) all students can and will learn, (2) success will lead to more success and improved self-esteem, and (3) a strong foundation in the "essentials" will foster academic success and enhance self-esteem. Following are scenarios meant to show the impact of a school philosophy on classroom organization and staff development decisions:

- If the philosophy at a preschool has been to focus on the transmission of knowledge and this changes to a focus on learning as a creative or constructive process, staff development will likely be followed by change in every aspect of the program, from organization of the day to selection and use of materials.

- If the philosophy at an elementary school now favors in-class flexible grouping to meet individual needs (Radencich & McKay, in press), previous organizational structures such as traditional ability grouping or cross-grouping will likely be dropped.

- If a middle or high school is adopting a Nancie Atwell (1987) philosophy of using coordinated reading and writing workshops, the same teacher might be assigned to both reading and language arts periods, with these periods scheduled back to back. This would undoubtedly necessitate training of teachers whose expertise might be in only reading or writing but not in both.

Some businesses and school districts provide models of mission statements and then ask their staffs to develop their own statements. They might use drawings, first individual ones and then consensus in gradually larger groups. This makes for powerful brain-based learning (Caine & Caine, 1991). Whatever the process and format used, it is helpful to find a way of putting down on paper a focus that can serve as a guide for programs.

Conclusion

This chapter has provided direction to supervisors and administrators regarding the need to know the history of administration and supervision, to be knowledgeable about the field from the past to the emerging future, and to build and use a philosophy of reading/writing instruction. With this armor in hand and with each other's supportive help, the supervisor and the administrator will be ready to use keys to effective leadership to open doors of curriculum and instruction change and, finally, to enter comprehensive reading/writing programs.

Analyzing and Improving Curriculum

*Curriculum development cannot be undertaken prior to, or
separate from, staff development. Instead, the curriculum must
evolve from the growing understanding of the staff.*

—Weaver, 1990, p. 282

The analysis and improvement of curriculum includes a number of issues. Those discussed here are curriculum change, elements in a K–12 curriculum, selection of instructional materials, implementation of a new reading program, management of materials, and dealing with censorship.

Curriculum Change

Responding to State and National Curriculum Initiatives

Current state and national curriculum and assessment initiatives will have an impact on district and school programs. If you are professionally active, you will be knowledgeable about such initiatives and will be able to use this

19

knowledge to help guide local curriculum efforts. Encourage teachers to accept invitations to contribute to some of these initiatives. Teachers who make their voice heard from the beginning will feel a greater sense of ownership in the products developed. Remind teachers that our job as literacy educators is political. As Shannon (1993) states: "All teachers are political, whether they are conscious of it or not. Their acts contribute to or challenge the status quo. . . ." (p. 2).

At the time of this writing, relevant initiatives include the National Council of Teachers of English and International Reading Association's development of the Standards Project for English/Language Arts (SPELA), America 2000, the National Assessment for Educational Progress (NAEP) state-by-state testing, changes in the formats of widely used standardized tests such as the Scholastic Aptitude Test (now Scholastic Achievement Test), and the New Standards Project of the Learning Research and Development Center (LRDC) and the National Center on Education and the Economy (NCEE).

The Process of Curriculum Writing

Curriculum writing is not easy. Writers must be knowledgeable about curriculum, know how to translate this knowledge into practical writing, be able to work with writing teams, and be dedicated enough to attend scrupulously to necessary detail. Curriculum writing must involve teachers who work with the grade level and the subject. This writing need not always "reinvent the wheel." Writing teams should gather and examine various curricula to help in designing their own. Burton (1991) recommends the following ideas for the curriculum development process:

- Admit that curriculum making is a political act. It reflects the problems and possibilities inherent in the values of the community.

- Committee members should stay somewhat naive. People who know too much may not be representative. The writing team can be a community of learners.

- Spend an inordinate amount of time on philosophy. This applies not only to the committee but also to the constituencies served.

- Create a collegial support network. A list can be provided of teachers with ability in different areas.

- Cross-reference people, professional writing, and policies. Rather than a scope-and-sequence chart, provide a cross-reference guide for learning experiences and for policy statements to which they relate. A possible inclusion in the guide would be how-to essays written by teachers in the district.

- Less is more. Burton cites Debbie Meier, a high school principal in New

York City, who states that the move from 1,000 objectives to 10 policies allowed teachers to develop classrooms that are experience-centered instead of objectives-centered, thus creating a high school that draws on the best features of a good kindergarten classroom.

Approaches to writing curriculum include the following:

- Large committee meeting for initial direction, followed by subgroups to draft grade-level curriculum, with representatives from subgroups then consolidating grade-level drafts

- Completion of one grade level before another grade level is tackled, with ongoing modifications as necessary in levels already written

- Committee of several subject areas working together to create integrated curricula

Several layers of review ensure curriculum that is solid. For example, with the Dade County (Florida) Public Schools' Competency-Based Curriculum (to be discussed), an assistant principal who was an expert in language arts but who had not been involved with the writing revised with the writers the progression of each objective. Then a committee of principals reviewed the revision. Finally, a pilot year-long use of the curriculum served as the basis for final fine-tuning.

Elements in a K–12 Curriculum

Harste (1993) writes that curricula are not courses to be run but, rather, conversations between disciplines, sign systems, and personalized knowing that are created, acted on, and re-created. This is very different perspective than the widely implemented scope-and-sequence view proposed by Ralph Tyler in his 1949 publication, *Basic Principles of Curriculum Instruction* (Burton, 1991). Clark and Peterson (1986) find that Tyler's rationale has "the logic of an industrial production system [and] underlies the most widely prescribed model for teacher planning." It views the curriculum from an ends–means perspective, with objectives always precisely formulated prior to activities.

Nancie Atwell (1987) supports Harste's rather than Tyler's notion when she writes that " 'curriculum' just doesn't fit anymore. A curriculum puts limits on learning, kids' and teachers', spelling out what may be covered as orchestrated from behind a big desk." When Atwell (p. 10) and a language arts team got together to write a K–8 curriculum guide, they decided that, rather than draw up skills sequences, they would start with a query: How do human beings acquire language? This approach went well beyond the traditional definition of a curriculum as a scope and sequence that provides a framework for the objectives and competencies to be mastered in each grade or subject. The term *scope and sequence,* to many, means a lockstep progression, with specific literature, skills, and the like tied to each grade level. Here, we use a broader definition of curriculum.

For some whole language advocates, even a broad definition of curriculum is offensive if it implies an imposed set of guidelines rather than a student-centered approach. But my experience leads me to agree with Yatvin's (1992, p. 16) concern that such advocates "avoid the question of whether anyone knows where all this is going in one school year, or eight, or twelve." I believe, as she does, that "experienced teachers do not operate on a student-driven curriculum alone. After all the textbooks, teachers' guides, and scopes and sequences have been abandoned, each experienced teacher still possesses a mental catalog of what students of a certain age should know and should be able to do. This catalog exerts influence over every activity in a whole language classroom." A curriculum catalog that is made explicit serves "not only as a guide for inexperienced teachers but also as a paradigm for all teachers to measure their classroom activities against."

Yatvin suggests that curricular decisions should be based on the following criteria: excellence and significance, student interests and needs, developmental learning, literary themes, and integration with content area subjects. She suggests that teachers select curriculum content that progresses:

- From short to long pieces

- From simple to complex structure

- From familiar to unfamiliar topics

- From highly predictable to less predictable texts

- From a narrow range to a broad variety

- From a single surface meaning to layers of meaning

Yatvin further suggests a focus on five whole language skills. She depicts each of these as a spiral of activities in two component strands as follows:

Skills	*Strands*
Comprehension	Getting meaning and expressing meaning
Literary knowledge	Awareness and performance
Technical skills	Decoding and encoding
Metacognition	Awareness and control
Information processing	Acquiring information and organizing/presenting information

The Policy Statement for the Upper Arlington City Schools in Ohio exemplifies a "less is better" K–12 curriculum (Burton, 1991). To replace their previous curriculum, which had 1,200 objectives across subjects and grades, this district now has 10 policy statements. The entire language arts curriculum is stated on one page—a page that even has room for a quote! The curriculum sections are as follows:

- The language arts policy statement that "Students will engage in meaningful reading, writing, and speaking activities for a variety of purposes and audiences" (p. 367)

- A one-paragraph rationale with professional references

- Subject objectives for each grade grouping: K–2, 3–5, 6–8, 9–12 (moving from three objectives in K–2 to five in 9–12)

- Suggested learning experiences and events for each grade grouping (moving from ten in K–2 to fifteen in 9–12)

- Assessment opportunities (six or seven for each grade grouping)

- Intervention possibilities (five to seven for each grade grouping)

The district sees this as an experience-centered rather than an objective-centered curriculum. It is a living document that will continually be revised on the basis of school input.

The importance of philosophy in the writing of this document should not be underestimated. Burton (1991) states that "until the names of Perrone, Apple, Carini, and Duckworth become as familiar to us as Smith, Goodman, Graves, and Calkins, we will be a bit like a professional tennis player having an overdeveloped 'literacy' arm and an underdeveloped philosophical one" (pp. 364–365). He feels that it is the philosophical arm that was most helpful in the development of this curriculum.

A curriculum different from that of Arlington City Schools is the Dade County Public Schools' K–12 Competency-Based Curriculum. The emphasis here is on mastery of a select number of competencies in each subject in each grade. Table 2-1 shows the entire language arts portion of grade 3, and one competency carried out through Grades K–12.

The Dade County Public Schools Competency-Based Curriculum is a detailed K–12 curriculum. A more streamlined picture of secondary reading programs alone can be found in the Position Statement from the International Reading Association on Secondary School Reading, adopted by the IRA Board in 1989. Reprints are available from IRA (P.O. Box 8139, Newark, DE 19714-8139).

TABLE 2-1 Portions of the Dade County Public Schools Competency-Based Curriculum

LANGUAGE ARTS: GRADE K

Component	Objectives	Competency

K.I Reading/ Literature	The following objectives support competencies A and B.
	
	1. Participates in shared reading activities using predictable language text and big books
	2. Begins to read simple words, labels, experience charts, nursery rhymes, poetry, predictable books, and other stories written by self and others
	3. Explores reading in flexible groups under the guidance of the teacher
	4. Looks at or reads books for a sustained period daily
	5. Listens to a daily reading from a wide variety of genres, e.g., picture and alphabet books, cumulative and other predictable charts and books, games, songs, nursery rhymes, simple poems, animal tales, stories about safety, finger plays, classic tales, puppet plays
	6. Begins to explore favorite authors and illustrators, including those whose work reflects cultural variations which focus on holidays, music, art, clothing, customs, values, and language
	7. Uses literature as a means of providing new experiences and gaining new insights
	8. Relates to own experiences; makes predictions by relating new information to prior knowledge, by previewing pictures and titles, and by using predictable text sequences
	9. Uses pictures to gain meaning from text
		A. After hearing a selection appropriate for story mapping, the student will demonstrate comprehension by retelling the story orally:
		  a. including main character(s) and setting
		  b. relating events in sequence
		B. After hearing two versions of the same story or after listening to a selection read aloud and viewing a film version of the same story, the student will identify similarities and differences:
		  a. through illustrations
		  b. by oral retelling

Source: Used with permission of Dade County Public Schools, Miami, Florida.

LANGUAGE ARTS: GRADE 1

Component	Objectives	Competency
1.I Reading/ Literature	The following objectives support competencies A and B. 1. Participates in shared reading activities using predictable language text and big books; participates in repeated readings such as buddy, echo, and varied forms of choral reading 2. Reads a variety of materials with increasing fluency, participating daily in flexible groups under the guidance of a teacher to: • read first grade level texts used for class instruction • read developmentally appropriate materials • participate in cooperative group activities 3. Looks at or reads independently, for a sustained period daily, selecting from diverse materials including wordless, predictable language, and picture books as well as stories, experience charts, books, and other writing by self and others 4. Reads at least one book per week from school, home, or public library 5. Listens to a daily reading on or above grade level from a variety of genres with a special emphasis on fairy tales and stories about families around the world Identifies and explores favorite 6. authors, illustrators, and titles and engages in the study of the works of a single author 7. Relates reading to own experiences, makes predictions by: • relating new information to prior knowledge • previewing pictures and titles 8. Reads, identifies, and understands key vocabulary words and concepts encountered in instruction	A. After reading a grade level story with the resolution omitted, the student will demonstrate comprehension by: a. identifying characters, setting and sequence of events using graphic organizer such as a simple story map B. After reading a story and reading/hearing a piece of non-fiction on the same topic (e.g., any book from Bridwell's Clifford series and an informational book about dogs), the student will distinguish between real and unreal: a. through drawings b. through oral and written response

Continued

TABLE 2-1   Continued

	LANGUAGE ARTS: GRADE 2	
Component	*Objectives*	*Competency*
2.I Reading/ Literature	The following objectives support competencies A and B.	A. After reading a grade-level story with the resolution omitted, the student will demonstrate an understanding of the relationship of characters, setting, and problem by:
	1. Reads a variety of materials with increasing fluency, participating daily in flexible groups under the guidance of a teacher to:	a. identifying characters, setting, problem/goal, and events using a graphic organizer such as a story map
	· read second-grade level texts used for class instruction	
	· read developmentally appropriate materials	
	· use appropriate shared reading and rereading activities such as buddy, echo, big book, and varied forms of choral reading	B. b. creating an original ending that is appro-priate to the story elements identified
	· participate in cooperative group activities	After reading at least two versions of the sae fairy or folktale (e.g., Cinder-ella versions such as *Yeh Shen, Prince Cinders*, and *Vasilissa*), the student will compare and con-trast story elements
	2. Reads independently for a sustained pe-riod daily, selecting from diverse materials including multicultural literature and sto-ries, as well as experience charts, books, and other writing by self and peers	
	3. Reads at least one book per week from school, home, or public library	
	4. Listens to a daily reading on or above grade level from a wide variety of genres with a special emphasis on folk tales from a variety of cultures, and stories of science and nature	
	5. Identifies and explores favorite authors, illustrators, and titles and engages in the study of the works of two or more authors or illustrators	
	6. Relates reading to own experiences; makes predictions and sets purposes for reading by:	
	· relating new information to prior knowledge	
	· previewing illustrations and titles	
	· scanning text	
	7. Reads, identifies, and understands key vo-cabulary words and concepts encountered in instruction	
	8. Maintains a reading response journal to show evidence of use of reading strate-gies	
	9. Integrates context clues (both meaning and sentence structure), structural analysis, pho-netic cues, and illustrations while reading	

LANGUAGE ARTS: GRADE 3

Component	Objectives	Competency
3.I Reading/ Literature	The following objectives support competencies A and B.	A. After reading a grade-level story the student will demonstrate an understanding by:
	1. Reads a variety of materials with increasing fluency, participating daily in flexible groups under the guidance of a teacher to: • read third-grade level texts used for class instruction • read developmentally appropriate materials • use appropriate strategies such as rereading, buddy, and other cooperative reading activities	a. mapping the story read b. mapping an original story which parallels the theme or genre of the story read, using story elements: title/author, setting, characters, problem/ goal, events, resolution
	2. Reads independently for a sustained period daily, selecting from a variety of fiction and nonfiction such as multicultural literature, informational selections, magazines, and writing by self and peers	B. After selecting a topic, the student will demonstrate application of reading skills by:
	3. Reads at least one book per week from school, home, or public library	a. completing a cluster of prior knowledge about the topic b. reading at least two selections and at least one reference source (e.g., encyclopedia, interactive video) dealing with the topic
	4. Listens to a daily reading on or above grade level from a variety of genres with a special emphasis on fables, tall tales, and mysteries	c. adding to the original cluster, highlighting new information through use of color and other means
	5. Identifies and explores favorite authors and illustrators, and engages in the comparison/contrast of the works of two or more authors or illustrators	
	6. Sets purposes for reading and makes predictions by relating new information to prior knowledge, previewing illustrations, and scanning text	
	7. Reads, identifies, and understands key vocabulary words and concepts encountered in instruction	
	8. Maintains a reading response journal to show evidence of use of strategies	
	9. Integrates context clues (both meaning and sentence), structural analysis, and phonetic cues to gain meaning from text	
	10. Monitors own reading by correcting miscues and rereading text when necessary	

(Continued)

TABLE 2-1   Continued

LANGUAGE ARTS: GRADE 3 (Continued)

Component	Objectives	Competency
	11. Demonstrates an understanding of story elements: setting, characters, problem/goal, events, resolution; compares and contrasts characters and setting in two or more selections	
	12. Responds to literature through a variety of activities including writing, arts, music, drama, and multimedia presentations	
	13. Uses information presented within and across selections including content area reading:	
	· restating concepts and passages in own words	
	· identifying the stated or implied main idea	
	· generating and responding to details such as who, what, where, when, and why	
	· placing events or steps in sequence using words that denote time (e.g., before, after, when; first, second, last)	
	· beginning to distinguish between fact and opinion	
	· recognizing and understanding cause and effect relationships	
	· drawing conclusions	
	· creating and sharing mental images as part of the comprehension process	
	Uses critical thinking (questioning,	
	14. interpreting, comparing, contrasting, analyzing) when participating in small group and whole class discussions about what has been read	
	Recognizes and uses figurative	
	15. language with a special emphasis on simile and onomatopoeia (e.g., kerplunk, swoosh)	
	Begins to identify author's purpose:	
	16. inform, instruct, persuade, entertain	
	Recognizes recurring themes in liter-	
	17. ature (family and citizens living and working together, sibling rivalry)	
	Recognizes and discusses biases	
	18. portrayed in pictures and in written and oral language	
	Recognizes and discusses biases portrayed in pictures and in written and oral language	

Component	Objectives	Competency
3.II Composition	The following objectives support competencies A and B.	A. In response to a prompt, the student will write a personal experience narrative of at least two paragraphs:
	1. Writes daily for a variety of purposes, both self-initiated and teacher directed, including poems, personal anecdotes, stories, book reports, interviews, surveys, letters, invitations, envelopes, journals, lists, questions, response logs	a. using prewriting strategies such as clustering, listing, or reading
	2. Uses various prewriting techniques independently such as reading, brainstorming, observing, charting, listing, imaging, and webbing to generate ideas for writing	b. using the writing process of drafting, revising, editing and publishing
	3. Writes first drafts independently with increasing fluency	c. including sequenced ideas and smooth transitions
	4. Begins to elaborate upon an idea by using a topic sentence, supporting details, examples, and vivid language to clarify meaning for reader/audience	d. using conventions of standard written English
	5. Revises pieces, independently or through conferencing with peers and/or a teacher, incorporating concepts from teacher instruction:	B. The student will demonstrate growth in literacy by maintaining a reading/writing portfolio which will include:
	· uses complete sentences and a variety of sentence structures and lengths	a. a variety of self-selected writing across the curriculum (e.g., narrative, persuasion, exposition, interview, speeches) with evidence of writing process
	· uses sentence combining to improve the flow of writing	b. evidence of use of reading strategies (e.g., predicting, webbing, reflecting on reading, noting difficult or interesting vocabulary) through a reading response journal, notebook, or other means
	· uses period in abbreviations	
	· uses appropriate punctuation	
	· organizes ideas in logical sequence, with most details focusing on a single topic	c. evaluations of own progress toward teacher/student goals over the course of a year (e.g., with notes giving rationale for inclusion of selected portfolio entries)
	6. Writes final edited pieces incorporating concepts from teacher instruction:	
	· uses commas in a series, between city/state, between month/year, and to set off nouns of direct address	
	· capitalizes the first word of a sentence, I, all proper nouns, first word of a direct quote, and initials in a name	

(Continued)

TABLE 2-1 Continued

LANGUAGE ARTS: GRADE 3 (Continued)

Component	Objectives	Competency
	7. Uses conventional spelling for a core of high frequency words in making an effort to spell correctly in daily writing 8. Spells correctly in published pieces of writing 9. Incorporates words from literature and content areas and attempts to spell them correctly 10. Begins to use appropriate proofreading and printed resources in editing own writing (dictionaries, thesauruses) 11. Produces pieces of writing of at least two paragraphs that convey message related to a prompt in narrative, expository, and persuasive modes 12. Begins to maintain a consistent and appropriate voice throughout communication using known, learned or imagined knowledge 13. Publishes work in a variety of ways (e.g., oral presentations, book displays, and mailing to authors, magazines, newspapers) 14. Chooses and evaluates pieces in a variety of genres which reflect best efforts and growth over the course of a year to place in a portfolio; sets goals for improvement with the help of a teacher 15. Uses the correct form for writing personal letters 16. Uses technology in the production of writing pieces 17. Forms cursive letlters correctly; makes the transition from manuscript to cursive writing	
3.III Vocabulary Word Study	1. Continues to expand vocabulary daily using a variety of diverse materials for reading, speaking, and listening; strengthens acquisition of new words through such recording activities as vocabulary notebook/ log, class list, card file 2. Participates in meaningful and rich word study when reading and writing that includes synonyms, anto-	A. The student will demonstrate acquisition and use of expanded vocabulary through: a. selecting words needed to write simple rhyming couplets, haikus, diamantes, and name poems b. selecting themes and generating at least two poems of different styles for each

Component	Objectives	Competency
	nyms, homonyms, words with multiple meanings, irregular plural nouns, compounds, contractions, base words with prefixes and/or suffixes, possessives, comparatives and superlatives, negative words, pronouns, and pronoun referents 3. Integrates phonetic, contextual, and structural analysis strategies to construct meanings when reading and writing 4. Compares words, discovering spelling patterns and relationships between spelling and meaning 5. Uses the context of sentence to understand unfamiliar words and appropriate meaning for words with multiple meanings 6. Uses graphic organizers to generate and classify words and concepts 7. Begins to understand and generate analogies	

3.IV Listening/
Speaking/
Viewing
	The following objectives support competencies A and B.
	
	1. Pronounces words clearly using standard English, appropriate body language and vocabulary, sentence length, and complexity appropriate for third grade level
	2. Participates in oral language activities daily:
	  · conducts interviews, introductions, and other social activities
	  · presents reports, news broadcasts
	  · retells, summarizes, dramatizes stories
	  · develops questions for peer response
	  · memorizes and recites poems, dialogue from plays, songs
	  · generates and follows multistep oral directions
	  · expresses and supports opinions and ideas to persuade, inform, etc.
	  · develops criteria and evaluates oral presentations by self and peers
	3. Evaluates oral presentations by self and peers using teacher/student criteria including conveying of meaning, engagement of audience, body
		A. After viewing or listening to a selection from multicultural literature, the student will work with a partner to analyze a character by:
		  a. planning an interview that explores ideas, values, and points of view of the selected character
		  b. role-playing an interview with the character
		  c. using teacher/student developed criteria for self and peer evaluations of all interviews
		B. The student will demonstrate effective speaking, viewing, and listening skills by
		  a. delivering oral presentations including exposition (e.g., reports, explanations, directions), narration (e.g., fables, fantasies, journals), recitation (e.g., retelling selections, poetry)
		  b. evaluating the oral presentations of self and peers using teacher/student-developed criteria

(Continued)

TABLE 2-1 Continued

LANGUAGE ARTS: GRADE 3 (Continued)

Component	Objectives	Competency
	language (eye contact, gestures, posture), articulation and pronunciation, standard conventions of English 4. Uses active listening and courteous, appropriate responding during class discussions; contributes effectively in cooperative learning situations 5. Gains a deeper understanding of the relationship between self and others through reading, viewing, discussing, and listening to a variety of multicultural materials 6. Listens and speaks respectfully to persons of all racial/ethnic backgrounds to gain and share information, ideas, values, and points of view reflecting their cultures 7. Listens for a variety of purposes: to recognize major points of emphasis; to identify details, sequence, and other literal content; to evaluate the effectiveness and style of the speaker 8. Formulates questions and begins to paraphrase/summarize information after listening or viewing 9. Understands purpose (e.g., entertain, persuade, inform) and message from oral and/or visual presentations (e.g., television, movies)	
3.V Information Literacy/ Study/Test-Taking/Skills	1. Uses all media and technological resources such as word processors, computers, library books, films, audiotapes, videotapes, interactive videos, newspapers, magazines, dictionaries, and encyclopedias as learning and communication tools 2. Begins to use organizational features of textbooks and reference materials such as table of contents, index, glossary, chapter titles, paragraph headings, italics, boldface print, diagrams, and illustrations as study tools 3. Uses home study strategies such as setting aside time and place for homework and managing time effectively 4. Uses graphic organizers (research	A. Working in a cooperative group, or individually, the student will demonstrate the ability to access and use information by: a. selecting a topic related to a current classroom theme in reading or content areas b. preparing a presentation using at least three sources to gather information c. making a multimedia presentation (e.g., computer, videotapes, drawings, dramatization, books, songs, posters) d. evaluating presentations using teacher/student developed criteria

Component	Objectives	Competency
	guides) to organize planning and research	

5. Practices and prepares for formal assessment including use of grade level material in simulated testing settings
6. Participates in periodic timed reading activities to increase reading rate, using fiction and nonfiction selections of varying lengths on third grade reading level
7. Begins to understand the use of effective test-taking strategies
8. Begins to develop a personal time frame for planning, drafting and giving some attention to revising and editing when writing to a prompt in a 30-minute period without assistance

LANGUAGE ARTS: GRADE 4

Component	Objectives	Competency
4.I Reading/ Literature	The following objectives support competencies A and B.	A. After reading a grade-level chapter book, the student will demonstrate comprehension by analyzing the main character:

Objectives:

1. Reads a variety of materials with increasing fluency, participating daily in flexible groups under the guidance of a teacher to:
   · read fourth grade level texts used for class instruction
   · read developmentally appropriate materials
   · participate in cooperative reading activities
2. Reads independently for a sustained period daily, selecting from a variety of fiction and nonfiction such as multi-cultural literature, informational text, magazines, and theme related selections
3. Reads independently at least one book per month from school, home, or public library, including a variety of genres and cultural perspectives at an appropriate reading level
4. Listens to a daily reading on or above grade level from a wide variety of genres with a special emphasis on legends, humor, and biographies/ autobiographies
5. Identifies and explores favorite

Competency:

A. After reading a grade-level chapter book, the student will demonstrate comprehension by analyzing the main character:
   a. using a graphic organizer such as a map/web to include quotes by and about the character, and the characteristics stated or inferred from actions
   b. writing a character sketch/ profile supported by information from graphic organizer

B. After selecting a topic, the student will demonstrate application of reading skils by:
   a. completing a list, graph, cluster, etc. of prior knowledge about the topic
   b. reading at least three selections and at least one reference source (e.g., encyclopedia, interactive video, or audio tape) dealing with the topic
   c. adding to the original cluster, integrating new and prior knowledge

(Continued)

TABLE 2-1   Continued

LANGUAGE ARTS: GRADE 4 (Continued)

Component	Objectives	Competency
	books and engages in the comparison/contrast of the works of two or more authors 6. Sets purposes for reading and makes predictions by relating new information to prior knowledge, scanning text, and previewing subtitles, graphics, and other illustrations 7. Reads, identifies, and understands key vocabulary words and concepts encountered in instruction 8. Maintains a reading response journal to show evidence of use of reading strategies 9. Demonstrates an understanding of story elements: setting, characters, problem/goal, events, resolution; compares and contrasts story elements across selections	d. writing at least three paragraphs on the topic, using the cluster as a guide

LANGUAGE ARTS: GRADE 5

Component	Objectives	Competency
5.I Reading/ Literature	The following objectives support competencies A and B. 1. Reads a variety of materials with increasing fluency, participating daily in flexible groups under the guidance of a teacher to: · read fifth grade level texts used for class instruction · read developmentally appropriate texts · participates in cooperative reading activities 2. Reads independently for a sustained period of time daily, selecting from a variety of fiction and nonfiction such as multicultural literature, informational texts, magazines, newspapers, and novels 3. Reads independently at least one book per month from school, home or public library, including a variety of genres and cultural perspectives at an appropriate reading level 4. Listens to a daily reading from a wide variety of genres, with a special emphasis on myths, adventure stories, and fantasy/science fiction 5. Recognizes recurring themes in	A. After reading a grade-level novel, the student will demonstrate cvomprehension by: a. writing a parallel multipage story using the same characters, but changing the time and/or place, and making appropriate modifications to the original plot b. illustrating and publishing the new story in book form B. After selecting a topic, the student will demonstrate application of reading skills by a. writing briefly and informally about the topic b. reading at least three selections of diverse types (e.g., newspaper article, encyclopedia entry, novel) dealing with the topic and using at least two types of nonprint media (e.g., video, film or filmstrip) c. adding to or changing the original piece of writing, integrating of new knowledge

Component	Objectives	Competency
	in literature (e.g., survival) by comparing and contrasting the approaches of different authors 6. Sets purposes for reading and makes predictions by relating new information to prior knowledge, scanning text, and previewing subtitles and graphics and other illustrations 7. Reads, identifies, and understands key vocabulary words and concepts encountered in their instruction 8. Maintains a reading response journal to show evidence of use of reading strategies 9. Responds to literature through a variety of activities including writing, art, music, drama, and multimedia presentations	d. writing at least three or four paragraphs on the topic based on prewriting and additional print and nonprint sources

LANGUAGE ARTS: M/J LANGUAGE ARTS1—GRADE 6

Component	Objectives	Competency
I Literature/ Reading	The following objectives support Competencies A, B, and C. 1. Reads, views, listens to, and discusses a variety of multicultural materials to gain new experiences and inights as well as a deeper understanding and appreciation of self and others. 2. Reads fluently a variety of materials at grade level, using appropriate settings such as flexible groups, rereading, paired and other cooperative reading activities. 3. Reads independently or as part of a class study at least one book per month, at an appropriate reading level, reflecting a variety of genres and cultural perspectives. 4. Listens to a diverse selection of literature read aloud on a frequent basis. 5. Sets purposes for reading and makes predictions by relating new information to prior personal and academic knowledge, previewing and scanning text and using text features such as subtitles, margin notes, and chapter divisions 6. Reads, identifies, and understands key vocabulary words, context clues, and concepts.	A. After reading selections from two different genres, selected from fiction and nonfiction, such as fables, folktales, legends, biographies, autobiographies, the student will create a graphic or write a response of at least three paragraphs which a. identifies the two genres and the characteristics of each and b. cites other pieces of literature, read in class or independently, which are examples of each genre. B. After reading a fiction selection at sixth grade reading level, the student will demonstrate an understanding of fictional elements and author's craft by creating a graphic or writing an essay of two or three paragraphs which: a. identifies the theme b. shows how characterization, plot, and setting as well as techniques such as foreshadowing, flashback, irony, and metaphor can

(Continued)

TABLE 2-1   Continued

LANGUAGE ARTS: M/J LANGUAGE ARTS1—GRADE 6 (Continued)

Component	Objectives	Competency
	7. Applies reading strategies within and across selections: • monitors own reading by correcting miscues, (pronunciation error) rereading, skimming, self-questioning, creating visual images, responding in writing, and summarizing • identifies stated and implied main ideas with supporting details • orders events or steps in sequential or chronological order • distinguishes between fact and opinion • perceives relationships (e.g., cause/effect, comparison/contrast, analogies) • draws conclusions and makes generalizations • makes judgments using details and examples from text	support the theme and contribute to the meaning of the story. C. After reading a *nonfiction* selection at sixth grade level, the student will demonstrate comprehension by selecting and completing the most appropriate graphic organizer, such as the Venn diagram (compare/contrast), flowchart/timeline (sequence), or main idea table (main idea-details)

LANGUAGE ARTS: M/J LANGUAGE ARTS2—GRADE 7

Component	Objectives	Competency
I Literature/ Reading	The following objectives support competencies A and B. 1. Reads, views, listens to, and discusses a variety of multicultural materials to gain new experiences and insights as well as a deeper understanding and appreciation of self and others 2. Reads fluently a variety of materials at grade level, using appropriate strategies, such as rereading, paired reading, and other cooperative reading activities 3. Develops the habit of reading as a lifelong activity by reading, either independently or as part of a class study, at least one book per month reflecting a variety of genres and cultural perspectives 4. Explores how literature is influenced by and reflects culture 5. Analyzes and evaluates reading selections using examples and inferences from the text	A. After reading a short story or novel, the student will write a response of at least three paragraphs which focuses on an analysis of: a. character motivation and actions as they relate to the cultural setting b. elements of the author's craft such as figurative language, foreshadowing, flashback, symbolism, and irony, and the way they contribute to an understanding of character(s) c. the author's point of view or perspective toward the character(s) B. After reading a *non-fiction* selection at the seventh grade reading level from a newspaper, magazine, or text, the student will demonstrate reading comprehension by: a. selecting an appropriate

LANGUAGE ARTS: M/J LANGUAGE ARTS2—GRADE 7 (Continued)

Component	Objectives	Competency
	6. Understands and paraphrases the stated or implied main idea in a reading selection 7. Analyzes passages/works to identify textual patterns, such as analogies, comparison/contrast, cause/effect, problem/solution, and detail/main idea 8. Applies reading/critical thinking skills, such as recognizing propaganda, drawing conclusions, making judgments based on text information, clarifying information, and using evidence from a selection to support opinion Analyzes and evaluates the author's 9. purpose and perspective (personal point of view or bias toward a topic)	graphic organizer such as a cause/effect diagram, a graph, a chart, a table, or a map b. completing the graphic with information from the reading passage

LANGUAGE ARTS: M/J LANGUAGE ARTS3—GRADE 8

Component	Objectives	Competency
I Literature/ Reading	The following objectives support competencies A and B. 1. Reads independently or as part of class study at least one book per month at an appropriate reading level from a variety of genres and cultural perspectives to gain an understanding and appreciation of self and others 2. Analyzes how literature is influenced by and reflects culture, including an appreciation of a variety of cultural vocabularies and dialects 3. Understands and paraphrases the stated or implied main idea in a reading selection 4. Evaluates statements of fact, inferences, and judgments/opinions in both reading and discussions about reading Analyzes passages/works to 5. examine textual patterns, such as analogies, comparison/contrast, cause/ effect, problem/solution, and order of importance Applies reading/critical thinking 6. skills, such as generating questions, recognizing propaganda, clarifying information, evaluating author's purpose and perspective toward a topic,	A. After studying myth and drama, the student will choose two selections from the same genre with a similar theme, and write a response of at least three paragraphs. The essay will compare and/or contrast the author's use of: a. literary elements (character, plot, setting, point of view, and/or tone) *or* b. elements of the author's craft such as figurative language, foreshadowing, flashback, symbolism, and irony, and the say they contribute to shaping the theme in each work. B. After reading a *nonfiction* passage from a newspaper, magazine, or text, on the eighth grade reading level, the student will demonstrate comprehension by: a. selecting an appropriate graphic organizer such as a cause/effect diagram, a graph a chart, a table, or a map

(Continued)

TABLE 2-1   Continued

LANGUAGE ARTS: M/J LANGUAGE ARTS3—GRADE 8 (Continued)

Component	Objectives	Competency
	and using evidence from a selection to support opinions 7. Understands functional reading material, such as newspapers, periodicals, manuals, instructions, schedules, common forms, maps, graphs, charts, tables 8. Reads and shares teacher suggested and self-selected books, for a sustained period on a regular basis each week	b. completing the graphic with information from the reading passage c. explaining the selected organizer in terms of the passage, either orally or in writing

LANGUAGE ARTS: ENGLISH I—GRADE 9

Component	Objectives	Competency
I Literature	The following objectives support competencies A and B. 1. Reads and discusses culturally diverse literature 2. Recognizes the connection between written works and other art forms and the cultures which produced them 3. Distinguishes among the major literary genres (e.g., short story, poetry, novel, drama, essay, and biography) 4. Identifies examples of figurative language (to include simile, metaphor, personification, oxymoron) and analyzes their use in a literary selection 5. Uses appropriate literary terminology to analyze literary selections (to include foreshadowing, tone, main idea, symbolism, and irony) 6. Identifies elements of literary work, including plot, setting, characterization, point of view, and theme 7. Identifies and analyzes the feelings, traits, and motives of characters 8. Interprets a literary selection and supports the interpretation with examples from the text 9. Relates literature to real life experiences 10. Develops the habit of reading as a lifelong activity by reading at least one book per month either independently or as part of a class study	A. The student will select one literary work studied during the year and at least one other art form produced by the same or different culture(s), and write an essay of at least three paragraphs which establishes the connection between the literature and the art form. The essay should a. examine how the literature and the art form illustrate values and/or beliefs of the culture(s) b. discuss how the techniques of the writer and the techniques of the artist in the other medium convey meaning B. Given a familiar literary selection with an emphasis on character, the student will write an essay of at least three paragraphs that a. identifies the genre b. discusses the methods the author uses to describe, develop, and reveal the character's feelings, traits, or motives

LANGUAGE ARTS: ENGLISH II—GRADE 10

Component	Objectives	Competency

I Literature	The following objectives support competencies A and B.
	
	1. Reads and discusses genres from a variety of world cultures
	2. Learns to appreciate and compare and contrast literature and other art forms from various cultures, religions, countries, and philosophies. Identifies universal themes and multicultural concerns in world literature
	3. Compares and contrasts a variety of genres, and recognizes distinguishing underlying patterns
	4. Reads selections written for a variety of purposes (e.g., narrative, persuasive, expository, imaginative, and informative)
	5. Understands the figurative language employed in literature (terms to include simile, metaphor, personification, oxymoron, hyperbole, and apostrophe)
	6. Recognizes the use of literary devices such as tone, mood, symbolism, irony, satire, imagery, allusion, foreshadowing, flashback, and uses the terms appropriately in oral and written analysis
	7. Analyzes fictional works in terms of plot, conflict, setting, characterization, point of view, and theme
	8. Identifies dynamic characters in a selection, and traces their changes in the story
	9. Uses appropriate reading strategies such as previewing and predicting to comprehend a selection
	10. Compares personal culture to the cultures represented in selected works
	11. Develops the habit of reading as a lifelong activity by reading at least one book a month either independently or as part of a class study
		A. Given one universal theme in world literature that has been discussed during the course of the year, the student will write an essay of at least three to five paragraphs that
		  a. relates the theme to the student's own values
		  b. supports the theme with examples which reflect the commonality of human experience and which represent at least two countries and/or two genres
		
		B. The student will select one piece of fiction that has been discussed in class during the year and write an essay of three to four paragraphs or more that
		  a. traces the development of a dynamic character
		  b. analyzes the plot, setting, characterization, point of view, and/or theme
		  c. explains the uses of literary devices and figurative language

(Continued)

TABLE 2-1 Continued

LANGUAGE ARTS: ENGLISH III—GRADE 11

Component	Objectives	Competency
I Literature	The following objectives support competencies A and B. 1. Reads and compares literary works in various genres which span the major periods in American literature and reflect a variety of cultures and points of view 2. Recognizes how works and/or universal themes in American literature are reflections of and reactions to contemporaneous historical events and cultural and social settings 3. Discusses figurative language and rhetorical devices in literary selections (to include extended metaphor, personification, hyperbole, undertatement, oxymoron, and apostrophe) 4. Discusses literary devices with respect to their importance in the develement of a work to include tone, symbolism, irony, satire, imagery, allusion, foreshadowing, flashback, dialect, and parody) 5. Analyzes a variety of works in terms of plot, conflict, setting, characterization, point of view and theme 6. Discusses techniques a writer uses for developing a character, and articulates how a character changes through the course of a work 7. Recognizes the functions of minor characters and subplots within a work 8. Identifies author's purpose/perspective in a literary work and recognizes rhetorical devices and propaganda techniques 9. Examines own values in light of those expresed in American literature and cites similarities and differences 10. Reads a variety of additional American literature selections to enrich his or her understanding 11. Develops the habit of reading as a lifelong activity by reading at least one book a month either independently or as part of a class study	A. Given several universal themes from American literature that have been studied during the year, the student will select one and write a multiparagraph essay of sufficient depth and length that makes connections between the theme selected, American literature studied or read independently, and the student's own values. The theme should be supported with examples taken from literature that: a. reflect a variety of American cultures and points of view b. span major periods in American history c. represent at least three different genres, including the formal essay B. Given two familiar literary selections with a common focus, the student will write an essay of comparison and/or contrast which a. has a declarative, controlling, and defensible thesis b. reflects all aspects of the writing process including cooperative discussion in pairs or small groups c. demonstrates an understanding of the use of figurative language, rhetorical and literacy devices, and relevant elements of literature

LANGUAGE ARTS: ENGLISH IV—GRADE 12

Component	Objectives	Competency
I Literature	The following objectives support competencies A and B.	A. After reading classical and contemporary British and/or European literature in addition to representative Asian, African, and Latin American literature, the student will write an essay which demonstrates

Objectives (continued):

1. Reads classical and contemporary British and/or European literature in addition to representative Asian, African, and Latin American literature
2. Understands and expresses how literature is a reflection of societal, political, and religious ideas of an age
3. Investigates literary themes and issues common to humanity in classical and modern literature
4. Recognizes the relationship of literature to the other humanities
5. Recognizes relationships between form and content
6. Recognizes how literary devices, to include figurative language, poetic devices, tone, symbolism, irony, satire, imagery, foreshadowing, and flashback) contribute to meaning in literature
7. Evaluates how the literary elements of setting, characterization, point of view, and plot contribute to meaning in literature
8. Draws inferences from literary works about the ideas and attitudes of the authors who wrote them
9. Identifies, compares, and contrasts philosophies, ideas, and themes of various works
10. Reads literary criticism as an aid to understanding literature
    Reads additional literary selections to enrich understanding

Competency (continued):

a. how a universal theme is portrayed similarly
b. how the theme relates to the student's own experiences

The theme should be supported with references to two works, one British or European, and one from another culture. Using the two works, the student should

a. identify the common theme
b. examine the different cultural influences on the development of the theme
c. explain how the student's own values influence his/her understanding of the theme

B. Given a familiar narrative selection such as a short story or long, narrative poem, the student will write a multiparagraph essay that
a. analyzes the relationship of form and content
b. shows how plot, setting, characterization, point of view, theme, and literary devices contribute to meaning

Selecting Instructional Materials

Selecting instructional materials is a critical task because, unfortunately, most teacher decision making is governed by textbooks. In 1985 Muther (1985c) found that 95 percent of decisions were based on textbooks. This figure probably has decreased somewhat but undoubtedly remains high. Moreover, this reliance on textbooks is the expectation of many administrators (Shannon, 1987).

There is a lot more to the process of selecting materials than meets the eye. The selection process can be a prime staff development opportunity for a faculty. Following is a description of issues pertaining, respectively, to the selection of core reading material, of language arts texts in the elementary school, of technology, and of other supplementary reading/language arts materials. For addresses of publishers, refer to the list of publishers in Appendix C.

Core Reading Material

- "This series has too many workbook pages. I won't vote for it."

- "I loved X series before. I want it again."

- "I hated X series. No way will I vote for their new book."

- "Look at the videos that come with this series! This is the series for me!"

Comments like these reflect narrow views that can impede faculties from getting a broad picture. Textbook selection today is complex, but it wasn't always that way. As Nila Banton Smith (1965) reminds us, choices in colonial America were limited to the *New England Primer* and a Holy Bible. Throw in a slate and a lunch pail and children were fully equipped for the school year!

Today, however, educators charged with the responsibility of text selection are barraged with a bewildering array of textbooks. And the consequences of their choices are monumental. First, the outlay of dollars does not leave any margin for error. Once a decision is made, it may well be set for five years or more as a result of the economic infeasibility of reordering. Second, the texts can and in many cases *will* dictate the curriculum. Therefore, a simple "flip test" as a cursory examination of sample texts is totally unacceptable.

Following is a smorgasbord of strategies from which schools can select during a text adoption process. Note that the learning that occurs through this process is probably even more important that the selection itself.

Textbook selection is best done by a committee. The more broad-based the committee, the greater the sense of ownership in the selection. This is crucial. The best text in the world will do no good if it sits on a shelf. At some level, textbook adoption committees should include administrators, curriculum supervisors, teachers, parents, and students.

1. *Outline a selection procedure.* Delineate an overall selection procedure. A proposed sequence of objectives and corresponding tasks can be presented at the first committee meeting, then discussed and amended until consensus is achieved. Communicate the procedure (including deadline dates) to parents, and develop a plan for keeping parents up to date with the procedure as it unfolds. Also, determine a mechanism for soliciting input from and otherwise communicating with the administrators, teachers, parents, and others who are not included on the selection committee.

An important component of the selection procedure is determining the role of publisher sales representatives. Decide if, how, and when they are to be involved. They can be helpful, but their flashy and biased presentations can sway committee members. Barnard and Hetzel (1986) call this glitz "the wine and cheese phenomenon." Another point to note: The last presenter always has the advantage.

If sales representatives are to be invited to make presentations, establish guidelines. Turn down all gifts from representatives to prevent any undue influence. Ask for specific evidence to support publishers' claims. Consider timing. How many minutes will each publisher be allowed for presentation? Should publisher representatives be present before, during, or after the time when the committee looks at materials? Should committee members at least begin to make up their own minds before seeing sales representatives?

2. *Conduct a needs assessment.* Consider several areas of need, including subject matter content (what content do we wish to teach?), social content (what values do we wish to impart?), difficulty level and user friendliness (are levels of difficulty and text features appropriate for the intended group of students?), and instructional design (how do we wish to teach the content?) (Young & Riegeluth, 1988).

A variety of methods can be used to conduct a needs assessment (Johnson, Meiller, Miller, & Summers, 1987). A survey (open- or closed-ended) of administrators, teachers, and parents can gauge their perception of needs. Focused discussion at meetings can clarify priorities and concerns. Thus, a group can brainstorm the aspects of the program that are of particular concern (e.g., user friendliness, quality of literature, integration of reading with other subjects, word recognition instruction, vocabulary development, comprehension instruction, assessment). Each aspect can be discussed to bring understandings closer together. The group's priorities are then ascertained and serve as the basis for text examination. This prevents situations in which one person evaluates the program on the basis of Factor A while another focuses on Factor B.

Muther (1988) provides a Forced Choice Analysis form that enables faculties to prioritize the issues that are most important to them in text selection. This tool can be invaluable in diluting controversy. When a school has decided on its three most critical issues, it becomes harder for any one person or clique to focus on a single pet issue. Otherwise, a divisiveness may develop, with one teacher voting because of the phonics component, another because of the literature component, and so on.

3. *Plan for a research update.* Because the textbook selection committee is likely to be composed of members with varying levels of familiarity with current research, planning for a research update is critical. Muther (1985b) suggests limiting the research update to brief statements of results and implications. The Florida Reading Association followed her advice and produced an attractive packet of half sheets, containing a research tidbit, the reference, and a classroom implication, each of which could be put into teachers' mailboxes once a week as basal adoption time neared (*Teachers on the Cutting Edge*, 1990).

4. *Define the ideal.* Information gathered from the needs assessment and research update can then be used to define and describe the ideal textbook. This vision of the ideal is particularly useful in guiding the committee as it sets up initial screening, in-depth screening, and final selection criteria (Young & Riegeluth, 1988).

5. *Conduct initial screening.* Only now do you proceed with an initial screening—that is, targeting three to five series to scrutinize thoroughly. A checklist based on the "vision of the ideal" can be helpful in this process. Bailey (1988) suggests that a checklist should be relatively easy to complete and should include items relevant to each of the assessed needs. If one assessed need is phonics instruction, for example, items might include teacher manual encouragement of the following: use of multisensory techniques (such as songs, magnetic letters, and small objects for sorting), integration of phonics with selections, and frequent opportunities for emergent readers to practice temporary spellings. In addition, the manual might include a professional article on good phonics instruction and a chart of the stages of temporary spelling.

Don't be swayed by labels! No matter how often this point is made, it never really seems to sink in. In 1990, the state of Florida asked basal publishers to categorize basal series as "traditional" or "integrated." Series that wound up in *different* categories were sometimes more similar than series *within* a category, but they were perceived quite differently by educators who allowed themselves to be taken in by the label. Don't trust the correlation or the table of contents. You have to get inside the books.

6. *Conduct in-depth review.* Conduct an in-depth examination of each series identified during the initial screening phase. As with the needs assessment, inspect four major elements of text: subject matter content, social content, difficulty level, and instructional design.

Because the in-depth examination is time-consuming, it may be prudent to appoint subcommittees to complete various examination tasks (Barnard & Hetzel, 1986). For example, one subcommittee can evaluate only the social content of all targeted series. Or each subcommittee might focus on one aspect of the subject matter content. An example of the latter would be a subcommittee to do a horizontal trace (Muther, 1988) of main idea instruction in the fourth-grade basals of each series, as is explained in the section on instructional design. Much can be learned through this kind of focus that could never be learned with a flip test.

Subject matter content. Young and Riegeluth (1988) recommend that content analysis include, among other things, an examination of the depth and comprehensiveness of content coverage and of the currency and accuracy of information. The guiding questions are: "What is being taught?" and "Is the content consistent with our curriculum requirements?"

One technique for comparing content coverage is a story sort for basal or literature textbooks (Muther, 1987) or a topic comparison for content area texts (Muther, 1988). With these procedures, a search is made for (a) a story that occurs—if possible—at the same level in three narrative texts (story sort), or (b) the same topic in three content area texts (topic comparison). These are then photocopied and compared. These procedures allow for a direct examination (without the distraction of color) of how different textbooks cover the same material. Muther (1988) also recommends doing a "kid rating" whereby the potential users of the book do the comparisons and provide their evaluations.

Social content. Social content evaluation is guided by the question, "What values are being imparted—overtly and implicitly?" Certainly the social content analysis of texts must reflect designated local needs and values as determined in the needs assessment. Seek texts that offer equitable representation of ethnic groups, genders, age groups, and the handicapped. Equitable representation is not a frequency count. It is necessary to examine materials closely and systematically to detect subtle biases (Young & Riegeluth, 1988).

Difficulty level. Students appreciate textbooks that facilitate learning. Following are ways to help determine text difficulty.

Traditional readability formulas can serve as rough gauges of text difficulty. Readability levels are often reported as grade levels. Two commonly used scales are the Fry Readability Graph (Fry, 1977) and the Raygor Readability Estimate (Raygor, 1977). Users must be cautious, however, and remember the following:

a. Typically, only two of the many factors that affect readability are measured by readability formulas.

b. The exactness of a grade level indicates a level of precision that we simply don't have. Indeed, different formulas may yield very different figures.

c. Materials artificially written to fit a formula are often more difficult than the level would indicate. For example, deleting "because" and chopping a sentence into two parts forces the student to make the causal inference (Pearson, 1974–1975) when "He was paid extra because he did a good job" becomes "He did a good job. He got paid extra."

See the list of common questions and answers in Appendix C for responses to the question, "What is the readability of this?"

Textbooks should also be examined to determine the degree to which they include features that enhance comprehension. Textbooks that include such features as headings and subheadings, vocabulary in boldface type, well-placed graphics, introductions, summaries, and glossaries are considered to be "friendly" or "considerate" to the reader. See the text friendliness checklist in Appendix C or other checklists for evaluating the friendliness of text (Irwin & Davis, 1980; Readence, Bean, & Baldwin, 1992; Singer, 1986).

The cloze procedure can help determine how well a textbook matches the reading level of students. A cloze test consists of a passage extracted verbatim from a target textbook from which words have been systematically deleted, as is shown in Figure 2-1. Students' ability to construct meaning from the textbooks is gauged by how well they can supply the missing words. Reading methods and content area reading textbooks describe the construction and administration of cloze tests (see, e.g., Readence et al., 1992). Note, however, that cloze tests are more a measure of language production than of comprehension per se.

See the description of the Degrees of Reading Power (DRP) test (1984) (Chapter 8) for an alternative in which choices for each deleted word are provided to students. Note also that readability data in DRP units are available for many textbooks to help gauge the student–textbook match. Even if you are not using the test and thus are not able to obtain student scores, you can use DRP readability values as one gauge in ranking texts by difficulty level. If DRP scores are not reported with new textbooks, you can usually get this information from the publisher. Once you have DRP values for the text, it will be helpful to know the following approximate equivalents from the DRP Readability Report: 40—Grade 1; 44—Grade 2; 49—Grade 3; 51—Grade 4; 53—Grade 5; 56—Grade 6; 57—Grade 7; 58—Grade 8; 59—Grade 9; 60—Grade 10; 61—Grade 11; 64—Grade 12.

Cloze passages are usually selections of 200–300 words in length that can stand alone. Cloze is generally not _____ below the third grade _____. It is most often _____ with every fifth word, _____, with every blank for _____ deleted word of equal _____. The first and last _____ are left intact. If _____ are fifty blanks, then _____ number right can easily _____ computed into a percentage. Only exact words are accepted; this provides for reliable scoring.

FIGURE 2-1 Cloze passage

The ultimate judge of whether or not a text is readable is the reader. A strategy has been developed to help students (in the middle grades and up) to conduct an independent informal evaluation of the level of text difficulty (Schumm & Mangrum, 1991). The strategy, known by the acronym FLIP, helps students evaluate text by taking text *F*riendliness, *L*anguage, and their own *I*nterest and *P*rior knowledge into consideration.

Instructional design. An evaluation of instructional design is guided by the question, "How is content taught?" Young and Riegeluth (1988) suggest that the instructional design of texts be evaluated on three criteria: the macro level, the micro level, and the message design.

Examine the instructional design of all major components of the text, including the text itself, the teacher's edition, and "core" supplementary materials (those that have direct impact on the quality of daily instruction—perhaps the tests that go with the series and/or the workbooks). Don't worry about supplementary materials that are not part of the core. If these extra supplementary materials are not budgeted, it's best not to be swayed by them. Instead, devote your energy to looking at the text itself and the supplementary materials that probably will be used.

Worksheets and related supplementary activities should be evaluated for task content, task design, opportunities for sufficient and appropriate review, clarity and consistency of instructional language, and opportunities for open-ended responses (Center for the Study of Reading, 1990). See the section in this chapter on "Other Supplementary Reading/Writing Materials" for further detail. Tests should include clear guidelines for administration, scoring, and interpretation; unambiguous directions and item content for students; and a distinct match between what is being taught and what is tested (Center for the Study of Reading, 1990). See Chapter 8 for a global view of assessment.

A *macro-level* evaluation provides an overall picture of the instructional design of the textbook, generally through the scope-and-sequence chart.

A *micro-level* evaluation determines how a particular skill is presented. A skills trace (Muther 1985a; Cotton, Casem, Kroll, Langas, Rhodes, & Sisson, 1988) is one way of doing this. With a skills trace, the evaluator isolates a particular skill and traces it through the series of books across a sample of perhaps three grade levels. This helps evaluate systematically how a skill is introduced, developed, and reinforced. Muther (1988) sees skills traces as being both horizontal (three series at a designated grade level) and vertical (three grade levels in one series).

At the micro level, it is also important to assess adaptations for learners with special needs in skill and concept instruction. The absence of suggestions for adaptation will put an unnecessary burden on teachers if instructional modifications are to be developed to meet individual needs. See "What to Do When the Textbook Is Too Hard" in Chapter 7 for suggested textbook adaptations.

As skill presentation is scrutinized, it is imperative to keep in mind the implications of Durkin's classic study (1981). Does the text teach and not just test skills? In other words, are specific instructional strategies provided: what to do, how to do it, when to use the strategy, and why it will help?

Format evaluation deals with an appraisal of page layout. Conn (1988) proposes an examination of headings and subheadings to determine the flow of presentation, and of individual units to see if they are focused and manageable. Other questions are:

- Does the page format facilitate learning?

- Are graphics in close proximity to corresponding text?

- Do teachers' manuals present information in a considerate, usable manner?

7. *Make the final decision.* One of the best ways to obtain information about the worth of a textbook is to communicate with professionals currently using the text through structured telephone interviews or through site visits (Muther, 1988). In the case of a district decision, at least three districts should be visited (the best route) or interviewed. The use of pilots is another possibility but is not recommended. Unless one teacher pilots all texts being considered, each teacher typically prefers the text that she or he piloted. And teachers can seldom afford to interrupt their teaching to pilot several texts.

Before the final decision is made, summarize and evaluate all data collected. Finally, review the initial designation of an ideal text. Then, *make a selection.*

Is this smorgasbord too heavily laden? You'll have to select among the strategies provided. But the more thorough your review, the more learning your faculty can engage in during the process and the more satisfied they will be with their choice.

Language Arts Texts in the Elementary School

Districts or schools studying whether to purchase language arts books for spelling, English, and handwriting must take several factors into account. Keeping their instructional philosophy in mind, they must evaluate existing curriculum and instruction, faculty readiness for change, and the content of new language arts books.

As teachers move toward meaningfully integrating the language arts, the need for separate books for handwriting, grammar, and spelling will decrease. But a school should at least have a few copies available, samples perhaps, to serve as reference tools. Beginning teachers might not know, for example, how to teach handwriting strokes. Teachers needing reassurance that no skills are being left out may find individual copies of the books to be a necessary security blanket. In general, however, schools are moving toward spending the dollars that typically have gone into the purchase of these materials on classroom libraries, manipulatives, and other resources.

Orange County, Florida, language arts supervisor Jackie Mathews provided strong leadership while placing the responsibility on schools with their 1993 spelling adoption. Her plan is a model for informed decision making. Mathews distributed to each school a packet that included:

- *Information on spelling research and practice:* (1) a paper on how Cambourne's (1988) conditions for learning apply to the teaching of spelling, (2) a list of recommendations based on spelling research, (3) a chart detailing developmental levels of spelling, (4) a list of spelling rules that should be taught, (5) an annotated bibliography of references on spelling, (6) a rating scale for choosing a spelling series, and (7) a framework for the formation of study groups and Wilde's (1990) "A Proposal for a New Spelling Curriculum."

- *A list of four options:* (1) the formation of a study group at the school to discuss research on spelling, instruction that best supports learning, methods of evaluating growth, and strategies for reporting the growth to parents: (2) a school committee to select a spelling series on the basis of district recommendations; (3) a school committee to select a spelling series from all state-adopted choices; and (4) a choice not to adopt a spelling series.

For teachers using a spelling basal, Opitz and Cooper (1993) provide weekly and annual plans on adapting the book for a second-grade spelling workshop. Their plan, which also has applications for teachers who select a word list without a spelling basal, has the teacher first constructing a chart listing the phonetic analysis and structural analysis patterns from each lesson. The teacher then records this information, along with the list of words on a student spelling profile, which is duplicated for all students. This form also provides space for pretest scores, for recording of pretest responses, and for posttest scores. A sample parent letter is included explaining that students choose as many words of their own as they pass on the pretest. Following a week of activities related to the words, sixth-graders test the second-graders. For further information on spelling, see the list of common questions and answers in Appendix C.

Technology in the Reading/Writing Program

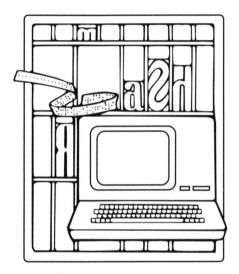

Technology is opening unthought-of panoramas into reading/writing instruction. Until the early 1980s, computers and software were the bread and butter of technology integration in the educational setting. The newest technological advances, however, have melted into the school environment with enthusiastic teacher and student response. Today's technologies include marrying the stand-alone computer with videodisc players, CD-ROM drives, scanners, video and audio digitizers, modems, and television. Thus, a new term emerges—*multimedia.* The expansive memory storage capabilities of today's multimedia technologies have transformed the standard educational drill-and-practice software of the past, driven by limited memory requirements. The new software provides an interactive environment. Teachers select software that enables the student to think creatively, problem-solve, and work in cooperative learning groups.

Technology changes so quickly that no list of recommended materials can remain current for long. For reviews, consult reading/language arts publications, as well as technological publications such as *Electronic Learning* (Scholastic) and *Technology & Learning* (2451 East River Road, Dayton, OH 45439). Following are some titles current at the time of this writing.

CD-ROM encyclopedias such as *Grolier's Multimedia Encyclopedia* (Grolier, IBM/MAC/Apple) brings reference work to life by using digitized pictures, animation, and video clips. Grolier's is appropriate for both elementary and secondary levels. An elementary reference tool called *First Connection: The Golden Book Encyclopedia* (Hartley, MAC) contains a built-in notebook for note taking and reads all or selected text aloud to the student.

Greater awareness of the multicultural dimensions of U.S. society has resulted in an interest in minority points of view, which can be found in a variety of newspapers and other publications. The *Ethnic NewsWatch* CD-ROM disc supplies access to and the ability to print this information. Articles in this secondary-level resource provide perspective on events by including original stories; editorials; and book, theater, and movie reviews. Students can browse through the database and research information by keyword, Boolean connectors, and/or date. For additional information on yearly subscriptions, call SoftLine Information (800-524-7922).

Valuable additions to the elementary library/media center or in the multimedia computer center in the classroom are literature-based CD-ROM packages. Three such products that integrate reading, writing, and listening are *C.D.'s Storytime* with 19 K–2 CD titles (Houghton Mifflin), elementary and secondary DISCIS Books with 10 titles (Discis Knowledge Research), and BRAVO BOOKS with a selection of 17 different K–2 interactive stories with accompanying little and big books (Computer Curriculum Corporation). Intermediate to middle school programs like *The Oregon Trail* and the new *Amazon Trail* by MECC (also available in CD-ROM format) and *The Lost Tribe* (Lawrence Publications), though primarily social studies oriented, can be used to enhance writing and reading skills in cooperative group decision-making settings.

Videodisc technology like CD-ROM has enabled students to become active learners who research, develop, and create their own reports and multimedia productions. Videodiscs or laserdiscs, as they are often called, can be purchased in two formats, CLV or CAV. CLV means constant linear velocity. A CLV disc is much like a videotape and can provide 60 minutes of video and audio on each side, with the ability to search for information remotely by time and chapter. CAV means constant angular velocity. CAV discs contain 30 minutes of audio and video information on each side, with two audio tracks for dual language selection and the ability to freeze frame, use slow motion, bar code read, and chapter and frame search. Some videodiscs labeled CAV III are published with accompanying software, usually in the form of Hypercard stacks, that allows interactive communication with the videodisc via the computer. Language arts videodiscs might feature elementary-level children's literature and films such as the *Legends, Fables, Folklore Series* (CAV), or enhance writing skills like *StoryTelling Sentences that Ask and Tell* (CAV), both by Coronet.

Telecommunications has become a communications tool that knows no boundaries. Using a modem connected to any computer, students can talk, research, and share information over telephone lines with other students and on bulletin boards. One of the most noteworthy is Prodigy (800-822-6922), a personal interactive communications service that allows users to navigate through more than 800 resource features. Taking this one step farther to a wide area network enables students to communicate with any worldwide Internet address wtihout the need for a modem at each computer station. Districts exploring the use of wide area networks are, however, limiting student access to prevent their becoming overwhelmed and to protect students from inappropriate addresses.

Useful for all age groups is a subscription to *WorldClassroom* (Global Learning Corporation), a global on-line computer education network that enables students to use real-life data in core curriculum projects to make decisions about themselves and their environment. To order, write P.O. Box 201361, Arlington, TX 76006.

With *National Geographic Kids Network* (800-368-2728), intermediate-level students are connected with a worldwide network of students performing real-world scientific procedures and investigating cultural, social, and environmental issues. Students problem-solve and collaborate using telecommunications. This package has scheduled units that run all school year.

Interactive media possibilities with CD-ROM and laser disk technologies make cross-curricular lessons a natural. Computers, particularly when used for purposes beyond drill and practice, can provide sensory involvement, continuous and timely feedback, and interaction. Computers can provide opportunities for simulations, problem solving, and word processing. When used with at-risk learners, computers can be especially attractive in that they can provide privacy, individualization, demonstrated achievement gains, cost-effectiveness, control of learning, flexibility in scheduling, open entry and exit, and a modern way to learn (Askov & Clark, 1991; Howie, 1990).

At-risk learners appreciate the ephemeral nature of writing that appears on an electronic screen, with the realization that it may be rethought and changed at any time. Older students often find new pride in learning "computers" rather than learning "skills" (Askov & Clark, 1991). These benefits, however, should be weighed against potential problems, such as the need for continual upgrading, lack of expertise, inappropriate programs, and feelings of displacement of teachers (Askov & Clark, 1991).

Selecting software and laser disks can be confusing for the novice. Often, teachers are reduced to using catalog descriptions or questionable advice to make decisions. If teachers are dissatisfied with the material, precious educational dollars are wasted. When selecting software and other nonprint media, use the following guidelines from the International Reading Association.

International Reading Association Criteria for Selecting Nonprint Media for the Reading Curriculum

Print media include printed materials in books, pamphlets, magazines, or newspapers. Nonprint media include any other means of conveying information, including television, radio, computer, music, games, audiotape, film, videodisc, videotape, and cable TV.

1. Materials shall support and be consistent with the general educational goals of the school district.

2. Materials shall contribute to the objectives of the instructional program.

3. Materials shall be appropriate for the age, social and emotional devel- opment, and interests of the students for whom the materials are selected.

4. Materials shall present a reasonable balance of opposing sides of controversial issues so that students may develop the practice of critical reading and thinking. When no opposing side of an issue is currently available, the nature of the bias will be explicitly discussed and explained to the students.

5. Materials shall provide a background of information that will enable pupils to make intelligent judgments in their daily lives.

6. Materials shall provide a stimulus for creative reading, writing, listening, and thinking.

7. Material shall reflect the pluralistic character and culture of society. Materials shall foster respect for women, minority groups, and ethnic groups.

8. Materials shall be of acceptable technical quality, including clear narration and synchronized picture and sound.

9. Materials should be selected on the basis of their aesthetic quality, providing students with an increasing appreciation of the world around them.

10. Materials should encourage affective responses and further humanistic concerns.

In addition to these generic suggestions for selecting nonprint media, more specific considerations should be made when selecting computer software. Radencich (1991) compiled suggestions for developers of computer software, and these sugges- tions can serve as a guide for consumers as well. They are organized into four categories: educational content, presentation, interaction, and teacher use.

Approved by the International Reading Association board of directors, May 1984. Reprinted with the permission of the International Reading Association.

Software Evaluation Suggestions

Educational Content

_____ Content is planned, sequential, and original.

_____ Concepts and vocabulary are of a consistent level of difficulty.

_____ Recall of prior learning is encouraged.

_____ Remediation is differentiated from review.

_____ Pretests are included.

_____ Evaluation components are included.

Presentation

_____ Presentation is logical and well organized.

_____ Facts are accurately presented.

_____ Grammar, spelling, and usage are correct.

_____ Response and loading time are quick.

_____ Sound enhances but does not distract.

_____ Graphics and color enhance.

_____ Screen display is clear.

_____ Menus are descriptive.

_____ Score is displayed.

_____ A help option is provided.

_____ "Crashing" safeguards are included.

_____ Exiting and reentering are easy.

_____ Sufficient component parts are included.

_____ Violence and sarcasm are avoided.

_____ The presentation is motivating and challenging.

Interaction

_____ The difficulty level can be controlled.

_____ Entries can be corrected.

_____ Waiting signals are clear.

_____ Cues and prompts fade to help the user answer questions.

_____ There is a range of appropriate responses.

_____ Intermittent reinforcement is provided.

_____ Specific feedback is provided for errors.

_____ Personalized responses are provided.

Teacher Use

_____ Minimal teacher monitoring is needed.

_____ Software can be modified to meet individual needs.

_____ Alternative learning opportunities are suggested.

_____ Data trail is provided.

Adapted from "Publishing Computer Software." by M. C. Radencich, in J. Baumann & D. Johnson (Eds.), *Writing for Publication* (pp. 176–178) (Newark, DE: International Reading Association, 1991). Reprinted with permission of the International Reading Association.

Other Supplementary Reading/Writing Materials

Supplementary materials should support genuine literacy tasks rather than fragment instruction. But the latter is what they all too often do. Frequent culprits in fragmentation are workbooks, dittos, and carefully paced programs in reading kits. This occurs despite a strong recommendation from *Becoming a Nation of Readers,* the Report of the Commission on Reading (Anderson, Hiebert, Scott, & Wilkinson, 1985), that time completing workbook pages be decreased. Jachym, Allington, and Broikou (1989) actually computed the cost of seatwork in terms of personnel time for duplicating, paper, and the like, and found that administrators underestimated the costs associated with seatwork. Costs added up to an average of $60 per student (a range among five schools from $29 to $102). If teachers insist on using workbooks, dittos, and kits, the following guidelines (Osborn, 1984, pp. 110–111) can be used.

Some Guidelines for Workbook Tasks

1. Workbook activities should match the instruction and learning occurring in the lesson.

2. Workbook activities should provide a systematic, cumulative, and meaningful review of instruction.

3. Workbook activities should match the most important learning occurring in the reading program.

4. Workbooks should provide relevant tasks for students needing extra practice.

5. The vocabulary and concepts of workbook activities should correlate with the experiential and conceptual background of the students and the series itself.

6. Language used in the workbook should be consistent with that of the instructional process.

7. Instructions for the completion of workbook activities should be clear and easy to understand. Students should be helped with practice examples to ensure that they understand the tasks.

8. The layout of the pages should be attractive and useful.

9. There should be enough content to ensure learning.

10. Workbook content should be accurate and precise.

11. Some workbook activities should be recreational in nature.

12. Students should respond in a consistent manner from one workbook activity to another.

13. There should be a close correlation between reading and writing response modes.

14. Discussions and illustrations should accompany workbook activities.

Aside from workbooks and kits, other types of materials that may or may not be supplementary materials include thematic units; trade books, perhaps with instructors' guides; sets of predictable books; and games. Potential buyers of supplementary materials can ask publishers' representatives for samples or demonstrations of the materials under consideration, or they can examine materials in the displays at professional conferences.

Controversial Instructional Materials

Controversial reading programs surface regularly. It is incumbent on instructional leaders to review such materials carefully and to read any published research and opinion on these materials before making decisions. The programs that engender the most controversy at the time of this writing are the following.

Hooked on Phonics. Claims of this widely advertised phonics program have been criticized by IRA (International Reading Association, 1991b), the Council of Better Business Bureaus (International Reading Association, 1991a), and others (Cunningham, 1992) including strong phonics proponent Jeanne Chall (Kantrowitz, 1991). I know of no published research on this program as of the date of this writing.

Mastery Learning/DISTAR. MF2-5SRA's Mastery Learning, based on DISTAR (Bereiter & Englemann, 1966) is a teacher-scripted program for reading instruction. It has been criticized as incompatible with process writing (Walmsley & Adams, 1993) and as relying almost exclusively on a single approach—a phonics approach that is of questionable value (Cunningham, 1992). For references to DISTAR success, see Meyer, Gersten, and Gutkin (1984).

Writing to Read. This IBM program has received much press, both positive (Nelms, 1990) and negative, with proponents citing gains in student writing and opponents citing methodological flaws in studies that have favored the program (Freyd & Lytle, 1990a, 1990b) and findings of no long-term difference between use of Writing to Read and of general good writing programs (Fairfax County Public Schools, 1988).

In evaluating controversial programs, the reviewer should consider the following:

- Has the material itself been carefully examined, or has the reviewer been guided by testimonials and advertising? If possible, the reviewer should interview teachers who use the material.

- Does the material make claims that seem too good to be true?

- Has there been independently conducted research to support the program? Has any research been published in a refereed journal? Has any research been longitudinal to measure results over a period of years?

- Were typical methodological flaws accounted for in any research? Was the selection of subjects random? Did students with and without the program receive instruction that was comparable in terms of factors such as length of time, amount of staff development, and teacher/pupil ratio? Is there evidence that the program was truly implemented as designed? Was there control for the novelty effect in terms of length of implementation or comparability between two novel programs? Was there control for regression toward the mean, the statistical phenomenon that results in the lowest scores automatically being higher (and closer to the mean) on a subsequent testing?

- Is it possible that some of the principles behind the program are effective but others are not?

- Is the program's cost (materials, staff development, class size) worth the investment?

It is the responsibility of a district supervisor to keep information on controversial programs and to supply the information to schools on request or as otherwise needed. Several Florida districts sent to all schools a set of articles regarding one controversial program, with a cover memorandum simply stating that the articles were provided for school review.

Implementing a New Reading Program

Effective use of new reading programs starts with preimplementation inservice training for administrators and teachers and orientation for parents. Staff development is most effective if conducted once teachers have their own materials in their hands so they can attach Post-It notes, paper clips, and the like. Escambia County, a small Florida district, has been able to spend an entire week training all teachers before implementation, to the point where teachers leave with a week's worth of personal lesson plans.

Many schools follow initial training with help, perhaps a couple of months later, when questions begin to arise. It is important also for support to continue throughout the life of the series, particularly for new teachers and administrators, but for those who have used the series as well. Make arrangements for using ongoing support services available from publishers. Monitor program implementation so that adaptations can be made as soon as possible.

Supervisors and school-based administrators who make a point of teaching lessons from a new series will be forever grateful that they did so. Doing this will not only help you understand the nuances of the program in order to be better able to explain them to teachers, but it will also help you feel secure and give you credibility when you help teachers with their implementation.

Aside from outside support, teachers must take responsibility, too, for their own learning. The favorite admonition of Becky Williams in her years as reading supervisor in Broward County, Florida, was, "Read your manual"!

See Chapter 3 for staff development suggestions.

Managing Materials

An organized program will have a system for managing materials. Here are some considerations for textbook management:

- What materials will be ordered? Workbooks? Trade books? Grade-level materials for all teachers? Extra easy materials to allow all students, as Bill Martin says, "to zoom through with joyous familiarity" (Cullinan, Greene, & Jaggar, 1990)?

- If workbooks are ordered, will they be used consummably? Caution should be exercised here. It has been estimated that, despite the questionable value of most worksheets (Anderson et al., 1985) the average first-grader completes 1,000 worksheets in reading/language arts.

- Will the texts be collected at the end of the year? The time involved in this process must be weighed against the need to be sure that all teachers have the materials they need in the fall. If teachers at a grade level or within a department handle sharing well, the collecting should not be necessary, and an inventory count should suffice.

- Will school-year texts be used in summer school also? Teachers may wish to save these texts for the following year. This can be advisable if the resulting summer program is more enriched than would have been the case with school-year texts. Thus, a summer focus on interdisciplinary themes would be much more enriching than a summer using old basal readers.

Dealing with Censorship Issues

When using trade books in the curriculum, districts and schools must be well prepared to deal with censorship issues. The following quotes paint the picture:

"Huck Finn and Holden Caulfield were again expelled from schools last year . . ."

"Parents said One Hundred Years of Solitude *by Nobel Prize winner Gabriel García Marquez should be removed from a required summer reading list for twelfth grade honors students because it was 'garbage' that depicted incest and was anti-Christian . . ."*

"So there was Little Red Riding Hood, merrily skipping to Grandma's house with a basket of goodies (including the evil flask of wine that Granny uses solely for medicinal purposes, of course) . . ."

With the diversity of values and viewpoints in our multicultural society, some conflict over values is inevitable. Newspapers abound with articles on censorship attacks. Many come from well-organized and powerful fundamentalist groups such as Citizens for Excellence in Education (CEE) (Hill, 1992). Hill cites a recent CEE publication, *Reinventing America's Schools*, as taking on educational reforms such as year-round schooling, outcome-based learning, site-based management, and multiculturalism. Hill cites as an example a conversation with Simonds, the author of the 1985 booklet on *How to Elect Christians to Public Office*, in which Simonds states that global education "seeks to alter a student's thinking and training away from patriotism, traditional family values, America's free-enterprise system, and capitalism." Marzano (1987), whose *Tactics for Thinking* has come under attack from CEE, points out six common educational innovations that have been criticized and labeled as New Age by Simonds and members of CEE: self-esteem programs, cooperative learning, global education, the use of imagery, gifted education programs, and whole language (Hill, 1992). Shannon (1991) writes passionately of his concerns over this type of censorship.

Instructional leaders cam help deflect censorship if they are aware of and address key censorship issues for schools (O'Neal, 1990):

1. *Self-Censorship.* Many teachers and library/media specialists attempt to censor prior to a controversy's emerging. O'Neal (p. 772) asks: "By providing access only to that literature that does not discuss sex, politics, violence, or question the role of the adult, what are we doing to children's minds?"

Publishing companies also exercise self-censorship. As editors of basal series include more authentic literature, they may find it difficult to include realistic fiction set in the present day. Pieces of literature such as Katherine Paterson's *Bridge to Terabithia,* which are frequently found on shelves of intermediate classrooms, do not make their way into basal readers. *Bridge to Terabithia* contains two small paragraphs that refer to the Bible.

2. *Policy.* Though not a panacea, library policies can be powerful. O'Neal (1990, p. 772) cites the example of Pinellas County, Florida, a very conservative community in which the school board had the courage to support unanimously the right for a controversial book to remain on their library shelves. Their stance indicated that, although parents have the right to restrict what their own child reads, they do not have the right to restrict what all children read. O'Neal feels that probably the strength of the Pinellas policy lies not only in its broad scope (guidelines both for the selection of books and for filing complaints) but also in its formality. Where policies work, they are endorsed by the school board rather than developed by a single teacher or librarian. Such policies tell parents that a district has thoughtfully considered the significance of controversial books and has provided alternatives for parents who object to their use.

3. *Roles of administrators/librarians/teachers/parents.* Nancy Spaulding, library and media supervisor in Round Rock, Texas (O'Neal, 1990, p. 773), celebrates those parents who monitor their children's consumption of media. She negotiates censorship with concerned parents; there is always some choice. Albert Meloy, superintendent of the Adrian (Michigan) schools, emphasizes the importance of respecting others' views even if those views seem bizarre. He points out that by showing respect and taking parents' concerns seriously, "you neutralize emotions that can lead to hostility" (Willis, 1992, p. 5). Marjorie Ledell, an education consultant and school board member in Littleton, Colorado, advises that schools "create as many open forums as possible." Often, protesting parents feel they have been shut out of educational decisions that affect their children (Willis, 1992, p. 5).

O'Neal suggests that collaboration among administrators, librarians, parents, and teachers take a number of forms. Parents and community members can inquire about how instructional materials are selected and used. They can also serve on committees dealing with book challenges, book selection, and book evaluation. Administrators can see that classroom libraries as well as school libraries/media centers be addressed in the district policy. They can also provide staff development on the content and procedures of the policy. Teachers can provide parents with book lists early in the school year and invite them to read the books themselves. They should work with their library/media specialist when selecting materials; should provide options; and, as warned by Lillian Gerhart, editor-in-chief of the *School Library Journal* (O'Neal, 1990, p. 773), should read from cover to cover those books they will be using as required reading.

For further support on this issue, join the censorship special interest group of the International Reading Association, or see *Common Ground: The National Council of Teachers of English and the International Reading Association Speak with One Voice on Intellectual Freedom and the Defense of It.* This pamphlet provides action plans and strategies for use at the local, state, and national levels. Single copies are available free with a self-addressed, stamped business-size envelope. Bulk orders are also available. Contact Public Information Office, International Reading Association, P.O. Box 8139, Newark, DE 19714-8139.

Conclusion

This chapter has focused on analysis and improvement of the curriculum. It is a task that cannot be underestimated. Edelsky (1992) reminds us that embedded in every textbook, every standardized test, every basal reader is a political perspective. Supervisors and administrators must not be afraid of being political and taking proactive stances in decisions that affect what our students will learn.

Chapter *3*

Analyzing and Improving Instruction

> We have come to understand that change comes from teachers' own initiatives, some of which we spark, some of which other persons or events ignite.
>
> —Rhodes and Shanklin (Weaver, 1990, p. 275)

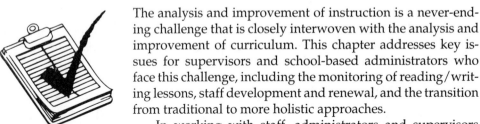 The analysis and improvement of instruction is a never-ending challenge that is closely interwoven with the analysis and improvement of curriculum. This chapter addresses key issues for supervisors and school-based administrators who face this challenge, including the monitoring of reading/writing lessons, staff development and renewal, and the transition from traditional to more holistic approaches.

In working with staff, administrators and supervisors must decide on overall tactics—to be or not to be assertive, or to be somewhere in between. Some school-based administrators find it wise not to rock the boat as they establish themselves in a new school. Others are comfortable immediately sending the message that reading/writing *will* be important and, with a lot of assertiveness as well as "warm fuzzies," quickly move a faculty to give their best. One principal started frequent grade-level inservice for all teachers. Those grade levels that were less responsive would continue to see on monthly bulletins that they were to gather in grade-level meetings. Because there was a lot of caring, too, the strategy proved successful. Different leadership styles and different faculties will dictate different tactics.

For district supervisors, the issue is similar. If you are visiting classrooms, you might encourage the principal to have teachers sign up. In that case, you will probably see only the most secure teachers. Or you might ask to see a range of teaching practices. If you engage in a program review, do you "soft-pedal" your findings, or are you more blunt? If you make several visits to a school, do you meet regularly with the teachers who are interested or do you keep trying with those who would rather be left alone? Again, consider your leadership style as well as the faculty involved.

Monitoring Reading/Writing Lessons

Administrators and supervisors who spend time visiting classrooms will learn much that will escape those who do not. Find ways of making both brief and extended classroom visits to support and to monitor teachers and students. Teachers who learn to expect such visits will become more comfortable with them as time goes on. Some, indeed, will post "visitor guides" that succinctly explain a teacher's philosophy and describe the activities a visitor can expect to see along with their rationale (Bird, 1989). Bird (1991) finds that visitor guides' real value lies in the incentive they have given teachers to reflect through writing what they really believe about teaching and learning.

Informal Monitoring

Much information about the culture of classrooms can be gleaned in quick visits. A simple look at posted student work, ongoing lesson plans, student involvement with the task at hand, classroom arrangement, and what the teacher is doing can give a trained eye a good picture of priorities, pacing, organization, and student engagement. But an extended visit provides an opportunity to observe the sequence and flow of activities, to question teacher and students informally, and to check out initial impressions.

Take advantage of visits for pats on the back. Tessa Gold, when she was principal at Rockway Elementary in Dade County, Florida, took snapshots of classrooms and posted them. The tradition continued after she left; it was not unheard of for a note to be written asking that "a snapshot be taken of my class whenever it is convenient"!

Formal Monitoring

For purposes of formal monitoring, supervisors and administrators might develop a short list of observable criteria. Vogt's (1991) observation guide will be most helpful for elementary schools and, with a few adaptations, for middle and senior high schools as well. The Program Review form in Appendix C can be used for a formal review of the school program. Program reviews focus not on individual teachers but on the strengths and weaknesses of the program as a whole. Program reviews can be done in house or by district teams of specialists. For an in-house review, a planning meeting can be held to explain the procedure to the entire faculty. Then selected faculty members can be trained in how to visit classrooms and interview faculty, parents, and students. After the review, the faculty is given feedback. A follow-up review can be conducted the following year to evaluate growth. For a district review, grade levels or departments can fill in the review form ahead of time so that their perceptions form part of the review process. Then, during the review, faculty representatives can be on hand to respond to visitors' questions.

When planning for formal teacher observations, school administrators should consider the message they send in their choice of subject areas to observe. When Tessa Gold first moved from Rockway to Kendale Elementary, she wanted the faculty to feel free to take risks. She told the teachers that she would do no observations that year in the reading/language arts block. That year, she monitored literacy through more informal means.

Self-Evaluation

Self-evaluation is, of course, an invaluable form of monitoring. Although the forms previously mentioned can be used for self-evaluation, educators at all levels may find Johnston and Wilder's (1992) Reading/Writing/Learning Self-Evaluation Form particularly useful because it was developed specifically for this purpose.

Staff Development and Renewal

"Inservice is something that everyone agrees some-one else needs" (Barnard & Hetzel, 1986, p. 65). Humor aside, one of your key ongoing jobs will be to foment professional growth and renewal among your colleagues. Some are hungry for any new information that they can get, but others must be coaxed.

Staff development to improve instruction starts with an understanding of the nature of adult learning. Palmer and Associates (1988) describe the process of adult learning as one of "intense curiosity coupled with problem solving" (p. 5). Adults make conscious decisions to accept or reject new ideas as they measure them against their experience. Lambert (1989) identifies four factors that facilitate teacher empowerment: *awareness* of available options, *freedom* to exercise choices, *authority* (shared leadership), and *responsibility* for professional development.

The following suggestions incorporate these factors of teacher empowerment in staff development efforts.

Guidelines for Setting Up Staff Development

Just as artists set out their materials with utmost care, so too must you prepare for staff development. Neilsen's quotes (1991, p. 676) paint a vivid picture of what can go wrong otherwise:

- Why is this article in my mailbox? Are you trying to tell me something about my teaching, or what?

- Who's got time to read this foolishness?

- This stuff is just common sense—I'm doing most of it already.

- So, what's this? Are we supposed to drop the latest trend and switch to this one?

Neilsen goes on to complain: "It's ironic. Isn't it? Our work as teachers is to foster a lifelong love for learning, to make learning contagious. But it seems, like the virus chicken pox, the virus is more acceptable in the young."

Barnard and Hetzel (1986, p. 65) do not mince words when they speak of the "dismal" history of inservice programs. Inservice has too often done something *to* people rather than *with* them. Much of it does not take into account the problems of teachers' isolation, their reluctance to change, or the needs of the adult learner. But even if your staff development is a class act, you will encounter resistance. There's often the feeling that if you need staff development, then you must be doing something wrong. This, of course, is unfortunate, because we can always profit from new twists in exercising the sophisticated art form of teaching. For middle and senior high school content area teachers, the resistance can be particularly strong (see O'Brien & Stewart, 1990).

Bird (1991) likens good staff development to the same principles she espouses for whole language instruction: trust that learning will take place, ownership of the goals and the means selected for achieving them, time for change, meaning for each participant—beginning where each is at, and interaction. These principles permeate this chapter.

Much of what is said in the next chapter regarding the change process applies also to staff development. Following are additional staff development guidelines written especially with school-based administrators in mind but applicable to supervisors as well.

School-Based Administrators' Tips: Staff Development

1. Start with an open-ended needs assessment and/or with your school's philosophy of literacy education. A needs assessment might allow for inservice delivery options (would like literature on the topic, a brief explanation, time set aside in meetings to read and discuss articles, a hands-on experience, or an ongoing training program). Ownership is essential! See Appendix C for a sample "Staff Development Needs Assessment."

2. Focus on the goal. With a firm philosophy or a mission statement in hand, the goal should be clear. Otherwise, it is easy to fall into the pattern of inviting several exciting speakers, each with a different focus. One assistant principal found that none of the previously developed district inservice components for reading met her goals, so she wrote an inservice component of her own. In one district, a team of district resource specialists focused on developing holistic teaching programs with six to eight teachers at a time for about six weeks. Focus is crucial if a goal is to be reached.

3. Consider establishing a professional growth committee. The mere existence of such a committee means the staff agrees that additional training is an inherent part of the profession of teaching (Barnard & Hetzel, 1986).

4. Determine whether inservice training is a logical answer to your need. Inservice training is appropriate when you are looking for an increase in knowledge or skill or an improvement in attitude, but is not likely to be helpful if the problem is, for example, a lack of materials or gross incompetence (Barnard & Hetzel, 1986).

5. Be certain there is a match between the goals and the type of session presented. Is the session intended to give information? develop skills? change behavior? (Korinek, Schmid, & McAdams, 1985).

6. Think carefully about any consultants you bring in. Yvonne Freeman (Weaver, 1990, p. 281) offers some points to consider: "Outside consultants may make a big difference even though their message . . ." may be the same as "what the school inservice people have been saying ('A prophet in his own land . . .'). Consultants must be prepared to make theory *palatable*. . . . It is important that consultants give teachers lots of classroom examples of real teachers in real classrooms." Make sure that any invited speakers know your needs and are willing and able to meet them. Also, if possible, listen to consultants speak ahead of time to ensure that their message and delivery are both appropriate and interesting.

7.   Be careful about using staff members to present. This can be effective at times, but the "good old boy" or "the one who got to go to the last convention" just may not be the one to conduct the program. Mention the proposed presenter's name; if you get groans, get someone else (Barnard & Hetzel, 1986).

8.   Send attractive agendas to teachers prior to meetings. Use borders or other clip art, and jazz up your titles. "Ring in the New Year!" is much more inviting than "January Meeting."

9.   Plan the schedule carefully. If possible, have meetings during the day, as in the business world, rather than after school. If there will be several sessions, space them out logically. Teachers may need time to apply something they have learned before they return for more information.

10.   Plan the location with care. If tables are needed, find a place where they will be available. Avoid rooms with malfunctioning heating or air conditioning. In one elementary school, meetings are rotated around different classes. For a couple of minutes at each meeting, the teacher highlights exciting events in that classroom. (This is a good way to motivate teachers to have something special to share.)

One middle school held a staff retreat in a hotel on a Saturday. The relaxed atmosphere was reminiscent of a social occasion rather than work. No phone calls interrupted the meeting. Another school starts the year with an informal planning session during a family picnic at the beach.

11.   Serve refreshments.

12.   Consider the advantages and disadvantages of mandated attendance and make a careful decision.

Here are two opinions:

Rhodes and Shanklin discuss a plan in the Denver public schools (Weaver, 1990) in which all teachers were required to participate in staff development but could choose their option each year. Some selected staff development that encouraged great change, others opted for staff development that eased them into reconsidering literacy instruction, and the most reluctant gradually began to take risks, with their confidence bolstered by the successes of colleagues who had risked change earlier. Rhodes and Shanklin point out (p. 275) that "not until teachers enjoy the power of making decisions and solving their own problems will they encourage students to do the same."

Mary Snow (Weaver, 1990) believes that Don Holdaway's conviction that "voluntarism is at the heart of change" represents his respect for adults as learners, similar to the respect he has for children as learners. "If we are not going to violate children by dictating the terms under which they will learn, we certainly shouldn't violate the adults who are responsible for them" (p. 277).

13. Personalize staff development when possible. Some sessions may be needed only by beginning teachers. Some may apply only to primary grades.

14. Try hard to attend major staff development sessions along with any other school administrators. It makes all the difference in terms of morale, attention, and follow-up. *Exception*: Stay away on occasions when you feel your teachers need an opportunity to vent without your being there.

15. Try hard to avoid combining a faculty meeting with a presentation and thus rushing a speaker into giving a too-brief presentation.

16. Avoid one-shot deals. Blackburn Elementary, the Florida winner of the International Reading Association's 1990–1991 Exemplary Reading Program Award in Manatee County, worked for two years with a regular consultant as they adopted a holistic approach to teaching. This allowed for ample opportunities for follow-up, practice, feedback, coaching, and celebrating. One highlight of their celebration was a bulletin board with conference ribbons from faculty members' many presentations! Plan for a long-term effort—three or four years minimum—for significant change (Michigan Reading Association, 1990).

17. For a multisession activity, reassess the program as the sessions progress. If it is not serving its purpose, it may be better to end the training than to subject teachers to a waste of time and energy (Barnard & Hetzel, 1986).

18. Model and encourage teachers to keep a journal, writing before, during, or after a meeting as a tool to aid reflection (Linda Henke, in Weaver, 1990).

19. Make use of summers when appropriate. Teachers at one middle school knew that a condition of summer school employment was participation in staff development. At one elementary school, summer school teachers regularly stay late for inservice sessions a couple of afternoons a week and go home early on other afternoons.

20. Provide teachers with an evaluation form and encourage them to comment on the most effective parts of the training.

21. After an inservice activity, try to ascertain if it was effective for the purpose intended. The ultimate judgment is in observing whether what was provided in training is in fact, being incorporated in the classroom (Barnard & Hetzel, 1986).

For more information on setting up staff development, see Sharp's (1993) workshop facilitator's handbook or the ASCD guide to school-based staff development (Wood et al., 1993).

What to Do Before, During, and After Classroom Demonstrations

Teachers often welcome classroom demonstrations by fellow teachers, school-based administrators, supervisors, or guest consultants. As Neilsen (1991, p. 677) says so well, "in literacy learning just as in marriage, parenting, or leadership, . . . demonstrations teach us more than words can ever say. And when we don't demonstrate what we advocate, our chances for a conversation based on trust go right out the window."

When demonstrations have not been requested by teachers, they must be handled with utmost tact. Sometimes demonstrations can be approached in this way: "Will you *let* me use your class to practice this strategy I've just heard about?" Sometimes they can be done first in rooms of department heads or grade chairs, so that no one sees the demonstration as something being done only for weak teachers. Indeed, when demonstrations are done first for stronger teachers, others may ask why they're not getting the same service!

Before a demonstration, the demonstrator should make appropriate preparations. For a requested demonstration, this might include the following:

- Making sure the teacher feels comfortable with the teaching style to be used and that the style complements the material being taught

- Suggesting a couple of strategies to model so that the teacher might evaluate which he or she considers more appropriate

- Carefully preparing the material and checking it out with the teacher to make sure the teacher's needs were understood correctly

- Planning follow-up time to discuss the lessson

- Preparing folded cards on which students can put their names to help with communication during the lesson

- Considering whether the lesson should be videotaped for purposes of discussion and for future viewing

For demonstrations intended for a group of educators, these procedures would, of course, be modified.

During a demonstration, the demonstrator should make sure that the observer(s) have all necessary material to understand the lesson (e.g., lesson plan, teacher's guide if appropriate). The demonstrator should feel free to consult with the class's teacher if necessary.

After a demonstration, a critique should follow. Student opinion might be solicited as well. A later date could be set for a lesson in which the roles were reversed.

Other suggestions for demonstrations will depend on who the demonstrator is. If, for example, the demonstrator is a reading resource specialist (RRS), an additional tip might be to grade any assignments given in order to send home the message that the RRS is there to lessen rather than increase workloads.

Keeping Educators Informed of Professional Growth Opportunities

A key weapon in your staff development arsenal is that of keeping educators informed of professional growth opportunities. This section provides some pointers.

When you try to "sell" professional journals or professional meetings, put yourself in the place of an advertiser. Think of what advertisers say, how they say it, and how often they say it. With a short and sweet message, advertisers tell you—over and over again—*why* you want their product. (Effective advertisers cleverly avoid antagonizing you with this repetition.) The following tips should help:

Tips: Informing Educators of Professional Growth Opportunities

District and School Site

- "Remove the label." Neilsen (1991) says that "using labels and trendy jargon" (e.g., "whole language") "can shut down a conversation as quickly as it began. . . . If we wear a role like the latest designer label, we may appear more like a copy than the real thing."

- Give highlighted articles to target educators. One supervisor hooked a legislator into reading something lengthy by highlighting enticing points.

- Get others to help you with the advertising so that teachers hear the same message from a variety of sources.

- Announce professional growth opportunities in a newsletter or, at the school site, through the public address system as well as through mailboxes or special sections on bulletin boards. At one elementary school, a whole bulletin board was dedicated to advertising an upcoming conference.

- Highlight teachers who are doing something special in newsletters or by encouraging them to present alone or with you at conferences.

- When resources are limited, consider carefully who you will target. Maybe the department head or the reading specialist doesn't need to go to a conference this time. Perhaps someone else needs a turn.

- Ask teachers who attend workshops and conferences to share with at least one self-selected buddy upon their return. Sharing reinforces learning. Although sharing with an entire grade level, department, or team can be optimal, it often ends up being superficial. Sharing with just one buddy may be more like gossip ("Guess what I just heard"), which gets more play and may result in greater learning.

- Copy the idea of one reading resource specialist: Put blurbs about reading in strategic places—like the restrooms. If this seems too outlandish, use the space next to the sign-in sheet. The district reading specialist put them in the board office restrooms!

School Site

- Ask that journals that are a few months old be moved from the school library/media center to the teachers' lounge. Some teachers are not likely to go to the school library but may peruse these journals in the lounge. As an alternative, ask that the journals be cut up so that articles can be filed thematically for further use.

- Provide release time and, if possible, expenses for teachers to attend conferences. Consider a fund-raising effort if necessary. One principal paid registration fees at a local conference for all teachers who had paid membership dues!

- Get a group of teachers to start traveling conversation books (Neilsen, 1991, p. 676) to serve "as forums for reading, writing, and talking with other teachers and administrators (parents and students, too!). The books—three-ring binders or sheaves with large clips—quickly grow fat and dog-eared as teachers exchange and respond to articles about literacy instruction, report on interesting professional news, and write about their classroom stories, challenges, joys, and frustrations."

Be on the lookout for possibilities to keep teachers informed. Publishers sometimes sponsor staff development events. In some districts, unions have assumed some responsibility for professional development (Hill & Bonan, 1991). And don't forget the simplest professional growth opportunity of all—the classroom. View teachers as active constructors of their own knowledge about learning and teaching (Nolan & Francis, 1992), knowledge that can be gleaned in everyday encounters with learning.

Teacher as Decision Maker and Teacher as Researcher

A sometimes unrecognized form of self-initiated renewal is action research. For many teachers, however, "research" is a four-letter word. The roots of this negative image are not hard to find. Researchers have communicated to teachers in subtle and not so subtle ways that it is the teacher's task to implement, not generate, research findings. Researchers have also communicated that teachers' research questions are not as well grounded as those of "experts" and that teachers' questions about their own classrooms are not particularly important. University researchers often present their findings in a format that is technical and uninviting (Schumm, Konopak, Readence, & Baldwin, 1989). Finally, when teachers cooperate as research subjects, they often are not provided with results.

In recent years, major strides have been taken in education to close the chasm between research and practice (Olson, 1990; Strickland, 1988). Indeed, the teacher-as-researcher movement has emerged to involve teachers in a more active role as members of the research community. Jerome Harste (1990) sees three major themes in this movement:

- Teachers have a voice which needs to be heard.

- Teachers and university researchers must communicate on an ongoing basis if research is ever to be reality-based.

- A new vision of a community of learners (children, parents, teachers, administrators, and university personnel) must emerge.

The advantages of involving teachers as researchers are many:

- It creates among teachers and researchers a problem-solving mindset that helps teachers when they consider other classroom dilemmas.

- It improves teachers' decision-making processes.

- It elevates teachers in their professional status.

- It reduces teacher isolation.

- It empowers teachers to influence their own profession at classroom, district, state, and national levels.

- It eliminates the weakness of relying on the leader alone as a reflective practitioner; one person often cannot directly observe the consequences of choices in a complex organization (Senge, 1990a).

- It offers the ultimate advantage of providing the potential for improving education for children.

By now, many of you may be thinking, "This all sounds great, but how can I convince already overtaxed teachers to become involved in research efforts?" Indeed, action research isn't for everybody. But for teachers who do raise questions, it helps to remind them that "most of the knowledge that defines the field [of English language arts] today has come from work that began with teachers asking questions in their own classrooms. . . . Some of the most valuable classroom research begins with small questions, with the wonderings of individual teachers as they engage in day-to-day work with their students" (Kutz, 1992, pp. 193–195). Judson (1980) points out that teachers who truly reflect about their classroom practice essentially experience the scientist's *"acute discomfort* at incomprehension . . . the rage to know" (p. 5, emphasis in the original).

Teacher research is being increasingly seen as a unique genre of research:

> *Experimental researchers strive for valid and reliable measures in order to assume generalizable results; naturalistic researchers seek trustworthiness and authenticity in order to uncover the social rules for the situations they describe. In contrast, teacher researchers seek to understand the particular individuals, actions, policies, and events that make up their work and work environment in order to make professional decisions. . . . (Patterson & Shannon, 1993, pp. 7–8).*

Action-based research can occur in many different forms, ranging from informal to highly structured. It may simply be telling a story. After all, what is a narrative about a classroom if not storytelling?

> *Story-telling is the mode of description best suited to transformation in new situations of action. . . . A reflective teacher builds her repertoire of teaching experiences, not as methods or principles to be applied like a template to new situations, but as stories that function like metaphors, projective models to be*

transformed and validated through on-the-spot experiment in the next situation (Schon, 1988, p. 22).

For example, Atwell's (1991) third annual edited volume, *Workshop The Politics of Process*, starts with a letter to parents from a fifth-grade teacher in which she reflects on her child's first day of school each year, her own childhood memories, and stories from previous years of teaching. For her, action research begins with reflection, a skill that has not often been the focus of programs for educators (Fox & Singletary, 1986). Reflection may occur through a journal, perhaps a dialogue journal, to organize thinking about one's teaching. Examples of dialogue journals might include sharing by a superintendent and a supervisor or principal; by a principal and a supervisor, fellow principal, or teacher; by a teacher and a peer or a student. Reflection may occur through video and audiotaping. Sixth-grade teacher Pat Yencho (Bird, 1991) thus studied her literature study sessions. Bird writes of other teachers taping and then reflecting on their writing workshops.

Reflection can involve a teacher working independently or a teacher collaborating with students, a fellow teacher, an administrator, or a university researcher. But the core of classroom action research is simply trying out something different in the classroom and reflecting about the results (as teachers do on a regular basis), and then taking it one step further by recording the results—in short, figuring out what works!

Judith Green (1987) has suggested a seven-step plan for action research:

1. Identify an issue, interest, or concern.

2. Seek knowledge.

3. Plan an action.

4. Implement an action.

5. Observe the action.

6. Reflect on the observations.

7. Revise the plan.

No complicated statistical procedures are used unless the individual teacher elects to do so. Action research is what many risk-taking teachers have done for years. See Hubbard and Power (1993) if you need a source for research design and data analysis aimed at teacher-researchers.

If you or your teachers are interested in initiating an action research program, how might you get started? Perhaps you can encourage a couple of teachers to network by observing each other's classrooms. Or foster a collaboration in which a teacher and a student teacher record and share systematic classroom observations (Kutz, 1992). Or encourage teachers to work with their students to create collaborative research communities. Beyond these initial strategies, other possibilities can be tackled. Some school districts and local professional organizations are now offering grants for classroom-based research (see "Grant Writing" in Appendix C). Many university professors are now structuring course components to provide initial training in research procedures. Professional conference programs include collaborative presentations between university researchers and teachers. Ethical guidelines for such collaborative research have been proposed (Allen, Buchanan, Edelsky, & Norton, 1992). There are university researchers who are anxious to meet other professionals willing to plunge into this exciting new world.

Professional publications are now available that outline basic tenets of the teacher-as-researcher movement, provide examples of existing efforts (Brandt, 1991; Olson, 1990; Samuels & Pearson, 1988; Santa, Isaacson, & Manning, 1987; Pinnell & Matlin, 1989), and provide specific suggestions for how to put your thoughts into print (Baumann & Johnson, 1991; McDonnell, Frey, & Smith, 1991). The International Reading Association has organized a teacher-as-researcher special interest group and has run columns on action research in its newsletter, *Reading Today*. The National Council of Teachers of English provides teacher-as-researcher grants. Following are some examples of action research projects:

- One example of an individual teacher's research effort is that of Marcia Truitt, a reading resource specialist at American Senior High in Dade County. She was the first recipient of the Florida Reading Association's Action Research Award. She sought to find out whether reading comprehension would improve if students had the opportunity to take a novel home and highlight main ideas and details. She reasoned that because high school students are not allowed to write in their texts, they do not develop the highlighting skills necessary for success in college. Although her results were inconclusive, Truitt had at least taken the first steps to answer a question that was of interest to her. With the help of her supervisor, she wrote up her results and then shared them at a conference.

- When Philip Balbi was a second-grade teacher at Biscayne Elementary in Dade County, his class included three students who had experienced little success in reading, two of them limited-English-proficient. Balbi's findings revealed that using a language experience approach proved beneficial in improving the students' reading and spelling. His research was eventually shared at conferences and was published (Balbi, 1986).

Teacher-as-researcher projects are not for everyone, but on every faculty there will be at least one teacher who is ready for this challenge.

Staff Development Models That Have Worked

Following is a breakdown of some models of staff development that may serve as starting points for your school or district.

Gradual Release Model. Good teaching implies a gradual release of responsibility from teacher to student. It is as applicable to an instructional leader working with other educators as it is to any other teaching situation. Think of a teacher initially taking charge of all stages of learning, from modeling and guided practice to application, and gradually releasing responsibility in reverse order for application, then guided practice, and finally modeling (Gordon, 1985). This responsibility is released with the learner first explaining a line of reasoning, then answering questions and finding evidence, and finally actually asking the questions.

A variation of this model that one reading resource specialist found to be successful started and ended a series of inservice sessions with a whole group. In between, the RRS models lessons in individual teachers' classes, and these lessons are critiqued. The teachers use the same strategies at later dates, and these lessons, too, are critiqued. Teachers receive inservice credit for all their participation. If there is no RRS, the model could be carried out by another instructional leader.

Mary Snow (Weaver, 1990) states that teachers learning new strategies need a period of self-regulated practice during which, without being observed, they role-play themselves into being a new kind of teacher. This period, too, can be seen as part of a gradual release model.

Coaching. The athletic metaphor of coaching is a fitting one for an instructional leader. When a team of teachers works together to study new skills and polish old ones, coaches can lend support. Coaches provide companionship, give regular technical feedback, help determine appropriate use of the new skill, help to gauge student response to the new technique, and provide emotional support as teachers try new skills in front of students (Alvermann, Moore, & Conley, 1987; Joyce & Showers, 1982).

Coaches need not be single individuals. For example, when one principal has a stronger and a weaker contiguous grade level meet together to discuss their program, this experience can be seen as tacit coaching. Coaching can be mutual. One district director tells of her early teaching experiences, when a teacher would ask a colleague to watch a lesson with some specific focus in mind. If the behavior was monitoring the questioning of girls versus the questioning of boys, the observer would watch and tally only this information on a class map. After the lesson, this information would be discussed. At another date, the favor might be returned.

Coaching has reflective thinking at its core. A study in which two groups of teachers were taught reflective thinking and only one received follow-up coaching found significant differences in teacher behavior (see Sparks-Langer

& Colton, 1991). The research of Joyce, Hersh, and McKibbon (1983) states that, with the *presentation* of theory, there is a maximum of 10 percent retention; adding *demonstration* yields another 10 percent retention; adding *practice* and *feedback* results in 20 percent retention or less; only when coaching for application is added does this figure rise to a maximum of 75 percent. These are powerful figures to support the need for coaching.

Testimony on the value of coaching comes from a Canadian teacher who was amazed at the ease with which he could subsequently speak frankly with a colleague:

> *I remember here thinking, my goodness, I'm, not [faking it] at all, I really am being open and honest, and I was amazed because this represents a change even from the first preconference where I had a feeling of awkwardness about opening up, and now [three observations later] I'm opening up without any degree of discomfort. (Grimmett, Rostad, & Ford, 1992, p. 199).*

Grimmett and colleagues explain that what the teacher implied is that he had been reluctant to open up with a supervisor. Among their other powerful quotes is the following:

> *I feel very supported and very good about this [collegial consultation] happening. It boosts me up, and that is really valuable. I'm not alone in this world. . . . [My advice to other teachers is] find a compatible partner and do it. The rewards are unexpected and powerful. (p. 199)*

Even with coaching, however, results are not guaranteed. Marzano (1987) found in one study that staff development does not result in high levels of implementation of the teaching of thinking processes "even when the staff development program is considered highly useful by participating teachers in a fashion suggested by Joyce and Showers." He states that effectiveness requires that staff development efforts often must "somehow engender a 'paradigm shift' among educators" (p. 9). The Michigan Reading Association (1990, p. 40) lists three criteria essential to such a major restructuring:

- The effort must be *experiential* in that teachers do not simply learn how to teach strategies, but also experience these strategies as learners.

- The effort must be *reflective*, helping teachers analyze their own understandings.

- The effort must also *encompass the broader issues* in the present curriculum and in current assessment practices that constrain effective strategic instructional practices and inhibit the development of the most effective learning environment.

Sometimes coaches are used not only for assistance, but also for assessment, as in Ohio's PAR (peer assistance and review) model (Zimpher &

Grossman, 1992). Potential pitfalls of these models come from administrators who see assessment as their responsibility and from teachers who resist differentiation among teacher roles. Efforts to temper these problems include careful training and use of terms such as *mentor*, which emphasize the assistance rather than the assessment. But the jury is still out on the ultimate effectiveness of plans that use teachers to assess their peers.

Teaching Episode Model. Schumm and Vaughn (1991) used a teaching episode model in which teachers first used dictaphones with think-alouds every time they thought about what they would do in the next week's lesson. The lessons were then videotaped. Finally, teachers participated in stimulated recalls with a university researcher in which the videotapes reminded the teacher of the sequence followed during taping, and allowed the teacher to stop the tape at any segment to explain his or her thinking at that point in time. The same procedure could be followed with the university researcher replaced by an administrator or supervisor.

If there is insufficient time for the school administrator or the supervisor to go through this process, grade chairpersons, reading resource specialists, or department heads could adapt it by first modeling the entire process by planning, executing, and debriefing themselves. Then, with willing volunteer teachers, they could (1) listen with each teacher to his or her audiotaped think-alouds, (2) help each teacher with the videotaping, and (3) go through the debriefing together.

Model Classrooms. Some of the most effective staff development—and some of the least effective—can take place when teachers visit classrooms of their colleagues. This strategy has been used at least since the second half of the nineteenth century (Tanner & Tanner, 1987). Yvonne Freeman (Weaver, 1990, p. 281) advises us that "what teachers see when they visit may surprise or disappoint consultants and administrators, but teachers must be allowed to take away from their experiences what they are ready to notice." On the negative side, "the innovator who gives the appearance of 'having arrived' can quickly become the staff pariah unless he or she is willing to admit to growing pains, mistakes, and false starts" (Neilsen, 1991, p. 676). Thus, the host teacher must be chosen carefully. On the positive side, however, a visitor can walk away from a colleague's room with renewed ideas and zest. This is most likely to occur when:

- The visitor knows what to look for (visiting by pairs of weaker and stronger teachers helps to ensure that the visit is focused).

- The possibility of visiting is open to all teachers and not just to those "in trouble."

- The host teacher is one selected by the visitor.

- There is an opportunity for each visitor to observe more than one teacher in order to have a broader range of target behaviors to choose from in selecting ideas to incorporate in his or her own classroom.

- Host teachers are not necessarily exemplary but are comfortable with some target aspect of instruction and are glad to share this with others.

One elementary school systematized inter- and intraschool visitations by apportioning a month to each grade level. Another arranged for visitations by all teachers when they were initiating a new plan for reading/language arts instruction. Regardless of the plan used, some provision for demonstrations can be a most valuable component of any staff development plan.

Making the Transition from Traditional Approaches to Holistic Instruction

Making the transition from traditional approaches to holistic instruction is a time-consuming process. Suggestions throughout this book should help in this process. Reutzel and Cooter (1992) have written a text aimed at helping teachers in the throes of this transition, a transition that may or may not be equated with "whole language."

Regardless of whether the transition is equated with whole language, it is a transition that is unrealistic to expect of everyone. In the words of one fourth-grade teacher, "I don't think that whole language will ever be understood by a great majority of teachers. . . . It's a philosophy, but it's also a style . . . a style that fits some teachers" (Walmsley & Adams, 1993). Walmsley and Adams organized survey results from 71 teachers regarding the "Realities of Whole Language" into the following headings:

- Whole language instruction is very demanding.

- Whole language alienates and divides.

- It's hard to manage whole language instruction.

- Administrators send mixed messages about whole language.

- Whole language is not compatible with traditional forms of assessment.

- Whole language is hard to define.

- Whole language will survive, but only among the dedicated few.

Part of the difficulty is that the transition involves changes in teachers themselves. An assumption underlying holistic programs is that teachers are model readers and writers for children, a status that may need developing (Atwell, 1987). Graves (1990) suggests that teachers must discover their own literacy if they are to demonstrate and encourage literacy in their students. The same goes for those who mentor teachers.

Another reason that the transition is difficult is the existence of administrative constraints. When teachers explore, does the administration grant institutional waivers? Refrain from holding teachers accountable with standardized test scores? Value goals set by teachers for their own self-improvement?

As with any transition, it is important to take one step at a time. Sometimes it is a matter of starting things off well the first week of school. Teachers might be inspired by Hood's (1989) detailed kidwatching in her "picture" of the first day of her kindergarten class, Jacobson's (1991) summary of her first two days in a second-grade class, or Coles's (1991) description of his first day in a seventh-grade class. Coles, who sees his students for a half day, greets students at the door the first day and throughout the year, allows each student to select a well-stocked desk, and minimally outlines routines. The class discusses expectations and fills out a questionnaire regarding educational experiences, interests, hobbies, and future goals. The students then browse and select a book from the 500+ titles in the classroom library. The students prepare for an activity that requires them to interact in pairs or small groups by discussing and exploring ways to work with others. The class later evaluates the process. Students free-write about a topic of their choice after discussing the nature of free writing and alleviating anxieties. The teacher joins the class as a fellow writer. The teacher reads a short story to the class as part of the daily routine. The students are invited to suggest other materials for him to read. The morning concludes with students being asked to bring personal reading material for silent reading time.

Viewed with a larger lens, transitions involve faculties evaluating where they are and where they would like to go. Faculties undergoing a transition to more holistic instruction may wish to use or adapt the following scale (Hysmith, Lamme, Mason, & Willis, 1990) developed by Blackburn Elementary in Manatee County, the Florida winner of the 1990–1991 International Reading Association's Exemplary Reading Program Award. Resources used in the development of this scale were Hall and Hord (1987) and Heald-Taylor (1989). Note that progression through the stages may not be linear. Teachers may embrace some portions of holistic programs but not others.

Blackburn Teachers' Involvement in School Improvenent: Whole Language

Low Involvement

Non-use

- Teacher has little or no knowledge of whole language.

- Teacher is aware of whole language only by name.

- Teacher is doing nothing to become familiar with whole language strategies.

- Teacher resists change or trying something new.

Preparation

- Teacher is acquiring information about whole language.

- Teacher is exploring its value system and its demands on time and resources.

- Teacher is curious—listens in on informal discussions about whole language or reads something that is given to him or her about whole language.

- Teacher comes to networking sessions or attends a conference.

- Teacher begins to ask questions about whole language strategies.

- Teacher notices that he or she is already using some whole language strategies.

- Teacher visits a classroom where whole language strategies are practiced.

Moderate Involvement

Experimentation

- Teacher tries a specific whole language strategy.

- Teacher is mildly apprehensive—has had some success, but questions if this new idea will work. Teacher fears that students won't learn their basic skills.

- Teacher begins to ask "What do you do when . . . ?" questions.

- Teacher relies on basal materials.

- Teacher sees numerous obstacles against whole language—time, resources, classroom, management, evaluation.

- Teacher begins to team with other teachers in planning whole language programs.

Mechanical Use

- Teacher focuses most effort on the short-term, day-to-day use of whole language, with little time for reflection.

- Teacher asks. "Am I doing it right?" kinds of questions.

- Teacher makes changes to meet his or her needs more than to meet student needs.

- Teacher gives evidence in the classroom that a few whole language strategies are being used regularly (Big Books, display of student writing, a writing center, children's books).

- Teacher continues to use many traditional strategies, such as phonics lessons, basal reader, and teacher-directed writing lessons.

- Teacher is more often seen conducting whole class lessons than coaching individual children or small groups of children.

- Teacher has a gut-level fear about whether this will work.

- Teacher relies heavily on literature guides and kit materials.

- Teacher begins to conduct workshops for others on whole language.

- Teachers begin to receive visitors to their classroom programs.

Routine Orthodoxy

- Teacher stabilizes use of whole language.

- Teacher makes few, if any, changes in ongoing use.

- Teacher gives little thought to improving use of whole language or to its consequences.

- Teacher continues to use some traditional strategies.

- Teacher suspends reading whole language professional materials.

High Involvement

Refinement

- Teacher bases variations on knowledge of both short- and long-term consequences for students.

- Teacher can explain why he or she is using specific whole language strategies.

- Teacher adds more whole language strategies to program. Few traditional strategies remain.

- Students share ownership of the room, displays, and curriculum.

- Teacher regularly purchases children's books for his or her own personal library.

- Teacher combines own efforts to use whole language with those of colleagues (e.g., music, art, physical education, Chapter 1) to achieve a collective impact on children.

- Teacher invites others into the room and seeks feedback from them about what is going on.

- Teacher reads professional journals and books on whole language topics.

- Teacher joins professional organizations.

- Teacher begins to read and write for self while students are similarly engaged.

- Teacher uses high-quality, current children's literature.

Renewal

- Teacher reflects on his or her own teaching and modifies instruction in an effort to improve whole language strategies.

- Teacher reevaluates the quality of the use of whole language.

- Teacher seeks modifications of whole language to achieve increased impact on students.

- Teacher regularly reads professional literature and current children's books, applies what is read to classroom teaching, and shares it with others.

- Teacher regularly attends professional meetings or is an integral part of a support group.

- Teacher explores new personal goals and new goals for whole language.

- Teacher questions orthodoxy.

- Teacher feels secure about evaluating children by observation and portfolio assessment.

- Teacher is primarily a coach to individuals and small groups; whole class instruction is minimal.

- Teacher encourages student input into curriculum design.

- Teacher writes and learns along with the students.

- Teacher writes articles for professional journals on whole language and prepares written materials to share with visitors to the classroom.

- Teacher receives many visitors to the classroom program.

- Teacher conducts classroom action research projects and shares the results.

Neilsen (1992, p. 642) reminds us that in the "endless, swirling dance of doubt and determination, details and dreams" that is teaching, sanctimony does not work. And sanctimony can be so common as teachers move toward whole language:

"He's a very traditional teacher, you know. Not reflective, or student-centered. His desks aren't even in groups. He needs to change, like us."
"I know what you mean. Every teacher should be a whole language teacher."

Other poignant voices of experience in making a transition toward "whole language" are those collected from around the United States by Weaver (1990). A few of these comments follow.

- From Ardis Tucker (p. 278): "My concern is that in many cases, people are using materials and not understanding their purpose. This leaves them with limited strategies for developing and modifying their own classroom program. When problems occur, they are not able to identify specific causes, and thus abandon the whole language perspective."

- From Jane Bartow (p. 269): "The important thing that happened in our school was that this effort . . . was always open for others to join in. No one came across as a know-it-all, so that others would be afraid to risk or wouldn't want to join."

- From Yvonne Freeman (p. 281): "New teachers who are able to implement whole language successfully may need assistance in learning how not to 'put off' their more experienced colleagues."

Weaver concludes the chapter by advising that

as many of us have found, making a commitment to implementing a whole language philosophy means, perhaps first of all, making a commitment to continued professional growth ourselves. This includes, but is not limited to, reading professional literature, and taking risks: that is, experimenting with putting new ideas into practice, and continually evaluating and reconsidering what we are doing and how we're doing it. Each of us must determine for ourselves what "making a commitment" involves. (pp. 284–285)

I heartily concur.

Conclusion

This chapter has provided guidelines for analyzing and improving instruction. It has included sections on monitoring reading/writing lessons, staff development and renewal, and making the transition from traditional approaches to holistic instruction. For further ideas on self-renewing schools see Bruce, Wolf, and Calhoun (1993). The task of analyzing and improving instruction is truly an art. Treat it with respect, but don't be daunted. Getting to teach and work with people is probably what got you into teaching in the first place. So get to work and enjoy!

Chapter 4

Using Keys to Effective Leadership

Our administrator has been a good model of holistic teaching, emphasizing a love of literature. She reads to classes. She gave awards to each child who successfully published a book, thereby exciting a large number of children to write—and a somewhat smaller but very significant number of teachers to get writing workshops into the academic schedule. Our administrator has been encouraging, freeing, delighting in our development as a school.
—Jane Bartow (Weaver, 1990, pp. 269–270)

Identifying leadership skills can be a fuzzy process. Good leaders come in many shapes and sizes. This chapter provides a range of suggestions, some of which will fit your style better than others. Use and adapt those that seem appropriate for you.

Collaboration with Other Professionals

There is no more important topic in administration and supervision than learning how to collaborate with other professionals. Whether they are colleagues in parallel positions or those above or below you in the organizational structure, you will need to work with people who are and are not reasonable, democratic, selfless, secure, dedicated, organized, personable, or knowledgeable. Simply getting to know and accept a colleague's idiosyncrasies can go a long way toward achieving positive working relationships. Understanding that our greatest strength is also our greatest weakness can be helpful as well.

When you find it difficult to deal with some of your colleagues, find a strategy that fits and give it a try. Following are some possibilities:

- Consult with a mentor to help you decide whether to make a concern known.

- Develop a tough skin.

- Take your colleague out for lunch or just find time for a chat.

- Refrain from invading your colleague's turf.

- Learn stress management techniques.

- Feed your colleague's ego and "kill" your colleague with kindness.

ASCD's video entitled *Adult Conflict Resolution* provides further ammunition. In it, Ellen Raider explores through dramatizations a six-stage framework for negotiating the conflict:

1. Plan the negotiation and recognize the difference between legitimate needs that can be negotiated and emotional positions that can't.

2. Create a climate for negotiation by establishing trust, avoiding blame, and building rapport.

3. Inform and question so that each side can clearly state its needs and understand the needs of the other side.

4. Look for common ground by focusing on shared problems that both sides can work on together.

5. Brainstorm possible solutions that address both sides' needs.

6. Choose the best solution that is most apt to satisfy the needs of both sides.

You will need to work with colleagues to accomplish almost any goal outlined in this text. When trying to effect change, the task may be particularly challenging.

Effecting Change: The Human Agenda

As a change agent you will be a combination of politician, energizer, manager, detective, salesperson, and hero (Carnine, 1988). Sometimes we are indifferent

or resistant to change, but we may not recognize this in ourselves. It has been said that the only people who like change are wet babies. It's not that we need change for the sake of change, but, like plants, either we are growing or we are dying. We cannot stand still. Inasmuch as teaching is an art, we never fully achieve mastery. It is not so much the product but the process of change that is important. You should thrive on change that results in growth.

Trust that, working with others, you can be a powerful instrument of change. John Manning (Samuels & Pearson, 1988, p. v) tells us that the realities of social, cultural, and educational improvements are more closely related to individual accomplishments than to national movements. He reminds us that it was the accomplishments of Martin Luther King, Jr., that defined the noble goals of passive resistance to racial segregation, and that it was the stubborn will of Eleanor Roosevelt that kept alive the liberal conscience of the American people before, during, and after World War II. You should be among whose who ask not "Why?" but, rather, "Why not?"

Littky and Fried (1988) say that to be lured out of their inertia people need change agents, people with great gobs of energy and enthusiasm, people with a passionate vision who have fires of school reform burning in their bellies. They warn that enthusiastic amateurs can get their heads handed to them. Even more likely, you may be patronized—thanked for your earnest efforts and sent back to where you belong. On the other hand, you *will* win some battles.

Why Is Change So Difficult?

Despite the truism that "you don't have to be sick to get better," there is often much resistance to the idea of change. Here are some reasons that change is difficult:

- In teaching, we have no absolute answers as to what will work. Research findings may seem to say one thing one year and another thing the next. When research findings are used, they are sometimes translated into checklists of desirable behaviors for teachers, regardless of their appropriateness to the teaching situation (Anders & Levine, 1990). Often, being forced to follow prescribed behaviors promotes cynicism and resistance to change (Fraatz, 1987).

- The act of teaching is continually oversimplified (Anders & Levine, 1990). Some skills require as many as 25 practice episodes to master (Good, 1981; Showers, Joyce, & Bennett, 1987). Furthermore, change will often involve more than Piaget's assimilation; it may well involve replacing one paradigm with another. This process requires time.

- Change involves risk taking, and not everyone is a risk taker.

- Change hurts and results in stress, something we have enough of already. Because of the stress inherent in change, change efforts often are restricted to safe areas, such as the purchase of a new set of materials (Pincus, 1974), rather than more stressful areas such as new classroom grouping structures that affect discipline and classroom control. From District #112 in Minnesota: "Teachers are taking tremendous risks, but are naïve about the fact that change hurts. . . . Teachers think people should be safe, shouldn't get hurt" (King & Ericson, 1992, p. 122).

- Schools, as opposed to private industry, may lack competition for clients. In most public schools, there is no struggle for survival. Like the domesticated cat, a school is fed and cared for. Its existence is guaranteed (Carlson, 1964).

- Change may result in attacks to the implicit curriculum. For example, O'Brien and Stewart (1990) describe how teachers often see the structure of the secondary school as immutable. Secondary teachers, who are stereotypically more discipline-centered than they are child-centered, may fight changes such as content area reading or interdisciplinary instruction because they support an implicitly unchangeable curriculum.

- Teachers may be unsure about administrator commitment (Anders & Levine, 1990). Administrators may (1) not give a clear expectation for change, (2) not have a reputation for following through, (3) view change only as something being implemented in response to "central office pressure," or (4) give mixed signals regarding what is important.

One way of looking at blockages to change is Carnine's (1988) description of discrediting, delaying, distorting, and, ultimately, discontinuing tactics.

- *Discrediting*: Innovations are usually discredited through activities such as:

  — Attributing their success to unique factors not found in other settings ("Sure, let's just see that work with *my* kids!")

  — Objecting to the values represented by the innovation

  — Questioning, criticizing, and ignoring any evaluation that judges the innovation to be effective ("Just goes to show, you can prove *anything* with research.")

> — Claiming that the innovative practice has already been incorporated into current practices

> — Simply ignoring the innovation's success

- *Delaying*: The widespread adoption of an educational innovation can be at least ten times slower than the already slow process of adopting a new drug (Carlson, 1964).

- *Distorting*: Although a process of adaptation seems reasonable for an untried innovation, adaptation may become a euphemism for distortion. A district may adapt only part of an innovation and then attribute the subsequent failure to the entire innovation. Or a practice may be implemented in name only.

- *Discontinuing*: Rowan (1977) found that innovations that had nothing to do with instruction had the greatest likelihood of survival. Those that dealt with instruction were terminated most quickly. Sometimes termination of a program is a reflection of political rather than pedagogical realities.

Meyer, Scott, and Deal (1979, p. 3) explain that schools are not organized around a knowledge base for delivering quality instruction:

> *It is most crucial for a school, in order to survive, to conform to institutional rules—including community understandings—defining teacher categories and credentials, pupil selection and definition, proper topics of instruction, and appropriate facilities. It is less essential that a school make sure that teaching and learning activities are efficiently coordinated.*

Fraatz (1987), a sociologist who did extensive observations in schools and gave us an enlightened outsider's perspective, discusses why it is so difficult for district-level personnel, for principals, and for others to effect change. What follows is an oversimplification of her thesis, but a key problem for administrators is that you can be effective only if you have cooperation. To achieve that cooperation you need to compromise, often to a fault. Because administrators rely so much on teachers' good will, Fraatz finds teachers to be the real power base in the school. Onore and Lester (1985) also argue that "if change is ever to occur, it is the teachers themselves who must carry it out" (p. 11). Teachers have the power to ignore you. You cannot be effective without them, but they can often be effective without you.

Stages of Readiness for Change

Do you remember the first time you heard some new term like *whole language, metacognition,* or *cooperative learning*? Were you instantly ready to implement the new notion in a variety of settings? Of course not. We all go through stages of readiness for change. Stages of concern (Hord, Rutherford, Huling-Austin, & Hall, 1987) move from awareness to informational, personal, management, consequence, collaboration, and refocusing. The challenge is to realize that others will be at different stages of readiness at different times.

If you didn't know better, you might suppose that change is easy once people have "seen the light." This is not the case. Gilbert (1978) illustrates this point with the story of a training course for Korean War soldiers on how to avoid trenchfoot and frostbite, greater sources of casualties than gunshot wounds. The point of the lecture was "Keep Your Socks Dry!" Even after watching movies of toes falling off, soldiers simply would not go to the trouble to keep their socks dry. If you think you're immune, think about the food you eat or the tobacco you smoke even though you know better!

A simulation game entitled *Making Change for School Improvement* (Hergert, Mundry, Kolb, Rose, & Corro, 1988) helps players apply their knowledge about the change process. The people described in the game conform to the following set of adopter types (Rogers, 1971): innovator, leader, early majority, late majority, and resister. One key assumption underlying the game is that interventions must be related to the people *first* and the innovation *second*.

Tips: Determining the Need for Change

When evaluating the need for change, consider the following:

- State the change you want to introduce.

- Identify the state of affairs that helped you to conclude that a change is desirable.

- Decide what others in the school have to gain or lose if the change effort is successful. Say the desired change is for teachers to spend more time with a low group than with a high group. Knowing that it is more satisfying to many teachers to work with the high group, you will be prepared for possible resistance.

- Determine what effect would be felt by the whole organization if the change were successful. Consider the price tag in terms of dollars, time, and faculty morale as well as student achievement.

Strategies for Change

You know that students must be strategic learners, that they need to learn when, where, why, and how to apply each strategy that they learn. The same applies to change agents. You cannot expect that simply because you are competent, you will be able automatically to effect change. Use strategic wisdom in planning: Know what to do and what not to do; know why you are doing something; and know when, where, and how to do it.

Tips: Strategies for Change

- Create a real awareness of the need for change, not merely through an impersonal, cognitive-level approach using hard data, but through individual interviews and group consensus as well. Barnard and Hetzel (1986) concede that personal interviews are time-consuming but assert that there is no better way of sensitively creating awareness than through one-to-one communication.

- Remember that change will be accepted more readily when there is both ownership (Lambert, 1989) and knowledge regarding the change effort. Without these, educators may try your idea without understanding why they are doing so. If it is not immediately successful, it may well be promptly dropped. To win people over to change, you may spend more time on rapport building than you spend in actual assistance. Ownership is greatest when educators have control of when and how they implement the change (see Wollman-Bonilla, 1991).

- Avoid imposing a solution on a group by using cue words that indicate your obvious wishes. If this occurs, you will have accepted ownership of the problem, and motivation will decrease (Barnard & Hetzel, 1986). Also, staff may feel manipulated and may rebel. One faculty, when listening to a supervisor explain the merits of three basal series, clearly sensed the preference for one and complained that if the supervisor's feelings were so strong, she should have been up front about this rather than engaging in a pretense of an impartial comparison.

- Try to work with an interested group rather than an individual. Because change is stressful and stress actually results in the brain's inhibiting creativity and openness to change, you will have a better chance of success when there is group support (Caine & Caine, 1991).

- Set a collaborative tone. The idea is to learn from one another.

- Use people's personal agendas. Some respond to praise, others to the opportunity to lead. Remember that we all march to different drummers.
- Don't let too much time elapse between staff input and action. Staff must feel that *some* action is underway and that their input is essential to a solution (Barnard & Hetzel, 1986).
- Assign involvement to each staff member, with the more important tasks assigned to those who demonstrate greater obligation, and lesser tasks to the less committed or more skeptical. Thus, those who accept ownership are regarded with the responsibility and recognition that result in self-satisfaction, and the others are not isolated from the activity.
- When possible, allow staff to pursue their solutions and even to fail, "for the only failure that lacks dignity is the failure to try" (Barnard & Hetzel, 1986, p. 61).
- Reward effort generously. Give credit where credit is due. Everything you do to reward effort will be much appreciated. A handwritten note, a memo in an employee's file, a public thank-you, even a pat on the back can go a long way. Two cautions: Your praise should be specific and honest, not general and overdone. Also, be careful not to hurt feelings when praising star performers in the presence of others.

Following are two models that incorporate strategies for change, the Rosabeth Moss Kanter model and the sales agent model.

Rosabeth Moss Kanter Model. Rosabeth Moss Kanter (1989), a professor at Harvard, author of *The Change Masters,* and consultant for Fortune 500 corporations, uses *Alice in Wonderland* as a metaphor for the change process. Like Alice in the croquet match, she says, we may feel as if we're sometimes trying to drive evasive hedgehogs through constantly moving wickets while the Queen of Hearts bellows new and contradictory orders at whim. How do you convince colleagues to design a more appropriate curriculum with constantly changing mandates or curricular guidelines?

Kanter lists some "F's" for change, among them that Change, she says, should be *focused, flexible,* and *friendly*:

- *Focused.* Kanter cites the example of Brigham Young, who didn't say, "I'll go West for awhile, and if that doesn't work I'll try another direction." Nor did Martin Luther King, Jr., say, "I have a few ideas; let's start a few committees." Rather, such leaders had focused visions and tenaciously pursued their dreams.

- *Flexible.* As educators, we are masters of flexibility. Kanter gives a business example of flexibility: a CEO who had his board of directors arrested by security guards, taken out of the board meeting, and helicop-

---

Tips: Adaptation of Rosabeth Moss Kanter Model

- *Be focused.*

  - Post your district/school philosophy (or goals) on the wall if that's what it will take to stay focused.

  - A slogan can help achieve focus. Think of "Just Say No to Drugs." In Florida, "We Make a Difference" campaigns ("Teachers Make a Difference," "Students Make a Difference," etc.) have been effective.

  - An Action Plan will help you keep on target (see Appendix C).

- *Be flexible.* Our resources may not vary, but we can vary the way we arrange them. One office clerk was a reading zealot. When she was on lunchroom duty, she read to the previously rowdy students and told them "knock-knock" jokes. You could have heard a pin drop in the cafeteria.

- *Be friendly.* It's hard for people to fight a friendly face. Your friendliness will go a long way toward effecting change.

---

tered to a new location. His point? They were not to be bogged down by old ideas. The new location symbolized a fresh start. Kanter speaks also of kaleidoscope thinking—rearranging resources to form a myriad of possibilities. We should not, however, be so flexible that we lose focus.

- *Friendly.* Contrary to popular belief, the route to success is not "each person for him- or herself." We need each other to effect change.

Kanter then adds two more "F's" for good measure: *family* and *fun.* We should remember to keep room in our plans for our families and for fun. Kanter cites the Massachusetts Institute of Technology as an example of a place where fun—via a playful, irreverent attitude—fosters a great deal of creativity.

Sales Agent Model. Your role as a change agent is partly one of sales promotion. You send information into the free marketplace of ideas in the hope that it will be purchased. You act as a traveling salesperson who tries to drum up business through personal techniques as well as through the quality of the product. You offer advice in response to a client-initiated need, and ultimately a product or service is negotiated (Gallagher, Goudvis, & Pearson, 1988).

Use techniques of the business world when dealing with educators' "sales resistance" (Burgett, 1976). This includes speaking the customer's language. It's smart to avoid the use of the term "whole language" in a school that is using some holistic instruction but dislikes the "whole language" label. With middle and senior high content area teachers, we've translated "reading strategies" into "learning" or "thinking" strategies.

Sometimes your sales efforts will have greater effect for an ambitious, demanding program than for a routine project. Educators are willing to take on the extra work if they believe their efforts will make them better professionals and help their students (Samuels & Edwall, 1976).

In engaging in change strategies, be they general strategies or specific models such as the Rosabeth Moss Kanter model or the sales agent model, conflict will be inevitable. The following section will give some pointers on conflict resolution.

Conflict Resolution

To avoid conflict is to avoid change. "The challenge is to minimize conflict and use it as a creative force" (Barnard & Hetzel, 1986, p. 59). The first step in

Tips: Force Field Analysis

Follow these pointers:

- Define the change goal precisely enough that action can be planned.

- List forces for and against change. Examples of the former include clearly set goals; time, effort, and product worth the amount of change accomplished; and change seen as betterment of self, students, professionals, and program. Forces against change can include cynicism, lack of trust, and lack of motivation.

- Decide which forces are most important, hardest to deal with, and most amenable to change with your influence.

- Choose a strategy. Decide on action that is required to: (1) weaken or eliminate hindering forces, (2) strengthen helping forces, or (3) add new helping forces.

resolving conflict is to acknowledge its presence and face it. Schutz's simile (1961, p. 305) says this well: ". . . overt discussion is like a cold shower: It is approached with apprehension, the initial impact is very uncomfortable, but the final result justifies the tribulations." One strategy for dealing with conflict borrowed from the business world is Force Field Analysis (Kast & Rosenzweig, 1974). Use this technique to help you identify the forces for and against change in your situation. You will always have both; the key is to maximize the former and minimize the latter.

Following is an example of Force Field Analysis:

Goal. You are an elementary principal enlisting the faculty's support in implementing a whole language curriculum in the computer lab. (*Note:* You recognize that computers belong in classrooms, but your district requires labs.)

Forces Against the Change

Faculty are unsure about the program's potential for effecting positive change.

The computer lab aide may be reluctant to maintain the added communication with the teachers that would be needed for an effective program.

There is little knowledge at the school about how to make this work.

There is little time for training on this program.

The assistant principal is seriously ill and will not be able to help.

The PTA/PTO doesn't want any such newfangled program to interfere with the current computer lab operation

Forces for the Change

There is no rush to start the program.

Faculty will be informed about the change and given a chance to vote on it.

There is sufficient hardware and software.

School-based management has had the effect of increasing openness to change.

There are contingency funds that can be used.

You have a good rapport with all concerned parties.

Strategy. After weighing the items in both lists, you consider whether to use persuasion or coercion, knowing full well that sometimes what is needed is a combination of both. Coercion can be a powerful tool—think of school attendance as a driver's license requirement, for example. But you opt to emphasize persuasion. You smile as you think of people you know who got much more accomplished with a carrot than with a stick—for example, the supervisor who left a rose on her superintendent's desk every week and who received unbelievable support for her programs. Your thoughts and actions are as follows:

1. You recognize that the faculty can probably be convinced once they know more about the program. You know that once the faculty is "sold," it will be easier to turn the PTA around.

2. You can take advantage of the forces working for you by setting aside contingency funds for substitute teachers so that staff development will be possible during the school day, when teachers are more receptive. Knowing of this fund availability will influence some teachers' votes. Moreover, teachers can be reassured that the program will not begin until they have received the proper inservice training.

3. You know that it is a good strategy to enlist the help of reluctant staff members. For example, you take advantage of your good rapport with the computer aide and your understanding of her hidden agenda (reluctance to spend additional time communicating with teachers). You work out a form for written communication and emphasize that the use of written communication will cut back on the time needed for oral communication. You also offer to help as a communications link. You may not completely change the aide's views, but at least you have neutralized the situation.

4. You meet with key PTA players and key faculty members soon after the teachers agree to give the program a shot. You invite the PTA members to visit the lab once it has been in operation for one month. You promise to meet with the PTA members after their visit to the lab if they so request.

5. Recognizing that it is always comfortable to go back to old ways, you systematically monitor and support this change throughout the school year.

For more information on the force field problem-solving model, contact Organization Design and Development, 101 Bryn Mawr Avenue, Suite 310, Bryn Mawr, PA 19010.

Although Force Field Analysis will help deal with broad plans to combat resistance to change, additional tactics will be needed for individual resistance. Hostrop (1973, p. 136) recommends the use of dyads. He points out that "groups of two show markedly dissimilar characteristics to similar groups of larger size. Dyads are markedly low in showing disagreement and unfriendly behavior, but markedly high on showing tension and asking for information. They appear to take extra care to avoid conflict and to persuade one another gently. [Using] groups of two . . . frequently resolves mistrust, leads to mutual understanding, and improves the likelihood of goal realizations." As an instructional leader, when you are a member of such a dyad, you will sometimes be able to overcome individual resistance.

Fifty Excuses for Why It Won't Work

We can always find excuses for why something won't work. Use the following list (from the Connecticut newsletter of the Association of Children and Adults with Learning Disabilities) as comic relief if you want to avoid hearing excuses:

1. We tried that before.
2. Our system is different.
3. It costs too much.
4. That's beyond our responsibility.
5. That's not my job.
6. We're all too busy to do that.
7. It's too radical a change.
8. There's not enough help.
9. We've never done it before.
10. We don't have the authority.
11. There's not enough time.
12. Let's get back to reality.
13. That's not our problem.
14. Why change it? It's still working O.K.
15. I don't like that idea.
16. You're right, but . . .
17. You're two years ahead of your time.
18. It isn't in the budget.
19. We're not ready for that.
20. Sounds O.K. but impractical.
21. Let's give it more thought.
22. That's my bowling day.

23. That doesn't affect me or my child.
24. Nobody cares about that.

25. We've always done it this way.

26. It might not work.

27. Not that again!

28. Where'd you dig that one up?

29. We did all right without it.

30. It's never been tried before.

31. Let's shelve it for the time being.

32. I don't see the connection.

33. What you are really saying is . . .

34. Let's not be the first.

35. Maybe that would work in your class but not in mine.

36. The administration will never go for it.

37. It can't be done.

38. It's too much trouble.

39. It's impossible.

40. You're not here to think.

41. Can't teach an old dog new tricks.

42. Let me think about that and I'll get back to you.

43. Let's wait until the next administration.

44. State says (I can't remember who) we can't do that.

45. We can't fight city hall.

46. That's old/new business and can't be discussed now.

47. That's too serious a subject.

48. No one is interested.

49. It's too early to think about it.

50. It's too late to start.

Excuses notwithstanding, change can be rewarding. Wollman-Bonilla (1991) quotes one experienced teacher: "For the first time in my life I feel like shouting from the tops of buildings about something that's happening in my classroom!" (p. 120) and asserts that, with effective staff development, many more teachers can be moved to feel this exuberance.

To the original roles of change agent as politician, energizer, manager, detective, salesperson, and hero, we must add the role of juggler. As you juggle all these roles, keep a close eye on the task at hand. Return to this section for a periodic refresher course as your constituents progress through stages of the change process.

Mastering Group Dynamics

Up to this point, this chapter has focused on mastery of the change process. The focus will now move to other keys for effective leadership. The first of these is mastering group dynamics, a must for any administrator or supervisor. This section will discuss group dynamics models, school-based management, effective meetings, and committee craft.

Group Dynamics Models

In mastering group dynamics, it is critical that you prevent the problems that arise when groups get into personality issues or form "camps" that side together regardless of the issue. DeBono's (1986) six thinking hats and Deming's quality circles (Manning & Curtis, 1988) are models that help eliminate these problems.

With the six thinking hats, each group member in turn "wears" a hat of a given color to look at an issue from a different perspective. Group members who do not switch hats with the group run the risk of appearing foolish. The hats are as follows:

- *White*: information—available? needed? missing?

- *Red*: intuition—feeling, emotion

- *Yellow*: logical positive—benefits? savings? advantages?

- *Green*: creative—alternatives?

- *Blue*: metacognitive—in charge of the thinking process

- *Black*: critical—caution (to avoid stereotyping, black is replaced by gray or purple in some versions)

Taking one perspective at a time guarantees careful examination of all perspectives before a decision is made. This is in contrast to the usual approach of trying to see every perspective at once and thus often overemphasizing one (such as critical) and underemphasizing another (such as logical positive).

Another valuable group dynamics strategy is quality circles. Manning and Curtis (1988) cite an agreed-upon definition of a quality circle as "a small group of people who voluntarily meet, on a regular basis, to learn and apply techniques for identifying, analyzing, and solving work-related problems" (p. 7). Quality circles are generally groups of 5 to 12 persons who meet for about an hour once a week to discuss issues about quality of work and quality of work life. Quality circles are based on the work of Deming in the Japanese auto industry. They operate on the premise that those closest to the job can best ascertain problems and suggest solutions.

One key quality circle procedure is round robin brainstorming, with each participant limited to one observation at a time. No ideas are evaluated at first. After everyone has had a turn, the brainstorming continues, with each participant in turn adding another comment or passing, until the issue is exhausted. After problems are brainstormed, the group votes to prioritize the issues. Issues that are dealt with are analyzed according to the five "Wh's" and "how" (e.g., Where does the problem occur? Why does it occur?). Subsequent brainstorming can focus on problem solutions. Managers are expected to respond quickly, either following up the group's suggestions or clearly explaining why it is not possible to do so (Manning & Curtis, 1988).

Use the six thinking hats, quality circles, or other plans to master group dynamics. These strategies will help with any group work, be it for school-based management teams or for meetings or committees of any type.

School-Based Management, Shared Decision Making, and Team Building

School-based management is based on the business concept of solving problems by those most closely affected and those most likely to have the best ideas about how to solve them. This approach aims at achieving high morale and good relationships with management, with a resulting increase in productivity. I have watched firsthand the rise of school-based management in Dade County, Florida, the district that has become most widely known for these efforts in a rapidly growing number of schools. Dade County's experience shows that districts moving toward school-based management will face some hurdles but also some pleasant surprises along the way.

Supervisors in districts beginning school-based management may find changing procedures. Supervisors used to open policies toward school visitations may find that they must wait for an invitation. Supervisors used to central purchasing or district mandates on purchasing may find that their direct influence on purchasing decisions is reduced to persuasion. Yet, tradition being the powerful force that it is, districts in which schools have traditionally relied on district recommendations may find that the district's indirect influence is considerable. With Dade County's 1990 basal adoption, schools were given the choice of three series but could request a waiver if they desired a different series. None did.

Regardless of the degree to which your district implements school-based management, any move in that direction will require the support of supervisors. Supervisors who have established a track record of being knowledgeable and helpful may well be called on even more than previously as schools look for ideas to implement or for validation of their plans. Supervisors who have not yet been able to establish such a track record can find ways of letting schools know of their availability, perhaps through recommendations from a well-respected colleague.

In actuality, school-based management is the way many schools already operate. Those faculty members who are interested in participating in decisions do so. Yet schools in which teachers are given a large voice in important decisions are often the ones least interested in officially being labeled school-based management schools. Teachers often do not want the extra responsibilities of committee work on day-to-day matters that they would just as soon leave to the administration. Committee work takes time, which is pulled either from instructional time or from the hours before and after school. And committee work can be ineffective, particularly when members have not been trained in problem-solving skills (Duke, Showers, & Imber, 1980).

On the positive side, however, school-based management has been responsible for pulling many faculties together. Some schools have used district intergroup management teams to help with team building and have used quality circle training in instituting and carrying out innovative programs. Sometimes these programs have required waivers from district and state requirements. A middle school might want to delete a sixth-grade reading requirement in favor of a program that integrates reading across the curriculum. An elementary school might want to eliminate an assistant principal position to fund another priority, or hire a private foreign language company to run the foreign language program.

Think of school-based management as a logical parallel to "whole language." Both involve empowering teachers to make decisions that will affect them. Some may want the privileges without the responsibilities, but many will welcome the added challenge. Work with your colleagues to see if you can make school-based management work for you.

Conducting Effective Meetings

Think of all the poorly run meetings you've attended and a number of tips for conducting meetings will come to mind. Follow these suggestions whenever possible. See also the sections on staff development in Chapter 3 and the "Tips for Making Presentations" in Chapter 5.

Tips: Conducting Effective Meetings

Give advance notice.

Hold meetings in comfortable settings and at convenient times.

When possible, schedule meetings with self-imposed deadlines so they do not go on endlessly.

Have only essential people at the meeting—small groups tend to work better than large ones (Barnard & Hetzel, 1986).

Serve refreshments.

Start on time and people will learn to arrive on time.

Start by defining the purpose of the meeting.

Allow time for introductions if appropriate.

Keep and promptly disseminate minutes.

Stick to an agenda, but allow discussion time as necessary.

Use humor to relax the group.

Don't spend time on lengthy discussions that can be worked out by a committee.

Watch for nonverbal cues indicating agreement or disagreement, a desire to speak, impatience.

Don't talk too much.

Interrupt if necessary to keep to the topic.

Summarize and bring closure.

Thank people for meeting.

Information disseminated in writing isn't always read, and information delivered verbally isn't always listened to. Remember that it isn't meetings that people resent but, rather, wasting time (Barnard & Hetzel, 1986). One principal simply stopped having faculty meetings when her faculty complained. Instead, she provided all information in writing. When the faculty did get together, it was more for sharing, as in a college seminar. Similarly, Bird (1991) reports on the Fair Oaks Elementary primary and intermediate teachers, who meet as separate groups twice a month on Thursdays, when time is built into the schedule for this purpose. Teachers spend about two hours talking and sharing concerns, questions, breakthroughs, and triumphs. Bird reports that she has learned the importance of not imposing too much structure. "Go with the flow" is now the school's motto for these meetings.

Committee Craft

Many of the tips suggested for conducting meetings are needed for committees as well. If you are supervising a committee, another skill you will need is the ability to monitor and sometimes nudge the committee without being over-bearing. Committees sometimes start with zeal, but other priorities get in the way. Thus, periodic requests for updates can help committees keep on track. Action plans (see Appendix C) can be helpful in this process. Additional pointers (Barnard & Hetzel, 1986) follow:

Tips: Committee Craft

- Decide if a committee is the best format to accomplish a given task. If the principal already has an outcome in mind, a committee should *not* be formed.

- Consider whether enough time and/or expertise are available to allow a committee to function effectively.

- If you are a school-based administrator, consider whether you should be a member of school committees. If so, (1) take care not to dominate proceedings, (2) volunteer for some of the more mundane assignments, and (3) help develop leadership skills by providing a model of good participant behavior.

- In forming the committee, consider the need for having a group that (1) is representative, (2) has something to gain by completing the task, and (3) has sufficient time and the appropriate expertise and knowledge. Appropriate representation also means including both skeptics and advocates to maximize ownership in the committee recommendations.

- Ensure that committee members appreciate the significance of the committee's work.

- Monitor whether committee members are completing their task and communicating regularly with their constituency.

- Assure that the purpose (in writing) and the chair are settled before the first meeting to avoid wasting committee time on these matters.

- Arrange for appropriate closure.

Barnard and Hetzel (1986, p. 3) state, "Given the often deserved disrepute into which committees can fall, a thorough understanding of the operation of committees is vitally important to effective leadership."

This chapter has discussed two keys for effective leadership, effecting change and mastering group dynamics. Following is a description of three more keys, using no-cost options to improve instruction, marketing programs, and long-range planning.

Using No-Cost Options to Improve Instruction

When economic conditions are tight, it becomes necessary not only to take lemons and make lemonade but, sometimes, to make lemonade with nothing more than lemon rinds. Following are some pointers that may help:

- At the school level, brainstorm with *all* staff. Let all the ideas come out.

- Follow the principles of zero-based budgeting. Reconsider all budget lines to see where dollars can be moved. An obvious place might be cutting back on workbooks and ditto paper to allow for more trade books and writing paper. Subscriptions for magazines and journals might be reevaluated. A new state adoption of spellers or English books might be ignored.

- Use volunteer help in whatever guise it may be available: parents, teachers, retired educators, college students, business partners, senior citizens, students.

- Solicit support: from the community, parents, publishers' representatives, the district office.

- Write grants. See "Grant Writing" in Appendix C for tips.

Marketing Programs

As in successful business advertising campaigns, you will want to make teachers, administrators, and the community aware of your programs. Ideas for marketing and enhancing motivational reading programs can be found in Chapter 6. Other marketing suggestions follow:

Tips: Ideas for Marketing Your Programs

- Try to get media coverage. If you don't succeed the first time, don't give up! Keep programs catchy: A pajama party in which all elementary faculty and students wear pajamas and bring their teddy bears and favorite bedtime stories to school is newsworthy.
- Create bumper stickers, bookmarks, or buttons.
- Highlight your programs in a regular and attractive newsletter. School-based administrators can also use bulletin boards, perhaps reserving one for parent information. Parent communications should be translated if the population includes a substantial number of non-English-speaking parents.
- Find ways to inform your district hierarchy and your school board of your programs. One former district reading specialist owes the elimination of her job to the fact that she did not do enough of this type of marketing.

Long-Range Planning for Effective Leadership

Long-range planning is sometimes neglected in the rush of everyday life. Set up a system so that you don't neglect it. Perhaps you can mark dates in your calendar or planner when you will examine and update your written long-range plans. Of course, changing district plans can wreck your best laid plans. But, without long-range plans, you're not likely to go far in accomplishing challenging goals.

For school-based administrators, personal long-range plans will, of course, greatly overlap with long-range plans for the school. Long-range planning for Bryan Elementary (Dade County), Florida's winner of the 1991–1992 International Reading Association Exemplary Reading Program included several years of school-based management, regular curriculum meetings, and creative budgeting, which paid for a reading specialist and large classroom collections of trade books, all of which resulted in a school with a united and strong faculty all pulling in the same direction. On the other hand, lack of long-range planning can result in unnecessarily erratic inservice schedules, frequent changes in direction, and a general lack of purpose. Long-range planning *is* worth the effort!

Conclusion

This chapter has reviewed some keys to effective leadership. These have included strategies for effecting change, mastering group dynamics, using no-cost options to improve instruction, marketing programs, and long-range planning. Review this chapter periodically to hone your leadership skills.

A Comprehensive District Reading/Writing Program

The first portion of this book addressed issues of concern to both school-based and district-level instructional leaders. The second portion of this book focuses on the comprehensive reading/writing program at the district level. This information is presented in a single chapter.

The District Role

*Probably our hardest lesson has been shifting responsibility
and decision making to teachers and administrators.*
                    —Rhodes and Shanklin (Weaver, 1990, p. 275)

A district reading/writing program must be comprehensive enough to give schools the direction they need, yet flexible enough to allow schools to make their own decisions. This chapter will not list specific components of a district program, which will vary from place to place. Instead, district administrators may want to look at the list of components for school programs (Chapter 6), and develop a plan to support those that are pertinent to their own district.

Providing Leadership to Schools

General directions regarding leadership are provided throughout this book. This chapter will focus on leadership from the district office. As was shown in Chapter 1, the concept of district leadership has evolved over the years. Following is a series of quotes on the evolution of supervision that should be amusing as well as thought-provoking:

A teacher, on the other hand, who deserves the name, is to some extent an original; that is to say, he views and explains subjects in a way peculiar to himself and the natural working of his own mind. . . . To require him to surrender his individuality, and to do his work after some favorite method of ours, is easy, and as preposterous as easy. To see that he does his work well, whatever be the mode, or if he does it ill, to show him where the defect is, and how to remedy it, and yet allow him the freedom so essential—requires more soundness of jegment [sic], and delicacy of discrimination than are always at command. (Worcester, 1857, pp. 9–10)

They merely enter the school, spend a short time in hearing brief recitations in the various branches, and just glancing at the writing books, slates and children; then, after making a few common-place remarks, they retire. . . . These visits seldom occupy more than one-fourth of a day, while it is impossible to form a just estimate of most schools in so short a time. In some instances, the visitors make it a point to visit thre schools in half a day! (Barnard, 1858, p. 142)

Going into a school, I try to put aside everything like authority, or superiority, and to approach the teacher in a proper spirit of helpfulness. Then, I endeavor to see the school from the teacher's standpoint, and, if necessary, to have the teacher see her school as it appears to me. (Greenwood, 1888, pp. 519–520)

Rice's genuine dismay and disgust of what was going on in American schools in the 1890s had evolved into grim determination that teachers and administrators must be made to do the right thing. (Kliebard, 1987, p. 23)

Lacking a half-million dynamic teachers, are we not forced to put into our schools a dynamic curriculum? (Rugg, 1926, p. 7)

Supervision has as its object the development of a group of professional workers who attack their problems scientifically, free from the control of tradition and actuated in the spirit of inquiry. (Commission on Supervision, 1930, p. 4)

The supervisor is an organizer of opportunity and . . . good supervision is the facilitation of opportunities. (Wilhelms, 1946, p. 222)

Supervision should become more group oriented rather than individually oriented. (Nolan & Francis, 1992, p. 51)

Acquiring an understanding of the learning-teaching process demands the collection of many types of data, over extended periods of time. (Nolan & Francis, 1992, p. 58)

Supervisors cannot wear their office on their sleeve, nor can they be "puffed up" about what strengths and abilities they possess. Rather, they keep a low profile, functioning like "well-worn shoes" (not noticed when entering a room, but having a definite sense of purpose) and they allow the strengths and abilities of the group members (including their own) to emerge. (Grimmett, Rostad, & Ford, 1992, p. 195, reference by Nancy Austin)

My vision for supervision is a simple one—it is of a day when supervision will no longer be needed. (Sergiovanni, 1992, p. 203)

These quotes tell us as much about what supervision should not be as about what it should be. The following sections, of course, deal with the latter.

Staying Well Informed

To earn the trust of your colleagues, you must stay well informed. Special professional groups such as the International Reading Association's Supervisors and Reading Special Interest Group can be most helpful. You will also want to own and use an extensive professional library. (See "Professional Resources" in Appendix D.) You must have research at your fingertips. When someone asks you questions, you will quickly lose credibility if you always have to take the time to look up an answer. There are sources that school-level personnel might find too technical, but with which you need to be conversant. These include journals such as *Reading Research Quarterly* and *Journal of Reading Behavior,* as well as books such as Adams's (1990) *Beginning to Read* or the annual *Yearbook of the National Reading Conference.*

You will, of course, not know *everything* off the top of your head, but the more you do know, the more efficient and effective you will be. This relates not only to reading/writing research but to innovative programs as a whole. Revolutions in a field are most often begun by someone from outside the field who brings a fresh perspective (Kuhn, 1970). For example, Dade County (Florida) Public Schools adopted General Motors' Saturn idea, letting anyone's new school plan compete through written proposals. Likewise, you will find that you can transport ideas from other fields into your reading/writing program.

Staying well informed includes keeping up with what is happening in your schools. Do you know your schools and your reading specialists well enough to play matchmaker when there is an opening? Do you know your principals well enough to know when you can cautiously run interference to help with a teacher complaint, and when you had best not intervene?

I find it a powerful measure of my knowledge of my schools to go into faculty meetings regularly confident enough about the questions on the session's topic that might be raised to structure the session comfortably around a K-W-L (Ogle, 1986). With this security, few surprises come up under the "what you *know*" and "what you *want* to know" columns. Discussion of what is brainstormed from these columns leads to completion of the "what you *learned*" column at the end of the session. Keeping on top of things will help make you a leader who inspires respect.

Staying well informed is a precursor to using what you know to support your schools and sharing your knowledge effectively. The next section will discuss how this can be done.

Serving as a Role Model

You will be seen as a role model by your principals and teachers. Take this responsibility seriously. If there are evening or Saturday morning professional organization meetings, you need to be there frequently. If you must pay your own way to conferences, let this fact be known. I found that keeping my own portfolio helped my credibility when I talked about portfolios. I found teachers more willing to set up literate environments in their classrooms when they saw me set up a literate classroom in a conference room over and over again for a series of inservice sessions.

Providing Direction and Support

A primary responsibility for any district administrator is to provide direction and support. As with mail carriers, "neither rain nor snow nor gloom of night" should keep you from your mission. Establish plans of action that are optimistic but not unrealistic depending on your resources, your other responsibilities, and your district's priorities. If you can engage the backing of your supervisor(s) for any commitments you make, you will have a better chance of fulfilling them without having new responsibilities suddenly superseding previously made commitments.

Making Presentations. You may be asked to make presentations to the school board, fellow district administrators, principals and assistant principals, schools, and parents and community members. When you do so, remember that your body language strongly affects the way others respond (Kindsvatter, Wilen, & Ishler, 1988). An audience will react more to the way in which they see something presented than to the actual words you use. It's been said that teaching is 95 percent presentation and 5 percent content. Most audience members will make up their minds about you by the time you're a few minutes into your presentation, so be well aware of your nonverbal communication.

If your audience is multicultural, be aware of cultural differences in nonverbal communication such as in appropriate distance and eye contact (Evertson & Emmer, 1982; Power, 1988). If at all possible, insist that participants sit so you have eye contact with each and every one. Move around if you can get away from a podium. Stand by teachers (or administrators) who aren't paying attention.

The following tips will help you deliver top-notch presentations. See also the sections on staff development in Chapter 3 and conducting effective meetings in Chapter 4.

Tips: Making Presentations

- Know the prior knowledge of the audience so that you can plan relevant sessions. Make sure that you and the audience have a common vocabulary. Don't cover material more rapidly than your audience can absorb it.

- Use concrete materials. It's far better, for example, to place the magnetic letters on the overhead projector or on a cookie sheet than to simply make a verbal suggestion that teachers do so.

- Know yourself. If you are not a funny person, don't try to be funny. A bad joke is worse than no joke at all (Goldstein, 1992).

- Establish personal rapport. Chat with participants as they walk into the room. Distribute name tags. Consider using an icebreaker. Attend to individuals during the presentation. Especially if the sessions will be ongoing, help participants bond with each other (e.g., writing about a special teaching experience and sharing it with a small group, with some subsequent whole group sharing).

- Involve participants as soon as possible. Don't just have them sit passively! Invite involvement by putting on each table a tub with paper, pencils, Post-It notes, and scissors. Find times when you can ask honest questions rather than lecture (Goldstein, 1992). Use shouted choral responses when appropriate.

- Make staff development an event. One staff development specialist in Lake County, Florida, uses themes. She might distribute Lifesavers for a session on classroom survival. University of Miami/Dade County Writing Institute presenters greet participants on the first day in rooms lined with poignant blown-up quotes from teachers, students, and famous people.

- Use music, laughter, and metaphors as tools for brain-based learning (Caine & Caine, 1991). A tape recorder can play music as participants enter or exit, during breaks, or while participants reflect in writing. A session for kindergarten teachers can be set up with an enormous flower mural to highlight the "kinder-garden" metaphor.

- As Neilsen (1991, p. 667) points out, "Given an opportunity to air their frustrations, even the most bitter of comments in an open, nonthreatening atmosphere does wonders for the group and for the crusty cynics. If we don't take the comments personally, but instead empathize with the frustration and hear it out, we can move beyond confrontation to conversation." One form of listening is reading written questions that participants may be unwilling to voice orally. A staff development specialist in Lake County, Florida, uses index cards ("care cards") for this purpose.

- If possible, learn to be a storyteller. Supervisors can add this to their repertoire of talents. Storytelling can enhance presentations immensely!

- Follow the "Audiovisual Tips" and "Handout Tips" in Appendix C.

In your presentations, as in any teaching, you must find the right balance between content (*what* is taught) and process (*how* it is taught). It is easier for you, in a way, than for the classroom teacher, because much of your content *is* process. Say that you want to teach both a K-W-L (Ogle, 1986) and cooperative learning. You can do the K-W-L *on* cooperative learning *and* you can have the teachers *do* cooperative learning in the process. Both K-W-L and cooperative learning are the content that you want to get across, but they are also processes that the teachers will use in delivering their own content of, say, science information. This use of strategies that you want teachers to utilize in their classrooms is called the Strategic Overlay Model (Kelly & Farnan, 1990).

You could start by pairing teachers and telling them how a Think-Pair-Share (McTighe & Lyman, 1988) works. Next, they can be given two minutes to THINK about what they *know* of cooperative learning and what they *want to know* about it, and two minutes to PAIR and discuss this with a partner. Participants then SHARE what they've brainstormed with the instructor, who fills this in in the first two sections of the K-W-L on the board. Finally, you go on to teach cooperative learning and then to work with the group to fill in the "L" *(learned)* portion. Thus, you have taught both the content and the process of K-W-L, Think-Pair-Share, and cooperative learning.

Your willingness to spend time on process (e.g., taking the time to have participants self-evaluate their participation in a cooperative learning activity) will serve as a model for teachers, who sometimes do need to sacrifice content for the sake of process. One middle school teacher had to spend an entire period having students move into groups, out of groups, into groups, out of groups, and so on. The rest of the year, she was able to concentrate on content. Initial emphasis on process can pay off in greater learning of content in the long run.

Have your calendar with you when you make presentations. You may well be cornered and asked to make related presentations at later dates.

Important / *Reading Tchrs promising candidates should have these qualities* ↗

Helping to Select and Nurture Reading Teachers. Supervisors sometimes are able to help select reading teachers. I keep a file of teachers who are looking for a position and interview those who appear promising. Thus, when a principal calls, I am ready. Hagerty (1990) provides a series of questions for candidates with regard to their knowledge base, interpersonal skills and attitudes, teaching ability, and organization/management skills. She suggests that principals, teachers, and supervisors make hiring decisions as a team. When teachers in my district know that I will be part of the interviewing team, they network and engage in a cram-a-thon to learn all that they can. Teachers should know that obtaining a reading job in your district requires a solid knowledge base and active involvement in professional organizations. Keep a list of local membership and nudge nonmembers when you can get away with it. I have been known to do "book talks" on selected *Journal of Reading* articles with middle and senior high teachers, without providing copies. The message teachers pick up on is, "If I don't have this already, I need to get it."

Responding to Ongoing Miscellaneous Requests. One inevitable aspect of your job is to respond to ongoing requests. These can be quite varied: "What can I do about my child who can't read?" "What is the difficulty level of this material?" "What materials should I order?" "What do you think about this program?" "Do you know of any jobs I might apply for?" "I'm taking a class and . . ." Prompt, caring responses are a must. Sometimes responses will require gentle probing. I've found, for example, that requests for materials often reflect a need for instructional strategies in the designated area (such as vocabulary) rather than materials per se.

As you put your schedule together, try to ensure that you are neither out so much that you can't complete required office work, nor sitting in your office with little to do. Schedule some office time that you try to keep inviolate.

A common request is for school visits. These may include speaking at PTA/PTO meetings, working with grade groups, visiting individual classrooms, addressing the faculty, helping plan a school initiative, or attending a function. You should have a plan for response to these requests. If you are in a large district, you might group a feeder pattern of schools (those whose students feed into one senior high school). Or you might have to weigh whether it is more important to visit many or all of your schools during a given period of time—recognizing that this may be a Band-Aid approach—or to concentrate your efforts. If you do not, you may find yourself engaging in what Bird (1991) refers to as the gas station model of professional development. She describes it as follows: "I ran from class to class, seldom stopping even for a bite of lunch, 'filling up' the teachers with demonstration teaching, feedback on their teaching, outlines of holistic instructional strategies, professional articles, and anything else I thought might keep them going until my next service stop the following week. By June I was thoroughly frustrated" (p. 324). When forced into this "gas station" model, Bird found herself writing letters to teachers to discuss what she would have liked to talk about had there been more time.

Some requests will need to be met conditionally. For example, demonstrations that require time for preparation as well as execution might be acceded to if a requesting administrator agrees to (1) be present for the demonstration, (2) have a number of teachers there, and (3) have a plan for debriefing. I received one request for teaching an audience of school-based administrators an entire reading/language arts block to model appropriate flexible grouping strategies. This meant visiting a school first to make arrangements, writing a four-day lesson plan around one core selection, teaching the first day without an audience, and doing the demonstration the second day. Thus, I was able to tell administrators what was accomplished on day 1 and what would be accomplished on days 3 and 4 so that they could see the flow. This proved to be a good but time-consuming experience. To meet such a time-consuming request, you might want to attach some conditions, such as assurance of a minimum audience size.

Requests for one-shot presentations may need to be explored. The requestor may mistakenly believe that one visit will solve a difficult problem, or may be afraid of asking for too much of your time. When more support is needed, you might suggest that you'd be willing to meet with grade levels first to determine the needs of each level, then return to visit classes and meet with the faculty as a whole. I have found this model to be effective. Teachers are more open to classroom visits after an initial nonthreatening meeting, and classroom visits give us ideas of what else needs to be discussed in a faculty meeting.

Parents frequently ask for names of tutors. Know your district policy on this issue. Even if no policy exists, tread carefully; your motives in recommending someone can be questioned. If you do make a recommendation, select more than one name from your files of people whose work you know you can recommend. If your district does not allow recommendations from district staff but only from professional organizations, make it clear that any recommendations you make are in your capacity of professional organization member.

Become known as someone who responds promptly to solicited requests. The resulting support from schools is most rewarding.

Providing Unsolicited Support. Another aspect of your job involves providing unsolicited support. For example, when you do professional reading, you may find yourself writing Post-It notes to duplicate this article for Teacher X, recommend that chapter for "Bigwig" Y, or lend that book to Principal Z. Or you might disseminate a summary of an article (Bird, 1991). Keep your colleagues in mind—you'll see how often you can provide support. Maybe you can offer to:

- Provide the local reading or language arts council or TAWL (Teachers Applying Whole Language) group with a speaker or a suggestion for an activity (e.g., reading day in the mall, administrator of the year award, or book-and-author luncheon)

- Serve as an advisor to this group

- Write inservice components so that administrators/teachers can receive credit for attending local council meetings

- Help a teacher going to a conference select good sessions to attend

- Review proposals for presentations/awards before they are submitted, and then help presenters prepare for their session

- Compile and share a list of local authors

- Work with applicants for school-based administrative positions, perhaps with dialogue journals or helping applicants gather personal portfolios

- Plan an evening to show parents writing displays from the entire feeder pattern at each senior high school

One type of unsolicited support is given by playing the role of cheerleader. One aspect of this is simply lending a sympathetic ear. Another is actively celebrating by means such as the following:

- Call the press.

- Pass on information about school or teacher successes to a school board member. One Dade County board member then gives imaginary "gold stars" at school board meetings.

- Suggest schools that are worth visiting because of their successful programs.

- During presentations, display collected albums/posters with photos and other evidence from local schools that show exemplary literacy practices in action.

- Encourage teachers/administrators to share their successes through publications and professional presentations; if necessary, participate.

- Make sure that "bosses" know of the successes of their subordinates—for example, by mailing a memorandum of congratulations.

Another type of unsolicited support is simply taking advantage of every opportunity to "sell your product." If you are on an interviewing team for assistant principals, the question you ask and the responses you expect can be instructive to other members of the team. If you are in a school on one mission, you may well find that other ways of helping will crop up. At a Teacher of the Year luncheon, you might be able to plant a seed in conversation with some key person.

Starting, Carrying Out/Supporting, and Evaluating Programs

Be on the lookout for program improvements that you can start, carry out/support, and evaluate—either at the district or the school level. Maybe the program is one of your own. The field of possible programs to start is, of course, infinite. Maybe you can visit a successful program in another district (or your own!) to evaluate its replicability. Perhaps you can help write a grant to start a teacher-as-reader program in which teachers gather to share personal reading, reading of books used in the classroom, or reading of professional books (Cardarelli, 1992). Or work with the PTA to have a "turn off TV—turn on to reading" night—launched with a march. Or work with a publisher to pilot a commercial program at a school. (But see the section in Chapter 2 on selecting instructional materials for cautions on pilots.)

Maybe you can "adopt" one school for intensive support to a particular program. School change is, of course, effected one school at a time. When Bob Kalinsky, Dade County's then-new principal for Frederick Douglass Elementary, asked me for ideas on how to turn around his inner-city school, I advised him to hire a top-notch reading resource specialist. He followed this advice and welcomed ongoing visits to the school. Later he added other outstanding resource teachers, two of whom chose to leave high socioeconomic areas to teach in a school where things were really happening. The school became a district model. Success simply bred success.

Examples of district-initiated programs include teacher-as-reader groups (Cardarelli, 1992) and teacher or administrator study groups (Klassen & Short, 1992; Short et al., 1992). In the words of teacher-participants, "There isn't enough time allotted to talk with other teachers and the study group provides some of that time." "We rarely get to develop collegial relationships. We need to learn to dialogue with others on professional issues. We need to share and reply rather than present and assess. I'm not used to having the chance to discuss practice in a nonevaluative way with other educators" (Short et al., 1992, p. 371). Such study groups represent changed roles for facilitators: "Understanding what it means to facilitate has been a major challenge for me. I struggled with how to share rather than present my own ideas and to encourage others to recognize and share their expertise" (Short et al., 1992, p. 374).

Another example of a successful district-initiated program was the summer school multigrade primary class in a shopping mall in Clay County, Florida. The at-risk students had a store booth as their real classroom and the whole mall as an extended one. Shoppers visited the whole language classroom as they shopped. The mall benefited from the extra business, the children learned and had a great time, and the community became better educated about whole language education.

One final example of a district program is the demonstration school program for new teachers in Buffalo, New York. The principal at each of two demonstration schools selects one demonstration teacher per grade level. A district specialist coordinates the program and sits in on demonstrations and follow-up debriefings. Visiting administrators are debriefed by the principal. The program has been successful for a number of years.

If you start a new program, plan up front for its evaluation. There is always a great need for more action research. Involve assessment support persons in your district if appropriate. If you cannot dedicate the necessary time to evaluation, see if someone else can—perhaps a local university.

Supporting Reading Resource Specialists

If you are lucky enough to have reading resource specialists (RRSs) who have release time from direct instruction to support overall school programs, you are fortunate indeed. For extensive discussion of this topic, see *Handbook for the K–12 Reading Resource Specialist* (Radencich, Beers, & Schumm, 1993). Two key ways in which you can support RRSs are by helping them to network on their own and by providing effective get-togethers.

Individual Networking. Although RRSs will build many solid collegial relationships at their respective schools, they will have a crucial need for networking with others in job-alike roles. Some networking will occur through the reading of ideas shared in the literature by colleagues, but a person-to-person network is, of course, irreplaceable. Following are some pointers.

Tips: Individual Networking

- Provide RRSs with a list of their colleagues and their work phone numbers. Encourage RRSs to visit each other for renewed perspectives. Let principals know you are encouraging this. Point new RRSs to colleagues who will be especially valuable to them.

- Encourage RRSs to network at local council meetings and at professional conferences. State affiliates of International Reading Association (IRA) special interest groups can be invaluable.

Tips: Get-Togethers

- Call sessions anything but meetings. "Sharing (or networking) sessions," "institutes," or "seminars" can spark more interest.

- Consider grouping RRSs at different levels together, at least those at middle and senior high school.

- Schedule sessions at a time that is most convenient for RRSs. Teacher planning days might be a good choice because some RRSs have class responsibilities part of the regular school day and would otherwise need substitute coverage. But don't overdo the use of planning days—they are also good times for the RRS to be in the building and working with teachers. If possible, set up a schedule for the year so that RRSs can plan ahead.

Get-togethers. Find ways to arrange for RRS get-togethers. Nowadays, when substitute dollars are in short supply and many middle and senior high RRSs are carrying partial teaching loads, I resort to occasional Saturday breakfasts. The crowd is not as big as during the work week, but the gatherings are nice social affairs as well as being informative. I have found these tips to be helpful for scheduling and carrying out get-togethers:

Following are a few formats for RRS get-togethers that I have found to be successful.

1. *Share and tell.* A sure-fire way to motivate the RRS to attend sessions is to provide "share and tell" time. Sharing can be dull if it goes on for too long, but otherwise it is beneficial to speakers and listeners alike. Call participants who are doing something even a little bit special and invite them to prepare a short presentation; this gets the ball rolling. The RRS may be more willing to undertake the extra effort if he or she knows that a pat on the back will be forthcoming.

Listeners can always pick up a pointer or two from the twists their colleagues may give to old ideas. "Share and tell" is also a way of keeping the interest of both old-timers and neophytes. These sharing sessions can blossom into presentations or articles that RRSs can contribute (together with the supervisor/director if necessary) to local, state, and national professional organizations.

2. *Role-play scenarios.* There's nothing like a role-play situation to learn the role of an RRS. Once the RRSs are comfortable with their leader and with each other, they can be asked to role-play touchy scenarios during gatherings. This is guaranteed to produce nervous mannerisms or giggles as familiar situations are enacted. The following ideas are not meant to imply that all experiences will be this difficult, but we all run into some of these!

- Try to convince a group of secondary department heads at a meeting that Sustained Silent Reading is worth teachers' time. Teachers feel that it would take away too much time from their teaching.

- Try to persuade a teacher to change a questionable method. Phonics as a sole means of dealing with decoding? Oral drills in teaching limited-English-proficient (LEP) students? Directions to just read the chapter and answer the questions? Round robin reading? Make the task a little harder by pretending that you've already worked with this teacher on this topic.

- Try to convince a principal in a low-scoring school that isolated skills work is not effective in raising student achievement.

- The principal wants you to start a reading lab. Make a case for the principal's letting you continue to resource the school as a whole instead.

- Try to work with a teacher whose performance has been found to be unsatisfactory. You've been asked to help this teacher, who is older than you are and who does not want your help. One of the teacher's problems is teaching vocabulary only by asking students to "look up words in the dictionary and write a sentence" for each.

- Begin your first inservice session on content area reading. The teachers' attitude is that they "don't have time for reading."

- Try to convince the library/media specialist to have some exciting events to increase library use. The media specialist's hidden agenda is that he or she does not want the library used more because this will create extra work.

- Try to convince teachers at an elementary grade level meeting that they should try alternatives to ability grouping. The school is adopting an integrated reading/language arts basal series with which it is virtually impossible to fit three ability groups into the school's 90-minute reading/language arts block.

- Picture yourself at your first meeting with a middle school team. Set a tempo for peer collaboration rather than assuming the role of instructional authority figure.

3. *Roundtable discussions.* Roundtable discussions are fail-proof ways of getting RRSs to network. Presenters are less intimidated when sitting around a table with a small group of colleagues than they would be if standing in front of a group. With several roundtables to choose from, RRSs can go to those that

best suit their needs. And, of course, the smaller roundtable setting promotes greater participation. RRSs can be asked ahead of time to lead specific roundtables, perhaps on cooperative grouping or newsletter writing or building classroom libraries. Optimum length will vary depending on the topic and the group; 30 minutes often works well.

4. *Formal presentations.* Inviting exciting presenters to talk to a group of RRSs can be a real shot in the arm! If this is expensive, costs can be shared with another district. Local professional organizations or textbook publishers might be able to help. Another resource is found in the best faculty members at local colleges or universities. And district supervisors/directors shouldn't forget their RRSs and other stars in their own back yard!

5. *Study groups.* Prior to a session, a group of RRSs can be sent literature to read on a topic of interest. The group can then discuss this material in light of their collective experience. Suggestions might be teacher-as-researcher columns in IRA's *Reading Today* newspaper, or Neilsen's (1991) delightful article on the woes of RRSs.

A supervisor/director who builds a cadre of strong RRSs will find enhanced programs throughout each school. Carefully planned meetings and other forms of networking as described here can make it happen!

Working within District Constraints

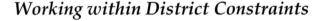

Just as each school has a culture, so does each district office. The district reading/writing program must fit into this overall culture. A new district administrator must be alert to learn all about this culture as quickly as possible. Weick (1982) suggests that the culture is the glue that holds loosely coupled systems together. In terms of your job, culture-related issues might include the following:

• Are there built-in tensions between top-down and bottom-up reform?

• What is the history of the reading/language arts

office, and what is the history of its relationships with other offices (e.g., exceptional student education, bilingual education, adult education, Chapter 1, the content areas)?

- Can the administrator work independently or not?

- Does the reading/language arts office have "clout"?

- Are there differences in the treatment of elementary and secondary programs?

- What are the district's relationships with the teachers' union and with parent/citizen groups?

- What are the legitimate channels for effecting change?

- What are the consequences if rules are "bent" in an effort to effect change?

New constraints may emerge if the district is in flux. If, for example, your district is moving toward school-based management, you will want to work toward "integrated decentralization," with both strong central coordination *and* strong local diversity (Murphy, 1989). Thus, you may shift away from monitoring and enforcing policy and toward providing services, facilitating, and coordinating. This involves a willingness to (1) negotiate discrepancies and inconsistencies between district and school goals, (2) help schools identify nonnegotiable areas and find ways to get waivers from state policy, (3) help principals and teachers reshape their roles and rethink their responsibilities, and (4) coordinate staff development when the needs identified by several schools overlap (Pajak, 1992). Other district changes, such as a move toward total quality management (TQM), will require other supportive responses from district staff.

Whatever the overall district picture, some constraints will be inevitable. On the next page are tips that I have found helpful for dealing with frustrating constraints. Every supervisor will have his or her own list. Evaluate the possibilities for your situation and your management style; use them carefully. If you can combine more than one, so much the better.

Each of these tips has served me well at some point; most have also been ineffective at other times. St. Francis of Assisi's prayer comes to mind: "Lord, grant me the serenity to accept the things I cannot change, the courage to change the things I can, and the wisdom to know the difference." A little strategic thinking can work wonders.

Working with Outside Resources

Although all schools work with outside resources, some specific issues in dealing with outside contacts are particularly pertinent to the district supervisor.

Tips: Working Within District Constraints

- *Try for a win–win situation.* I had seen the success of a literature conference elsewhere in the state and had envisioned a local literature conference, cosponsored by the school district and the local affiliates of reading, language arts, and library/media specialist national groups. All groups saw that cooperation would result in a bigger and better conference than would occur if one group tackled the project alone. All saw the potential benefits to conference attendees. Each group also had its own reasons for participating. The positives outweighed the concerns, and planning began.

- *If you cannot get something done in one way, see if there is another route, maybe an even better one!* For example, when I was restricted from writing memoranda to reading teachers, quarterly newsletters were born. When budget constraints later resulted in the demise of district newsletters, information was published instead in the reading council newsletter. To use a military metaphor (probably a bad idea here), you are losing the battle but winning the war.

- *Consider timing.* Toward the end of a year I proposed the establishment of administrator study groups. The response was a "no." When the idea was again proposed late in the summer, as energies for the new year were being deployed, it was enthusiastically accepted (Radencich, 1993).

- *Consider who would be the best person to introduce a new idea.* If you are not likely to get support for an idea, try to have it introduced by someone who is. For example, when I saw a need to provide district scoring for the Degrees of Reading Power Test (DRP) (1984), I brought it up before a committee looking at the overall district assessment picture. It emerged as a committee recommendation.

- *Network!* Two heads always work better than one. Colleagues within or outside the district may see possibilities that haven't occurred to you. Florida, for example, has been praised for the close relationship between the boards of the Florida Reading Association and the Reading Supervisors of Florida. Several supervisors on both boards network regularly.

  You may wish to establish a relationship with a mentor who can advise you on a regular basis. Such mentorship can work both ways. Following is a Florida example. When Susan Oestreicher, a Clay County specialist, faced the unpleasant task of responding to her superintendent's request to increase their standardized testing program, she obtained from a Lake County specialist a tool that had, in turn, come from the math consultant in the Orange County Public Schools. Oestreicher, in turn, was able to use this to convince her superintendent to institute a broad-based, meaningful assessment program (Oestreicher, 1992). (The tool was a pyramid of blocks that formed a picture of a whole child on one side and, on the reverse, had the name of a different type of assessment on each block.) Two years later, Oestreicher shared her report so that other district supervisors could use it to try to modify policies in their respective districts.

- *Provide open-minded key people with research support for your ideas.* Be selective. Highlight key points. If the research isn't read, I find that my providing it at least adds to my credibility.

- *Work through your local professional councils.* Much that cannot be done at the district level can be done through a professional group. If you cannot solicit donations from publishers for refreshments at meetings, ask local IRA or NCTE councils to sponsor meetings. Councils can also help by making oral and written statements to the school board, sending written information to schools, or serving on task forces.

- *Publicize your efforts.* If possible, send copies of your memoranda, even "blind copies," to key persons. I had held seminars for middle/senior high administrators in which articles read beforehand were discussed by the group (Radencich, 1993). The participants had requested that the seminars be replicated for other subject areas under the direction of a key staff developer. A memorandum to the associate superintendent responsible for all subject areas was copied also to the staff developer, who responded positively.

- *When you know your ground, be assertive!* Your confidence (or lack thereof) can make all the difference. When the Clay County superintendent mentioned previously wanted a traditional testing program, a firm explanation of the value of an alternative assessment model resulted in a multifaceted assessment program.

- *If you see no way to implement a desired change, put it on the back burner.* Changes in district hierarchies and priorities may allow you to resurrect the idea at a later date. I had received no support for a desire to start a Reading Recovery program (Pinnell, DeFord, & Lyons, 1988). But when the associate superintendent picked up information on the program at a conference, he became interested, and a modification of Reading Recovery was begun (Radencich, 1992b).

The Community

At the district level, you will receive requests from community organizations wishing to support literacy efforts. You may even initiate some of these contacts. Some common sense will help you here. Is the organization asking for money? Who will do the leg-work, if any? If schools are to be rewarded with a performance, can you see the performance first to be sure it is appropriate? Will all students who meet a criterion be rewarded, or will a reward go to only a few?

Above all, consider the district's beliefs and your own. Should students be rewarded for reading, or are you concerned with the research (Kohn, 1991) that shows the dangers of such plans? Kohn points out that when rewards are bigger than tokens, they often become the goals themselves; thus, people who originally enjoyed an activity (such as reading) stop engaging in it when a reward is instituted and then taken away.

If you do decide to participate in a program, help to shape it if possible. I once worked with a recreational center where the desire, over the summer, was to reward readers only from schools that were the center's "partners" in a districtwide business–school partnership program. A little persuasion resulted in acceptance of the idea that the public library system could also be involved, thus extending the program to a much larger population.

Be sure to thank any helping organization publicly. Perhaps the sponsor can be introduced at a school board meeting, or a thank-you letter can be sent from the superintendent of schools.

Publishing Companies

As a district supervisor, you will be visited frequently by representatives of publishing companies. You should meet with representatives to become familiar with their products. You will get to know which representatives will take care of their business quickly and which you will need to hurry along. Accept samples so that when schools call requesting your opinion about a product you can refresh your memory or even lend the sample to the school. As with any business dealings, a few cautions are in order:

- Be careful about what you accept beyond samples of materials. Publishers will often be generous with offerings of expensive dinners, publisher-sponsored conferences, and other "perks." Whether or not your district has rules about accepting gifts, set guidelines for yourself. It is important not only that you maintain your objectivity about commercial materials, but just as important, that there be no appearance of impropriety.

- Watch what you say to publishers' representatives. Supervisors learn from experience that during very competitive district adoptions, it is poor judgment to let representatives know about internal district disagreements.

- Be careful of your recommendations to schools. Too strong an endorsement can prompt suspicions of impropriety.

- Be fair. If you request a speaker from one company for one presentation, try to request one from a competitor the next time.

A cordial relationship with representatives will be helpful to the district as well as to the publishing company. Be sure to copy your representative's boss with any thank-you's you send.

Assessing Program Effectiveness

Another responsibility you may encounter is involvement with district assessments of program effectiveness. Whether you are directly involved in this process or not, you will be interested in the results. Information on assessment is provided in the next chapter within the context of comprehensive schoolwide programs. Following is additional information specific to the district supervisor.

Assessing Faculty

You are not likely to have to formally evaluate school administrators or teachers, except perhaps in the case of unsatisfactory teachers for whom an external review is required. If you are to perform an external review of a teacher, you will probably be trained to use your district's instrument. When you explain to a principal your perspective following a teacher's observation, staff development for the principal may be a fringe benefit. If no district instrument exists, or if you prefer (or are asked) to use a narrative style, you might consider describing the events in the class and then listing commendations and recommendations at the end of your report.

Assessing Schools

You will likely participate in program reviews of some type. It may be that you visit classrooms informally and then provide some verbal feedback to teachers and school administrator(s). Or you may be part of a formal district team that issues written commendations and recommendations, not for individual teachers but for the school as a whole. The Program Review Form in Appendix C or an adaptation can be used for formal program reviews. Whatever the form of the review, it is essential that there be sufficient follow-up support for implementing the recommendations, and that there be closure with a future program review, perhaps a year later. Further information on program reviews is provided in the section on "Monitoring Reading/Writing Lessons" in Chapter 3.

Assessing the District

Districts have been most commonly assessed with the standardized test scores that are printed in the newspaper. The problems with the tunnel vision involved in evaluating with only one measure—and a deeply flawed one at that—are well documented (Brown, 1989; Valencia, McGinley, & Pearson, 1990). School districts are now decreasing the the number of grades in which standardized tests in reading are administered. Many districts and states are now assessing writing through holistic scoring. National, state, and local efforts to include the use of portfolio and performance based assessment are increasing. Chapter 8 addresses assessment in detail.

Conclusion

In summary, this chapter has examined the role of the district supervisor. Although much of the rest of the book will apply to the supervisor as well, this chapter is specifically aimed at the supervisory audience. Key skills—providing leadership to schools, working within district constraints, working with outside resources, and assessing program effectiveness—were described. It is hoped that readers who are not supervisors will gain a newfound respect for a challenging and sometimes underappreciated role.

A Comprehensive Schoolwide Reading/Writing Program

The third portion of this book gives school administrators a framework for answering the question, "Does my school have a comprehensive reading/writing program?" The three chapters that make up this section deal with the components of a comprehensive program, organizing for instruction, and measuring whether the program is working.

Chapter 6

Components of a Comprehensive Schoolwide Reading/Writing Program

The schools have taken on every problem, every task, every reform at the heart of the matter of American civilization—from illiteracy to child labor to segregation to Vietnam to dope to sex and, if the schools' scores are low on these matters, no other institutions in the country even showed up for the test.

—James Herndon (1985)

What is the school's reading/writing program? Too often it is perceived to be a commercial series. But no matter how good a series is, materials can only be one piece of the pie of a comprehensive reading/writing program. This chapter's discussion of a comprehensive program includes issues of curriculum and instruction, the library/media center, the players both within and outside the school, and motivational reading/writing programs.

It is important that the comprehensiveness of a reading/writing program be evaluated beyond the elementary level. Middle and senior high administrators should not be lured by the incorrect assumption that "elementary school reading instruction is adequate and sufficient to meet the more sophisticated and challenging reading tasks of the secondary school curriculum" (Irvin, 1990, p. 199). In some schools, a comprehensive program extends to the preschool or the adult education level. For information on these levels, see Appendixes A and B, respectively.

Curriculum and Instruction

The interweaving of curriculum and instruction form the core of the reading/writing program. Chapters 2 and 3 of this book address curriculum and instruction, respectively.

The Library/Media Center

The library/media center, or "resource center" (Haycock, 1992), can be the heart of curriculum and instruction. An examination of the library/media center must first take into account the role of library/media specialists, a role that has changed (American Association of School Librarians and Association for Educational Communications and Technology, 1988). The job title tells part of the story. "Librarian" has been replaced with "library/media specialist," "librarian-teacher," or "teacher-librarian" (Haycock, 1992). Library/media specialists have seen other job changes as well. They must see themselves as media brokers and also as teachers. They must now often work with classroom teachers who are suddenly quite knowledgeable about children's literature. Interpersonal skills with adults have become increasingly important. Administrators may have to help their library/media specialists to embrace these new roles.

Administrators must make several decisions regarding use of the library/media center. The first relates to location of resources. If the budget does not allow for ample deployment of resources in both classrooms and the media center, administrators must decide the optimum location for different resources. If classrooms have the priority for trade books, students will have immediate access, and immediate access translates into use. Indeed, schools in Australia, where there is no position comparable to that of library/media specialist, work well with this arrangement. On the other hand, no single classroom can have the variety that a library/media center can house. And one runs the risk of creating very different environments for the "haves" and "have-nots" in schools where only some teachers have accumulated extensive collections. Aside from books, decisions must be made regarding other resources. Computerized encyclopedias, filmstrips, films, and other expensive materials will undoubtedly be housed in the library/media center. Blackburn Elementary in Manatee County, Florida, offers the best of both worlds by having students use the computer in their literature-rich classrooms to check on availability of materials in the library/media center.

A second decision refers to the choice of resources to purchase. Will the emphasis be on books or on other types of media? Do teachers give the library/media specialist suggestions? Are materials purchased according to need: Enough multicultural titles? Enough foreign language materials? Enough predictable books? Will priorities rotate, with, for example, material related to the reading/language arts program in Year 1 and material related to the new social studies series in Year 2? How are decisions made regarding which magazines and professional journals to purchase? On a broader basis, funds may be required for computerizing the card catalogue.

A final decision for administrators who are fortunate enough to have a library/media specialist (a diminishing commodity in the United States) relates to the respective roles of teachers and library/media specialists. Although they have similar goals for students, they often view their professional lives through different lenses (Dales, 1990). School administrators must look through the lenses of both. Administrators can examine the status quo with a number of questions (Dales, 1990):

- Is there flexible access to the library/media center so that students can visit at any time, or is there a fixed schedule for each class? With an active library/media specialist, a flexible access library lends itself to more interaction with classroom goals. Flexible access allows the library/media specialist to meet with a whole class and then follow up with small groups or to be available regularly for planning with teachers.

- If there is flexible access, do all the teachers take advantage of it, or do some neglect to provide this opportunity for their students?

- When entire classes go to the library, what happens? Does the library/media specialist read or tell stories? Do book talks? Help students check out books? Teach information skills? Use electronic encyclopedias and indexes?

- Do library/media specialists follow up and find out how a student personally constructed meaning from a particular book, or do they feel their job is complete once items are located?

- Do teachers help students discover everything that is published on a topic, or do they keep stagnant classroom collections?

- If teachers do cache materials in their rooms, is this an attempt to deal with inaccessible library collections?

- Are library/media specialists involved in the educational process or merely available if asked to answer a reference question or when called on to locate a particular text?

- Do teachers stay with students when they go to the library/media center as a class? Teachers might team-teach with the library/media specialist. Or they might bind student-authored books in the media production room, read articles from professional journals, find resources to support their classroom studies, and use their more intimate knowledge of the students to coach them on book selection (Lamme & Ledbetter, 1990).

- Do library/media specialists see their domain as the whole school or only the library/media center? They might boost a motivational reading program over the public address system, place recent back issues of professional journals in the faculty lounge to make them more accessible, or initiate a campaign to ensure that all students have public library cards.

- Do library/media specialists offer rotating classroom collections? Thematic groupings of materials? Space for student-authored books? Book fairs? Sessions to update teachers on current literature? Storytelling festivals with help for teachers in storytelling and prop making (Lamme & Ledbetter, 1990)?

- What are the consequences of a mismatch of expectations between teachers and library/media specialist? Dales (1990) points out that any rifts may be erroneously attributed to personality, when in fact it may be the organizational demands that are influencing behavior.

Once you have examined the status quo, it is time to work with all interested parties to consider improvements. Lamme and Ledbetter (1990) give several ideas that were implemented while Ledbetter was library/media specialist at Terwilliger Elementary School in Gainesville, Florida. New books did not circulate until each one was presented in a book talk to every potential reader. Ledbetter surveyed teachers for their favorite read-alouds and then made a list of core read-alouds for each grade level. She also designed book bags in which kindergarten children could take home read-alouds.

Some schools encourage parents to donate a book on their child's birthday with a nameplate celebrating the occasion. Others open the library/media center for students and families beyond school hours. Walter Frank, library/media specialist at Phillis Wheatley Elementary and then at Jackson Senior High in Dade County, published regular newsletters highlighting library/media center events.

When card catalogues are not computerized so that bibliographies are easily printed out, library/media specialists can create book lists by subject and update these lists as new books arrive. They can compile information files about authors, illustrators, pop-up book or puppet making, and the like. Collecting flannelboard patterns, tape recordings of good storytelling, and story character dolls (Lamme & Ledbetter, 1990) are other worthwhile endeavors. The possibilities are endless.

The Players in a Comprehensive Reading/Writing Program

Aside from the students—the most important players of all—those responsible for a comprehensive reading/writing program include the principal and assistant principal, the reading committee and other committees, the reading specialist, the library/media specialist, other professional support personnel within and outside the school, parents, and the community. The role of each adult player will be examined in turn.

The Principal/Assistant Principal

The principal or assistant principal must be not merely a manager (Tanner & Tanner, 1987) but also a leader in the reading/writing program. Wepner (1989) sees the leadership role as encompassing five areas: working with teachers, working with students, creating a school atmosphere, providing policy leadership, and building community support. She supports Barnard and Hetzel's (1976, 1986) belief that principals are the key to good reading programs and states that this role has been strongly supported by other principals (Manning & Manning, 1981; Rice, 1987).

The Reading Committee

You may find more support for a project requested by a reading or curriculum committee (Anders, 1985) than for one of your own design. A wise administrator will try to work through a reading committee consisting of influential people in the school—perhaps an administrator, a reading resource specialist, a library/media specialist, parents, students, grade chairs or department heads, a union representative, an exceptional education teacher, and other well-respected teachers. Structure meetings to allow for an open-door policy. Have the committee use an action plan like the one in Appendix C to guide their efforts.

Yatvin (1992, p. 34) recommends that schools using whole language have an oversight committee that can guide and coordinate the curriculum, with grade-level and grade-cluster teams that maintain the quality of classroom implementation. She sees the job of the oversight committee as follows:

- Write the school philosophy and a set of teacher guidelines that highlight the most important principles of the philosophy.

- Describe a general approach to teaching that can be used at all grade levels.

- Secure and distribute funds for classroom books and materials.

- Make an implementation plan that includes a timeline and divisions of responsibility.

- Develop a system for apportioning content-bound material among the various grade levels.

- Provide an introductory inservice training program for all teachers.

- Establish other committees to deal with ongoing issues and problems.

Teachers

This book emphasizes over and over again the vital role of teachers in achieving programs of excellence. This is true for *all* teachers. I have seen a school-wide read-aloud campaign at a senior high school where *every* department—you name it—was involved. I have seen a physical education teacher dressed in costume reading to elementary children over closed-circuit television. A particularly impressive example is Blackburn Elementary in Manatee County, Florida, where special area teachers were specifically courted so that they would be integral to their whole language program. As a result, the speech therapist teaches whole language lessons, and art and music rooms are "littered" with subject-related books, charts, and other print materials.

The interplay among teachers is what often makes the difference: teachers who trade materials and ideas as each starts a new theme in one elementary school, or a second-year teacher at another school who shares ideas from a workshop with his peer teacher from the year before. Such teachers truly exemplify communities of learners.

Library/Media Specialist

The role of the library/media specialist was described earlier in the section on "The Library/Media Center."

Reading Specialist

Many of the roles ascribed to others, such as the supervisor, the school-based administrator, and the library/media specialist overlap significantly with the

role that a school-based reading specialist can play. For a thorough examination of the role of the reading specialist, including sample weekly and year-long schedules, see Radencich, Beers, and Schumm's (1993) *Handbook for the K–12 Reading Resource Specialist.* Following are some key pointers:

The roles of reading teachers are evolving from pull-out or classroom remedial models to models that include resource specialists who serve the school as a whole or perhaps a number of schools. Fucello (in Wepner, Feeley, & Strickland, 1989) found that many states are beginning to require reading specialists to devote 50 percent of their time to the resource role. Indeed, the International Reading Association's *Standards for Reading Professionals* (1992) include close attention to the role of the reading specialist/consultant/coordinator, one that requires a wealth of both procedural and content knowledge. Not only should the reading resource specialist (RRS) have a wide array of ideas, strategies, and creative solutions readily available upon request, but he or she should also have the skills to offer such information to teachers in a collaborative, nonthreatening manner.

The following list of services is adapted from Barnard and Hetzel (1986):

- Help with student assessment.
- Provide instructional suggestions.
- Evaluate and help order new instructional materials.
- Demonstrate new materials and techniques.
- Develop needed special materials.
- Consult and tutor in individual cases.
- Share research findings and school success stories.
- Train and supervise paraprofessionals.
- Help organize and manage classrooms.
- Conduct workshops for faculty and for parents.
- Inform administrators of services provided for the school.
- Consult administrators and make recommendations on materials and programs.
- Analyze and interpret test data.
- Help meet school goals and objectives.
- Help identify learning problems and solutions.
- Report and share research findings.
- Train new teachers in instructional expectations.

- Provide the community with information on the purpose and progress of the reading/writing program.

Barnard and Hetzel (1986) identified characteristics of an effective RRS, which are adapted as follows:

- The RRS is a professional who avoids gossip at all costs, does not evaluate teachers, and is fair and businesslike with everyone.

- The RRS is a teacher, demonstrates new techniques and materials, and asks teachers to use their classrooms to try new approaches.

- The RRS has a smile and is friendly, respectful, and honest while performing his or her duties.

- The RRS listens; realizes that other people have ideas, biases, and feelings that should be respected; and helps people define and remove problems rather than having the answer for everything.

- The RRS is visible and is available to meet day-to-day teacher needs.

- The RRS has a positive approach and emphasizes what can be done, as opposed to giving all the reasons that something will not work.

- The RRS is adaptable and can adjust to teachers and principals with different philosophies and needs.

- The RRS is sensitive to public opinion; is aware of the importance of a public image; and works to project an image of sincerity, competence, and efficiency.

- The RRS is involved with everyone in and around the school.

Other Support Personnel

Other support personnel include secretaries, cafeteria managers, custodians, psychologists, visiting teachers, and counselors. Administrators should make good use of these personnel in enhancing the reading/writing program. In one district, an Exceptional Student Director involved her psychologists in a motivational reading program for the exceptional education students. Counselors might use bibliotherapy with the students they work with. Secretaries, cafeteria managers, and custodians might do read-alouds of their favorite childhood book or speak to classes during Career Week about the role of reading and writing in their lives. Together, all can project the climate of a literary community.

Parents

Parent involvement is a two-way street. We give parents mixed messages—we want their help, but we don't always make them feel welcome. Parent involvement can be particularly problematic for parents who experienced difficulty in school themselves and who therefore may avoid the school as adults. Use the following tips as you work with your staff to encourage parent support and involvement.

Tips: Parent Involvement

- *Expect all school staff, from the cafeteria manager to the custodian, to be ambassadors to parents.*

- *Use good psychology to encourage parents to attend PTA/PTO meetings:*

    — Have students perform.

    — Make arrangements for the children (such as a storytelling session in another room).

    — Remember the refreshments!

    — Address topics relevant to parents. Aside from the usual topics, such as understanding test scores, look for timely topics such as finding time to read to your child when you are a single parent. In some areas you might need a session on gangs, or AIDS, or crack cocaine. Do whatever it takes. Once the parents are there, you can supplement the program with literacy-related issues.

    — Involve the men in the family. Too often it is the mothers only who are expected to attend. One Chapter 1 school in Lake County, Florida, invited the men in the family—father, grandfather, older brother—to a special men's breakfast on Valentine's Day. Children were given books, which they read to the men or listened to as read-alouds.

— Use PTA meetings to model literacy behavior. For example, parents can go through the stages of the writing process with a piece of their own writing. Kitty Kaczmarek, a director of program/staff development in Arizona (Weaver, 1990, p. 273) recommends that, during meetings, parents read and discuss a "short and sweet" article written in language they can understand.

- *Have inservice sessions for teachers on how to communicate with parents.*

— Call parents early in the year, before there is any reason for a complaint. This establishes a positive rapport and may help avoid the assumption that any call from the teacher means bad news.

— *Listen* to parents! They have agendas just as you do. Find ways in which teachers can help parents with *their* agendas.

— Meet parents side by side. Sitting authoritatively behind the desk is as bad as sitting authoritatively behind educational jargon!

— Brainstorm with teachers on how to make parents feel a part of the school community so that they will be involved on an ongoing basis.

- *Involve parents with report cards.* Copenhaver (1993) suggests an evaluation form on which parents list three plusses they saw during the grading period, one wish for their child, and one "story" or insight about their child's learning at school or at home. One middle school teacher, Kathleen Jongsma (1993), had students write letters home about their progress and parents write letters in return. A more drastic measure for involving parents is to require that parents pick up report cards. This might be the only way to get parents of middle and senior high students into the school and make sure they see the report cards.

- *Ask teachers to involve parents with homework—both by taking the school into the home and by taking the home to the school.* Heald-Taylor (1989) suggests activities such as a family photo album with child-dictated stories to go with each photograph, and taped and transcribed interviews of family members. One elementary school used volunteer accountants to teach math to parents so they could help their children with their homework. See also Radencich and Schumm's (1988) *How to Help Your Child with Homework.*

- *Educate parents and keep them informed.* Appendix D includes a list of resources for parents. Use regular newsletters, flyers, or radio/television announcements for those who can't read. In multicultural communities, use the media from each cultural group. Use video training programs such as Edwards's (1990) "Parents as Partners in Reading" or those sold by professional organizations. Captain School in Clayton, Missouri, includes information about educational trends in its newsletter. Kaczmarek (Weaver, 1990) suggests topical literacy breakfasts and parent lending libraries. A secondary school in Brevard County, Florida, provided parents with a flip chart of information on study skills, interpretation of test scores, and the like.

- *Market your programs to parents.* Hand parents testimonials provided by other parents like the ones in Windsor et al.'s (1991) "Parents Supporting Whole Language." One elementary assistant principal in a lower-middle-class community provides a list of suggested magazine subscriptions for holiday gifts. She makes ordering easy by including age range, address, and price.

- *Involve parents in decision-making, advisory, or service committees.* Make clear the parameters of these committees' roles to avoid any misunderstandings.

- *Hold community school activities after school.* Parents who get used to coming to the school for flower arranging or aerobics may be more willing to come on other occasions. One inner-city Philadelphia principal went so far as to install washing machines for family use!

- *Find ways in which all parents can help out: working parents, limited-English-proficient parents—everyone!* Maybe they can do some paperwork at home. Maybe they can encourage neighbors to send their truant children to school. Maybe they can take off a day or give up a lunch break to come and speak on Career Day or to serve as a field trip chaperone. Maybe they can periodically stop by the frame shop to pick up leftover matting for use with hard-cover student-authored books.

- *Incorporate students' language and culture into the program.* Encourage community participation as an integral component of children's education (Keenan, Willett, & Solsken, 1993). One of these authors, as an urban teacher of a multilingual, multicultural class, had family members for 20 of 24 children bring knowledge to the class that contributed to themes under study. One mother baked bread with the children, another talked to them about the fast of Ramadan, while a third read them favorite family books and told of her experiences on a tobacco farm. One previously unreachable father shared his martial arts and his cartoons and portraits, while another played his African drums.

- *Plan activities that specifically relate to literacy.*

  — Parents can have a "lunch bunch" reading club (an award-winning PTA project) with small groups of students who read and discuss the same books.

  — Parents can receive literacy training while students participate in a homework club.

  — Parents can help with incentive reading programs, mounting displays, gathering rewards from the community, and the like.

— Parents can sign contracts specifying that they will read aloud to their children on a daily basis. Senior citizens and other volunteers can help fill out certificates *or* help plan a spaghetti dinner for children and parents who complete their contracts.

— Second-grade teacher Joni Weed (1991) allows students to invite family or friends for the "first public reading" of published pieces. Whenever the class has at least six completed pieces, a Celebrate Authors Day is held for this purpose.

— Parents can help with incentive reading programs, mounting displays, gathering rewards from the community, and the like.

If all else fails, take drastic action. Principals at Lillie C. Evans Elementary and Orchard Villa Elementary in Dade County, Florida, have marched with faculty members in the schools' inner-city streets waving signs, chanting slogans, and giving out literature to call for parent involvement. Headlines the next day spoke of parent apathy. The embarrassed community responded.

Community

There is no more vital stakeholder in a school than the immediate community. As more and more community agencies and businesses have become educationally conscious, providing grants for innovative projects and sponsoring recreational reading activities have become quite trendy. Pick up on the trend! If you need funding for a special program or activity, ask. The answer may be no. It may be no over and over again. But there is a yes out there. It just takes persistence.

1. *How to approach community agencies and businesses*: Be specific about what you want to do and how much it will cost. Let your potential sponsor know what he or she can gain from the collaboration. Maybe you can provide a public thank-you, or display student work in the corporate office, or get the project some publicity in the local paper.

2. *Public libraries*: Reach out to your public library and try to create. It may be joint projects, such as developing lists, reading incentive programs, visits from noted authors, library tours, and library card registration campaigns.

3. *Local newspaper, radio, and television*: Your local newspapers may be involved in "Newspaper in Education" activities or may have special thematic supplements available to schools. Make certain that you are on the mailing list and have a contact person at the newspapers. Be aware of the procedure for getting publicity and recognition for your special programs from newspapers, radio, and television. Of course, you will have a better shot with a neighborhood paper or supplement than with a major newspaper or television. The media are interested in off-the-wall projects. For example, one elementary principal agreed to spend a day on the roof if the school completed one million minutes of reading. Sure enough, she invited dignitaries to join her and wave to classes reading on the lawn below.

4. *Volunteers*: Volunteer efforts are on the rise in the United States. Many high schools and universities now require a community service component. Religious and service organizations and organizations of retired professionals have become actively engaged in volunteer efforts. Despite this upsurge of volunteerism, many schools are not prepared to accommodate volunteers who may show up at their door. Frequently, volunteers are delegated tasks such as running off copies or grading papers. These tasks are necessary, but some volunteers wish to make a contribution other than doing clerical tasks.

Some volunteers may serve on an ongoing basis to assist with particular teachers or children. Volunteers may also get involved in one-shot deals, lending an extra hand during special reading programs and the like. Local celebrities can also be enlisted for one shot read-aloud sessions. Think big! Again, many no's can lead to a yes!

There is more than meets the eye to having a successful volunteer program. If you are serious about enlisting volunteers, your efforts must be intentional and well structured. An effective volunteer program needs to incorporate plans for enlistment, training, placement, monitoring, evaluating, and recognizing.

1. *Enlistment*: Start with a multifaceted recruitment campaign. As prospective volunteers contact you for details, ask how they heard about your program and keep a tally of their responses. This will help you track the best method for future recruiting campaigns. Some suggestions for recruitment include:

- Letter to parents

- Ad in the newspaper

- Radio or television news spot

- School district volunteer office

- Sign-up table at a major school event (carnival, PTA meeting, etc.)

2. *Training*: For smooth functioning of a volunteer program, some training is essential. Make volunteers aware of their roles and responsibilities. Focus training on an overview of the school environment and routines. Detail procedures for signing in and out of the school. Clarify expectations. Clearly delineate procedures for maintaining student confidentiality and trouble shooting. Volunteers will take their job seriously if the school does. Depending on your plan to involve volunteers, your training can range from an informal chat to a series of training workshops. Here is an example of a workshop series for a volunteer read-aloud program:

> *Session 1*: Orientation (overview of the program, roles and responsibilities, introduction to the school environment)
> *Session 2*: How to read aloud to children
> *Session 3*: How to encourage students to respond to reading through writing, art, and discussion
> *Session 4*: How to select appropriate books
> *Session 5*: How to motivate the reluctant reader and writer

3. *Placement*: With large volunteer programs, placement can be particularly challenging. A strategy for placement of volunteers can be outlined. Animosity can arise if all teachers who *want* volunteers cannot *get* volunteers. Conversely, volunteers should not be assigned to teachers who prefer to work alone.

4. *Monitoring*: Often, once volunteers have been assigned to teachers or children, the volunteers are left to their own devices. A system for periodic monitoring of volunteers is necessary to make certain that they feel comfortable in their role and have the support they need.

5. *Evaluating*: Volunteers need the opportunity to evaluate the program. End-of-year or exit interviews would be one way to glean information about program pros and cons. This monitoring can be done by a staff member or an experienced volunteer whose responsibility is to serve as a liaison between the volunteers and you.

6. *Recognizing*: Volunteers give of their time and talent for altruistic reasons. But without ongoing recognition, they may begin to feel that their services are not valued. Thank-you notes from children, teachers, and you are always appreciated. Certificates, buttons, and recognition in the school newspaper are other ways to show that volunteer services are valued. Formal recognition of volunteers at a function at least once a year is also a must.

Motivational Reading/Writing Programs

It has been said you can lead a horse to water but you cannot make him drink. It has also been said you *can* make him drink—if you use a little salt. This section provides some literacy salt. Students will read if they are motivated to do so. Following is a collection of suggestions for implementing a motivational reading/writing program in your school.

Matching Students and Books/Magazines

Facilitating the student–selection match is crucial to a successful motivational reading program. As the school year progresses, most teachers learn about students' reading interests and attitudes toward reading. But to maximize the opportunity to match students and books early in the school year, it helps to ascertain students' interests and attitudes fairly quickly. Chapter 8 includes references to a variety of ways to determine such information: personal interviews, rating scales, open-ended sentence forms, reading reflection logs, and reading dialogue journals.

Initially, direct assistance from teachers is needed to help many students select books and magazines. Ultimately, however, it is important that students learn to make selections independently. As you have probably observed, during school library periods, many reluctant readers aimlessly roam around and then finally grab a book near the end of the period. Unfortunately, the book rarely if ever is opened. Many students simply do not know how to select reading material.

For elementary students, the so-called five-finger rule of thumb can be helpful in fostering independence in selecting books. The child is directed to read the first page of a book that looks interesting. While reading, the child puts one finger up for each work he or she does not know. If the child runs out of fingers before the end of the page, then the book may be too difficult. No such "quick and dirty" method is perfect, but this one can provide a good start. Teachers at all levels can use the "Strategy for Helping Students Find the 'Right' Book" in Appendix E. This sequence was written for middle school students but can be adapted to other levels. It can be given to teachers for classroom use, to the student body as a whole (perhaps on closed-circuit television or in a newsletter), or to individual students as needed.

What's on the Market? Keeping Up with Literature for Children and Adolescents

One way to keep up to date with literature is to have monthly book talks between the library/media specialist and teachers. These book talks, perhaps over a brown bag lunch, can be used to develop awareness of what's on the market, students' favorites within the school, and needs of teachers and individual students. A variation is to participate in a Teachers as Readers book-sharing club which gathers monthly to discuss books, perhaps in each other's homes or in restaurants (Cardarelli, 1992).

Another enjoyable way to keep up with what's new is by spending time in bookstores and libraries. Encourage teachers to take a pal and try this, perhaps on a Saturday morning. Book lists are usually available at your public library. See also "Suggested Readings for Students" and "Read-Aloud Lists" in Appendix D. One caution, however. If you share book lists with parents, be sure they understand that no book list is etched into stone. Lists are merely starting points from which readers should feel free to wander.

Schoolwide Literacy Activities

To establish a school culture that includes a community of readers and writers, organize schoolwide activities that highlight the importance of literacy. Ideas for schoolwide reading programs may emerge from your local community, or you can participate in existing programs sponsored by local, state, or national businesses or nonprofit organizations.

Focus on programs that provide intrinsic motivation, such as the use of reading and writing contracts (samples in Appendix C). Keep any extrinsic motivators small (buttons, stickers, etc.) so that the reward does not become the reason for the reading. Kohn (1991) warns that activities that are intrinsically appealing lose their appeal if they are nevertheless extrinsically rewarded and the extrinsic reward is then removed. For example, people who have always contributed to charity may stop if a tax incentive is instituted and then removed. The activity that once occurred for its intrinsic reward now loses its appeal.

One parent provided a powerful incentive for her two elementary children to read. She had the girls solicit donations for a family read-a-thon. Friends and family donated money for each book the girls read. The money was then given to the University of Miami Student Literacy Corps to buy books for children who could not afford them. With some imagination, similar programs that promote reading and teach students important lessons about citizenship can be implemented at the school level.

One effective schoolwide literacy project is the book fair. Students who might never pick up a book under other circumstances will often buy books at a book fair. One senior high reading resource specialist used the substantial proceeds she made from book fairs for school-related expenses throughout the year. This paid for her professional resources, for extensive Newspaper in Education activities, and for special requests from teachers. Book fairs can be held twice a year or even more often. Parents should be advised of the dates so that they can support the effort. Arrangements are made with one vendor. For addresses of companies that conduct book fairs or clubs, see the tips box in this chapter on "Sources of Reading Material."

Another effort that can be schoolwide is Newspaper in Education (NIE). NIE activities often focus on one month of the year, but they can be ongoing. Cheyney (1992) provides a wealth of NIE activities. Teacher idea guides are often available free of charge with orders from local newspapers, *USA Today*, or magazines such as *Newsweek* and *Sports Illustrated for Kids*. For addresses of

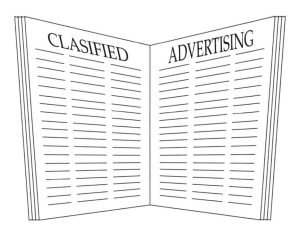

these sources, see the list of publishers in Appendix C. NIE activities are usually inexpensive. Depending on the activities that are planned, a class set of newspapers or magazines may be usable in more than one class.

There are three keys to a successful schoolwide literacy program. The first is *opportunity* for all students. A competitive program that appeals only to academically adept students is limited at best. The second key is *organization*. And the third is keeping *enthusiasm* sky high.

Twenty Suggestions for Schoolwide Literacy Activities That Give Everyone a Chance to Plug In

1. Reading sleepovers

2. Read-alouds by high-profile community members

3. Peer or cross-age reading programs

4. "Write to Your Favorite Author"

5. Character dress-up days

6. Used book sales or exchange programs

7. Student book reviews in the school newsletter or pockets for reviews in school library books

8. Audiotaping of books for younger children by volunteers or older readers

9. Reading of student-authored pieces on school television

10. Bilingual presentations of favorite stories (e.g., "The Three Little Pigs"/"Los Tres Cerditos")

11. Book fairs

12. Family folktale storytelling "bees"

13. Storybook/author door decorating activities

14. Special days - Comic Book Day, Celebrate a Book Day

15. "Literary clubs" that meet before or after school or at lunch

16. Monthly contests (e.g., designing a bookmark, slogan, T-shirt, etc.)

17. Lotteries in which faculty and students earn entries for every book read (Lubell, 1991)

18. Children's or young adult author of the month

19. Student-authored section in the school media center

20. "I Read to the Principal Today" programs, in which children whose names are drawn at random read to the principal and are rewarded with a button or a snapshot on a bulletin board

Businesses and Nonprofit Groups That Sponsor Literacy Programs

- MS Read-a-Thon (305-599-0299)

- Pizza Hut Book-It! (800-4-BOOKIT)

- Reading Is Fundamental (202-287-3220)

- World Book (PIE: Partners in Excellence Reading Program) (800-621-8202)

Tips: Organizing Schoolwide Literacy Activities

- Decide on a coordinator.

- Devise a rough plan.

- Enlist faculty support.

- Organize a committee. Involve parents, students, and teachers and other staff.

- Brainstorm a name for the program or, if linking with an existing program, personalize the name to fit your school. For example, Lubell's (1991) "Lotto Read" became "Cougar Challenge" at Rubén Darío Middle School and "Reading Raffle" at Miami Senior High School.

- Decide on logistics. Identify the tasks, personnel, and timeline.

- Identify ways to promote the program, such as flyers and school television.

- Execute your plan.

- Evaluate your plan and decide how to embellish it in the future.

Sources of Reading Material

Reading choices in the classroom should include more than discards from the school library and books the students have currently checked out. A good selection of newspapers and high–low books and magazines is always helpful. The International Reading Association's books on easy reading (Ryder, Graves, & Graves, 1989) and on magazines (Stoll, 1989) can be invaluable. See "What's on the Market?" earlier in this chapter for additional ideas. Once classroom libraries have been assembled, you can be instrumental in setting up a checkout system.

Following are some ideas for expanding classroom choices.

Tips: Sources of Reading Material

- Keep class libraries in plastic bins that can be rotated from class to class.

- Public libraries or school libraries will often lend teachers class sets of about 25 books to be kept for some time. Encourage teachers to take advantage of these opportunities!

- For beginning readers or limited-English-proficient students, it may be difficult to find enough predictable language books or other appropriate material. Options can include student-made books, books in the student's native language, and books accompanied by recordings.

- Teachers can bring magazines from home. Middle and senior high content area teachers or elementary special area (e.g., art or music) teachers can bring to class magazines or books related to their field. This can help teachers see SSR (Sustained Silent Reading) as a valuable use of class time.

- One secondary school rotated responsibility for reading material every four weeks. Thus, at some point during the science week, the science teachers took the students to the library so that they could get their SSR books for the week. Not only did this ensure that all students would have books, it also helped all teachers—rather than just the language arts teachers—have a sense of ownership in the program. Some would not otherwise have taken their students to the library this frequently.

- Book clubs can be an ongoing source of paperbacks. "For every dollar spent, and for ordering in certain slower months, or just for ordering at all, teachers receive bonus points for a variety of items: books, teacher equipment, even VCRs" (Barchers, 1990, p. 22). Addresses of book clubs follow:

Scholastic Book Clubs
2931 East McCarty Street
P.O. Box 7500
Jefferson City, MO 65102

School Book Fairs, Inc.
801 94th Avenue North
St. Petersburg, FL 33702

Troll Book Fairs
100 Corporate Drive
Mahwah, NJ 07430

The Trumpet Club
666 Fifth Avenue
New York, NY 10103

Weekly Reader Paperback Clubs
4343 Equity Drive
P.O. Box 16628
Columbus, OH 43272-6112

- Stacks of paperbacks can often be picked up at garage sales and flea markets for just a few dollars. Teachers can persuade used bookstores to offer an especially good deal for such a worthy cause. Book drives can yield large numbers of paperbacks that community members may be all too willing to discard. Older students can donate books that they have outgrown. Any books gathered should be examined in light of any censorship guidelines that may be in place at the school.

Writing Incentives

There is no better incentive for writing than seeing your writing in print. Find ways of publishing student work: letters to pen pals, book recommendations attached to library books, reading work over closed-circuit television, portfolios. One elementary school has a different student read a piece of his or her writing on the school answering machine each night. Classmates can call and tune in. One feeder pattern of elementary through senior high school students displayed their writing on the walls of the senior high school. Particularly noteworthy among the parents who attended the evening function were migrant fathers who saw the occasion as a true dress-up affair. For more ambitious publishing, see the list of publishers of student writing in Appendix C.

Audience can, of course, make the difference. Rankin (1992) writes of a special education student who was unwilling to be mainstreamed out of the special class if that meant ending correspondence with her pen pal. Thomas

(1992), when a principal at Bess Rankin Elementary School in Arlington, Texas, let high-risk students write her notes and deposit them in a special purple box for her response; students discovered the pleasure and adventure in writing and reading.

Conclusion

This chapter has addressed the question of what makes a comprehensive reading/writing program. As was pointed out earlier, a program is not equivalent to the set of materials in use. A program goes beyond school walls to involve an interaction among people, curriculum, and planning that makes instruction a cohesive whole.

Chapter 7

Organizing for Instruction

*The task of organizing a classroom is always new with
each group.*

—Debra Goodman (Goodman & Curry, 1991)

A comprehensive reading/writing program includes well-thought-out scenarios for instruction. Scenarios involve schoolwide climate; physical design
of classrooms; student placement and grouping; services for special needs
students; and the creation of yearly, weekly, and daily plans. This chapter
addresses each of these issues in turn.

Schoolwide Climate

A schoolwide culture of literacy must set the tone for instruction. Yatvin
(1992), a former school principal, suggests that school-based administrators
foster informal relationships among staff members. Principals and assistant
principals can lay the groundwork for growth of friendships and partnerships.
They can set up common planning times for teachers at the same grade level
or in the same department. They can create comfortable teacher work areas in
the library/media center, in the teachers' lounge, or even outdoors. They can
regularly schedule social events and professional sharing times. In the Cottrell
district in Virginia, Yatvin tells of quarterly evening get-togethers of teachers,
educational assistants, and even school board members. At these gatherings,
where two or three teachers present their ideas and everyone eats, attendance,
though voluntary, runs close to 100 percent.

On the other hand, climates can be negative. In one school, teachers whose
work is praised by the administrator become the subject of derision. In another

school, faculties avoid asking questions or otherwise participating during a faculty presentation, especially if the principal is in attendance. Administrators who inherit such environments have much work to do to turn them around to environments that will support literacy. They will have to attack the root of the problem. Teachers may feel a lack of trust, or they may feel that a previous administrator played favorites. Administrators in difficult situations may need outside help. In Dade County, Florida, the district office provides intergroup relations teams.

Physical Design and Appearance of Classrooms

Classroom arrangement can have a lot to do with student engagement. Visitors to the room make an initial judgment of the teacher on the basis of what they see. Until classrooms have a manageable structure, little else can be accomplished. And what goes on in the classroom is often intimately linked with the classroom's structure.

This section first addresses general issues regarding physical design and appearance, followed by specific issues related to elementary and middle/senior high instruction. The section concludes with pointers for the physical arrangement of students.

In providing help to teachers as they arrange their classrooms, remember that it is the teacher who will have to live in the room, so the teacher will have to buy into any arrangement. Your assistance may take several forms:

- Do your best to provide an environment that is conducive to learning. For example provide carpeting to cut down noise levels and foster cooperative learning.

- Discuss alternative arrangements or show teachers classrooms arranged differently. For example, teachers sharing a room might arrange to team-teach rather than separate the room with a divider

- Brainstorm ways to involve students in planning their environment. For example, students might decide how to organize trade books and then manage the organizational process

- Suggest sources for needed materials—for example, free carpet squares from carpet outlets, needed furniture that you have seen unused elsewhere in the school

Here are some questions to ask yourself:

- Are materials laid out for easy access?
- Can all students see the chalkboard?

- Is any provision made for heterogeneous and other flexible grouping?

- Is there a quiet space? Second-grade teacher Joni Weed (1991) finds "get-away" corners to be very important.

- Where is the teacher's desk positioned? A prominent placement by the door sends a message of teacher ownership, whereas placement in a corner may convey more student empowerment.

- If there is a thin divider with another classroom, is furniture arranged so that each teacher's voice will carry into his or her own room rather than into the adjacent room?

Once you have attended to the basic physical design, look at the overall appearance.

- Is your first impression one of a classroom "marinated" in literacy, or is it one of piles of dittos?

- Are the bulletin boards student-made rather than store-bought? How about student-made borders for bulletin boards?

- Are instructional materials and student work at eye level for students when possible?

You can rotate faculty or committee meetings among attractively decorated rooms. This strategy can work wonders in motivating teachers to keep rooms bathed in literacy.

Beyond questions of physical design and appearance of classrooms are those that relate to the school as a whole. A dull library and dreary hallways do nothing to enhance enthusiasm. You can enlist the aid of students, a rotating committee of teachers, a reading resource specialist, or an art teacher to liven things up. Visitors can readily evaluate school priorities if they see:

- Teacher writing as well as student writing on display

- Permanent murals painted by students

- An attractive library shelf of books written by students

- A rack with books and other material for students and parents to read when in the office—with a "Read while you wait" sign!

Specific Elementary Issues

Calkins and Harwayne (1991, pp. 11–12) admonish us to not "rush about filling the room with a variety of paper, bulletin boards, conference areas, editing checklists, and an author's chair—these will all come in time—but instead, to fill the classroom with children's lives." They suggest that, "instead of stapling scalloped edges and cardboard horns of plenty onto our bulletin boards, we might let youngsters use bulletin boards as a place for announcements, jokes, news about ticket sales, [and] displays of artwork, writing, quotes and posters, maps and photographs."

Authentic print-rich environments should be created one step at a time. Gradually, you may be able to help teachers come to see the need for elements such as the following. The list will, of course, vary by grade level:

- Does classroom management use print? Is/are there . . .

    - A mailbox(es)?– A message board?
    - Labels and printed signs?– Daily routines posted?
    - Helper charts?– Attendance charts?
    - Center assignments?– A calendar?

- Are there displays of words that might be helpful in writing?

- Is recent work from every student readily visible? If writing is displayed, is it individual writing, or are all the papers "carbon copies"?

- Has an effort been made to hang student writing at the students' eye level?

- If display space is limited, are creative solutions found (e.g., writing clipped to clotheslines or hula hoops hung from the ceiling; walls outside the rooms used as bulletin boards)?

- Do classrooms have learning centers: a listening center, a reading corner, a writing center? Are centers logically placed? For example, a quiet reading corner would not work well next to a noisier kitchen center. Are the centers well designed? If not, children will not use them.

- Does the reading corner stand out when someone first enters the room?

    - Does it display the covers of some books?
    - Does it have a comfortable feel to it—beanbag chairs, area rugs, an old sofa, a bathtub, a rocker?
    - Is it well stocked with a variety of age-appropriate and ability-appropriate material?

        - At least five to eight books per child?
        - Multiple copies of favorite books?
        - Appropriate reference materials (illustrated dictionaries, encyclopedias, maps, etc.)?
        - A variety of magazines (e.g., *Sports Illustrated for Kids*, *Highlights for Children*, a nature magazine)?

- Is the writing center well planned? Are there:
  - Index cards for students' own words?
  - Materials for making books?
  - Postcards, stationery, envelopes, and stamps?
  - Various colors and sizes of papers?
  - Various kinds of markers and pencils?
  - Spelling aids for high-frequency words? "bad spellers" dictionary?
  - Story stimulators and motivators?
  - A typewriter or computer?
  - Alphabet chart, tactile letters?
  - Writing folders?

- How about a day-to-day print center with newspapers, restaurant menus, coupons, and the like? Or an exploring center? Or a unit center focusing on a current theme? Or ad hoc centers that change throughout the year?

Try having contests for the best library corners or the best bulletin boards; be sure to use judges from outside the school. And remember to take photographs or arrange walk-throughs of winning rooms for all to enjoy.

Specific Middle/Senior High Issues

The design and appearance of middle/senior high classrooms give clues to whether cooperative learning is encouraged, whether student writing is celebrated, and whether reading of trade books/magazines/newspapers is a priority. Middle and senior high teachers sometimes must share classrooms. When there is no ownership in the classroom, its appearance may be no one's concern. You might suggest that teachers who share a room rotate responsibility for its decoration, and student help can be enlisted as well.

You can also attend to the appearance of the school as a whole. At one senior high school, a sports trophy case was used to display prizes for a reading lottery (Lubell, 1991). At this same school, bookworm displays with additions for each book read were unabashedly hung all over the outside walls.

Physical Arrangement of Students

Note where different students are placed within classrooms.

- Where are the lower and higher achievers sitting? If there are rows, students in the front and center of the classroom are more likely to be noticed and asked to respond than are those on the room's periphery

(Miller, 1988), so low-performing students might best be seated close to the teacher in the front of the classroom.

- Are students' seats grouped by reading level? This may be necessary if teachers are using ability groups and are in small rooms with no space for students to gather around a table or on the carpet. But grouping by reading level further aggravates the problems inherent with ability grouping.

- Are students grouped in cooperative heterogeneous groups—for example, two pairs of desks facing each other? This is a desirable arrangement because it allows stronger students to help weaker peers and promotes cooperation among all students.

- Are mainstreamed exceptional education students or disruptive students isolated? This can be helpful occasionally, but it is damaging to students' self-esteem when done for long periods of time.

Student Placement and Grouping[1]

Grouping students for the teaching of reading and language arts is one of the most challenging tasks a teacher faces. Teachers who are aware of the disadvantages of traditional ability grouping (Barr, in press) are searching for ways to create an alternative grouping plan. Following are descriptions of alternatives, first for elementary school and then at the middle/senior high level.

Flexible Grouping in the Elementary School

As an alternative to traditional grouping patterns, some elementary schools are exploring either nongraded instruction or grouping across grade levels for specific subject areas (Pavan, 1992; Slavin, 1992). Most, however, look for solutions within the grade level.

There is a temptation to search for a clear alternative to the three-block plan of traditional ability grouping. But alas, it is not so simple. No single-faceted plan, whether it is peer tutoring, small groups for repeated reading practice, skill groups, or whole class, will meet the needs of all students. As we move toward alternative grouping plans, we must be careful to avoid the rigidity that characterizes traditional ability grouping, and to offer students dynamic and flexible opportunities that are responsive to curricular goals and individual needs.

---

[1]Portions of this section are adapted with permission from M. C. Radencich, L. McKay, & J. R. Paratore, *Grouping Options: Keeping Flexible Groups Flexible* (Boston: Allyn and Bacon, in press).

What follows is a description of flexible grouping using one core selection with an entire elementary class, not the only way of structuring flexible grouping, but one that is becoming increasingly common and that requires much thought and skill for good implementation. Teachers attempting this model in classes with a broad range of student ability recognize that reading achievement depends not only on text level but also on the conditions of the learning situation. For further detail, see Radencich and McKay (in press). For models of flexible grouping, see also Reutzel and Cooter's (1991) adaptation of Atwell's (1987) Reading Workshop to grades 2 and above, Cunningham's (1991) first-grade model, Morris and Nelson's (1992) supported oral reading with second-graders, and Strickland's (1992) broad organizational framework.

Flexible grouping involves use of several grouping options, which will be described. These are categorized as (1) whole class, (2) teacher-facilitated needs-based groups, (3) cooperative groups, (4) pairs, and (5) individual teaching and learning. These options should be viewed as ad hoc groups, which are formed and dissolved according to need. The use of these grouping options may apply not only to the reading/language arts period but to instruction in the content areas as well (Pardo & Raphael, 1991). See Table 7-1 for suggested grouping options related to a list of typical classroom activities.

1. *Whole class instruction.* Whole class instruction meets several teaching goals, including: (a) introduction of new ideas and concepts, (b) review of recently taught skills or strategies, (c) development of a cross-curricular theme, (d) development of a "common experience" from which group discussion can emerge, and (e) direction for writing through Atwell's (1987) "state of the class" meetings. Whole class instruction effectively puts children in touch with the social nature of reading while creating a safety net to protect them from the risks associated with this learning (Reutzel & Cooter, 1992).

Whole class instruction can accomplish several specific literacy goals. For example, before reading, whole class grouping can be used for introducing new vocabulary, discussing background knowledge, modeling by reading aloud, making predictions, setting purposes for reading, and providing an audience (e.g., through author's chair). After reading, the whole class can discuss, analyze, and extend the selection. Whole class organization can also be used for storytelling, dramatizations of stories, sharing Big Books, sharing writing pieces, Sustained Silent Reading and writing, and creating language experience charts (Reutzel & Cooter, 1992). Whole class instruction is most effective when successful completion of the task is possible without decoding fluency.

Beyond literacy learning, whole class instruction may yield positive benefits in students' self-esteem as students of differing performance levels learn to succeed while working with each other. But despite the many advantages of whole class instruction, there are also disadvantages. Attention to individual needs is minimal; individual students may be less likely to participate; and

TABLE 7-1 Matching Activities to Grouping Options[a]

Activities	Whole Class	Small Needs-Based Groups (Teacher-Facilitated)	Cooperative Groups	Pairs	Individuals
Teacher read-aloud	X	X			
Demonstrations/ modeling	X	X			
Repeated readings:					
Choral/echo	X	X			
Readers'/story theater	X	X			
With taped story			X		X
"Mumble" reading					X
Buddy reading				X	
Second tier guided reading for emergent and struggling readers		X			
Journals	X			X	X
Self-selected reading			X	X	X
Projects	X		X	X	X
Writing process:					
Conferencing				X	X
Mini-lessons	X	X			
Author's chair	X		X		
State-of-the-class (Atwell, 1987)	X				
Learning centers			X	X	X
"Early bird"		X			

[a]Grouping options not limited to those suggested.

instruction tends to be teacher- rather than student-centered. Thus, it is difficult for teachers who rely too heavily on whole group instruction to be good "kidwatchers": recognizing what each child can and cannot do, and knowing which child is ready for a nudge and which child is not (Goodman, 1991). Further, even if teachers were to observe specific needs, the whole class framework simply does not allow teachers to direct a lesson to some students and not others.

It is critical that whole class teaching not take up the bulk of instructional time. "One big reading group" is not the idea. Rather, the usefulness of whole class instruction grows out of effective combination with the following grouping options, which better address individual needs.

2. *Teacher-facilitated needs-based groups.* Teacher-facilitated needs-based groups are intended to address the diversity of learning needs in every classroom. Needs-based groups are grounded in Vygotsky's (1978) notion of scaffolding, where meeting students' needs is not so much a matter of placing them in materials at a given level as of providing the scaffolding or instructional support that is necessary to help them achieve beyond that level. This notion has led teachers and researchers to explore ways of meeting those needs by changing the way we teach reading rather than by changing the materials we assign (Paratore, 1991).

Teacher-facilitated needs-based groups are particularly beneficial when:

- A few individuals need additional instruction on an ad hoc basis in any areas determined by teacher observation, student request, and/or testing.

- Hard-to-teach students or emergent readers require frequent, even daily extra help.

- Higher performing students need some direction or explanation in preparation for a cooperative or independent learning project.

Needs-based groups are more flexible than traditional ability groups, with students moving among different types of groups (e.g., skills need, interest) rather than being restricted to only a performance group with students of similar reading levels. Needs-based groups are most often formed by the teacher, particularly early in the school year. Often, however, students are able to make good decisions about the groups they wish to join.

Although needs-based groups are often thought of as remedial or "extra help" groups, it is important to emphasize that such groups may be intended to meet the special needs of higher as well as lower performing students. Research (Johnson & Johnson, 1992) supports the need of higher achievers to work together at times (see the section on using key research studies and reference literature in Chapter 1). In a meta-analysis of studies on ability grouping, Kulik and Kulik (1992) found that flexible grouping, combined with appropriate, differentiated instruction, led to academic gains for highly able students. However, Dooley (1993) reports that surveys of teachers and observations of gifted and average students reveal little differentiation in heterogeneous classrooms.

High achievers can benefit from curriculum compacting (Renzulli, 1977), a systematic process through which proficiency in the basic curriculum is assured, instructional pacing is appropriate, and time is made available for enrichment and acceleration. Thus, high achievers might participate in initial instruction as necessary but might then proceed to extend class reading, for example, by reading an entire book when the basal includes only a chapter, or doing in-depth explorations of thematic units or personal interests. High achievers could also be given alternative assignments to replace routine practices that are unlikely to benefit them (e.g., teacher read-aloud of the text before students read). As is true for the special needs of any students, modifications for high achievers should encompass both content and process.

Needs-based groups may occur before, during, or after reading of a selection, depending on the instruction to be provided. Sometimes they are skill/strategy groups. For example, comprehension-building activities that occur after students read might well focus on clarifying ideas and events or on confirming predictions. Specific activities might help students understand particular parts of the selection, focus on the author's main ideas, or summarize major events in the selection.

Teachers might conduct mini-lessons (Atwell, 1987) based on their observations, a formal curriculum guide, lessons in a basal, assessment information, or student request. The purpose of these mini-lessons could be to reinforce the strategy for those needing additional instruction or to extend the strategy to more advanced applications (Strickland, 1992).

One risk of needs-based groups is the tendency for a few children to become permanent members. Teachers often address this and maintain heterogeneity by including "visitors" to the group who might benefit socially more than academically. Including visitors and keeping performance groups as only one selection in a smorgasbord of grouping options helps avoid some of the problems common with ability groups such as less wait time, lower levels of questions asked, and slower pacing for students in low groups (Barr, in press).

When I discuss flexible grouping with teachers, I often start by talking about the parallel use of two tiers (levels) for students significantly below grade level. It's like a light bulb turning on. Teachers know they must *teach* these students and that no amount of stretching will make students comfortable in material several levels above their instructional level. Teachers know that some of these students' needs—often sight vocabulary and sound–symbol correspondences—are not directly addressed in higher level materials. For these students, the core selection may be on their listening level. They may be able to achieve fluent reading only with repeated readings of a portion of the selection. Thus, supplementary use of a second, easier level may be crucial primarily for reading fluency.

To elaborate further, in one tier, students may interact with the grade-appropriate text(s), listening to a read-aloud, learning concepts with classmates, contributing to story discussion, and writing in response. This enables them to maintain their "citizenship" in the classroom community. In addition, however, they regularly receive instruction and practice in easier texts, and on specific strategies and skills. A metaphor that helps bring across the point is that of a child stuck in a tube (Fields, 1993). While you pull from the top with grade-level material, you must also push from the bottom with comfort-level text. The comfort-level text can be use of predictable language books that children can "zoom through with joyous familiarity" (Bill Martin in Cullinan, Greene, & Jaggar, 1990). Or it may be general trade books and/or student-authored books. The use of lower level basals as "easy reading" is not recommended because of the possible negative impact on the child's self-esteem and motivation. If the class is reading from one core selection, it is helpful if the easier-tier material is thematically or otherwise related to it.

TWO-TIERED INSTRUCTION

Pull from top of tube
with grade-level materials

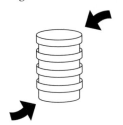

Push bottom of tube
with comfort-level materials

The use of an easier set of materials will be particularly necessary for emergent readers. Routman (1991), for example, recommends that, at the beginning of first grade, teachers meet students in small homogeneous groups as part of their instruction to help students move through books of gradually decreasing levels of predictability. Wright Group and Rigby collections can be used for this purpose. Cunningham and Allington (1994) write of an "after-lunch bunch" that met to read "for fun." The less proficient readers participated frequently, but not every day, and every child participated at least once during the week.

Following are examples of strategies and practices for before, during, and after reading that are particularly suited to small groups.

1. *Teacher-assisted before-reading activities:* Teacher-assisted before-reading activities can make the language and concepts more familiar through a read-aloud; make vocabulary more automatic through previewing, explicit instruction, and practice; or make events and their relationships more comprehensible through prereading discussion.

One widely used practice is the formation of a needs-based "early bird" group that may meet a day or two before the rest of the class begins the core selection. During this "frontloading" time, students may listen to a read-aloud and participate in initial discussion and practice of vocabulary that is essential to reading and understanding the selection. This group might be led by the classroom teacher, a special teacher (special education, Chapter 1, etc.), or a volunteer or aide. Some teachers ask the parent to provide this assistance at home. Early bird grouping represents a way of being proactive, intervening to prevent, rather than to remediate, failure. The result is that students who often struggle to keep up may now actually outshine their otherwise higher performing peers. Teachers who try early bird grouping enthusiastically report that "It works!"

2. *Teacher-assisted during-reading activities:* Teachers typically conduct the first reading in different ways depending on the nature of the group. If most students can read the selection alone, but a few cannot, the teacher might conduct a "whisper club" (Fields, 1993), reading a class selection to a group of less proficient readers while others read it to themselves. One teacher adapted this technique by having strong readers do the whispering. If most students cannot read the selection alone, the teacher might read it to the group while higher achievers use earphones at a computer or listening station activity, work in a quiet part of the room, or go to the school library.

3. *Teacher-assisted after-reading activities:* Among the most useful teacher-assisted after-reading activities for needs-based groups are repeated readings with passages about 100 words long, with an emphasis on speed more than accuracy (Samuels, Schermer, & Reinking, 1992). Use of repeated readings has received extensive support in the professional literature. A wide range of studies (Radencich et al., in press) indicates that even one rereading can increase both fluency and comprehension, but that both can increase further with additional readings, with three to five practice readings appearing to be optimal for the development of fluency, even with below-average readers.

Teachers may read selections aloud to a class or group, perhaps tape recording themselves in the process to provide rereading material for a listening center. Other alternatives include teachers dividing the labor and sharing their recordings, or asking high-performing readers to do the recording. Additional repeated reading activities that can be teacher-directed and are easy as initial rereadings include the following:

- Various forms of choral reading

- Echo reading, with the length of the chunks progressing throughout the year, perhaps from phrases to sentences or sentence clusters (Morris & Nelson, 1992)

- Assigning groups to each character in story theater and readers' theater

Types of rereadings that require less teacher direction and invite more pupil interaction include:

- Buddy or partner reading of the selection or of just a portion or an adaptation of the selection—first and last page, a single page or paragraph, a story summary, or a predictable version of the story (see the discussion of pairs later in this section)

- Assigning individual parts for story or readers' theater

Finally, successful use of small needs-based groups requires some system for classroom management. The time-worn idea of learning centers can be dusted off and reconceptualized to help teachers manage small groups simultaneously while offering some extra help and other challenging activities. Included in thematic or more general centers for early readers can be follow-ups to predictable books. Third-grade teacher Caryl Crowell (1991) includes in the centers in her multilanguage classroom materials in the students' native languages.

4. *Cooperative groups:* Of all grouping options, cooperative grouping may represent the best opportunity for everybody to have something to add to the group. Research (e.g., Slavin, 1991) indicates that children in cooperative learning groups consistently show increased achievement, self-concept, and social skills. Cooperative groups may provide a forum for sharing predictions and ideas or for discussing and responding to one or more selections with peers. Cooperative groups may be used either before or after reading.

Cooperative groups are typically formed with three to six students, but most often three to four. Tasks may be assigned, or students may select among several options. Tasks frequently culminate in a written group product. Examples include comparing predictions made prior to reading and actual story events, describing character traits and their impact on the story, listing predictions, summarizing a selection, or comparing a selection with one read previously. Tasks are structured so that there is face-to-face interaction among group members, and there is both interdependence among members (sink or swim together) and individual accountability (Johnson, Johnson, & Holubec, 1990).

Possible cooperative groups are as follows:

- Interest groups that work on problem solving and theme projects

- Literature response groups in which groups of students each read and discuss a different title

- Computer work groups in which rotating roles can be those of keyboard operator, monitor, and checker

- Story retelling groups in which each group member retells a story read to the group and fields comments

Cooperative learning is a grouping practice that has received abundant support from researchers and teachers. Most agree, however, that it requires thoughtful planning and execution. "The often-heard complaint that in cooperative groups a few students do all the work and all students get the credit is not valid in classrooms where teachers help students to divide up tasks and closely monitor their progress, any more than it is true in a well-run experimental laboratory where senior and junior scientists, technicians, and students work together toward the same goal" (Yatvin, 1992, p. 28).

Appropriate procedures for cooperative grouping may vary from culture to culture. Vogt, Jordan, and Tharp (1987) report high levels of peer interaction and helping among heterogeneous groups of Native Hawaiian students. When Vogt et al. attempted to use these same arrangements with Navajo students, however, they met resistance. They found better success when they restricted cooperative learning to single-sex groups because of the distinctness and separateness of gender roles in the Navajo culture. Au (1993) also contrasts Native Hawaiian interactions in which students persist in efforts to help peers even when the targeted students initially refuse assistance, with those of

Yup'ik Eskimo students, in which help is more subtle and less obviously intrusive.

Johnson, Johnson, and Holubec's *Circles of Learning* (1990) is an excellent source for more information on cooperative learning in general. Keegan and Shrake (1991) provide specifics about using cooperative learning to support literacy learning.

5. *Pairs*: Cooperative pairs are perhaps the easiest form of cooperative grouping to manage. Pairs allow for both "less negotiation and more opportunity to construct" (Berghoff & Egawa, 1991). Pairs can be ideal for literacy tasks such as the following:

- Finding and recording information

- Planning, co-authoring, revising, and drafting writing

- Interviewing a partner and responding to the book the partner has read

- Practicing skills and routines

- Testing each other on material each has studied

- Listing predictions in preparation for reading

- Completing everyday tasks that might have otherwise been independent seatwork

- Solving problems

Paired learning can occur through peer tutoring (Cohen, Kulik, & Kulik, 1982; Topping, 1989); reciprocal teaching (Palincsar & Brown, 1984; Palincsar, Brown, & Martin, 1987); partner or buddy reading (Topping, 1989; Wood, 1987), perhaps with students taking turns reading aloud to the class the one or two paragraphs they had been assigned to practice until they could read them aloud fluently (Pardo & Raphael, 1991); and use of a Think-Pair-Share (McTighe & Lyman, 1988). Cunningham and Allington (1994) describe the use of alternating "take turn" days in which pairs take turns reading and "ask question" days on which partners read each page silently and then ask each other a question about each page before going on to the next. Paired learning can fit into the classroom routine with little preparation and can be monitored with ease. It is a useful way to stretch instructional time and provide students practice reading connected text.

6. *Individual teaching and learning*: Although working with individuals is not strictly a form of grouping, it is addressed here because of its vital place in overall classroom organization. Individual teaching often takes place in one-on-one conferences. These serve not only to personalize instruction and to review skills/strategies, but also to monitor the progress of individual students (Strickland, 1992).

As opposed to individual teaching, individual learning takes place in any grouping situation. Particularly important for individual learning are times when students set their own goals/purposes, reflect on ideas and on their progress, apply and practice skills/concepts/strategies, do self-selected reading and writing, and engage in personal creative tasks. Strategies and activities that students may practice alone include journal writing, question generation, project development, and some types of repeated readings—following along with audiotaped selection, "mumble" reading (mumbling the words to oneself), and simple rereadings. When more teachers choose to use a single text with the whole class, there is a risk that some students may be held back or not be given enough opportunities to read and write on their own. Ample opportunities for individual practice and extension should not be neglected in the effort to build more collaborative learning environments.

In summary, flexible grouping at the elementary level is an art of combining different grouping options for different individual and literacy needs.

Organization of the Middle/Senior High School Reading/Language Arts Program

Organization and grouping at the middle and senior high school levels must cope with wide ranges of reading ability (Conley, 1989) and with "drip-feed" timetables that allow little continuous time for students to engage in a lesson and its associated group activities. Middle and senior high questions include: How homogeneous or heterogeneous should classes be? What about within-class groupings? Will there be a "school within a school"? Will all instructional periods be of equal length? Such decisions are, of course, made within the boundaries of the school's philosophy and goals. These decisions involve the orchestration of interrelated human, material, and procedural components (Samuels, 1981). Some areas to consider carefully in making grouping decisions are described here.

Research is by no means unanimous in recommending a grouping pattern of preference (see Barr, 1989, for a review). Middle and senior high students are generally placed homogeneously in all content areas according to teacher recommendations and scores on traditional norm-referenced group achievement tests such as the Stanford Achievement Test (1989) or on the Degrees of Reading Power test (1984). But these popular tracking plans have been heavily criticized in recent years. Fortunately, recommendations for grouping patterns that can enhance student achievement and self-esteem are now being promoted (Brandt, 1992) and should be considered. Much of what has been described in detail in the section on flexible grouping in the elementary school is appropriate for middle and senior high schools as well.

As a beginning, middle and senior high schools that place students primarily on the basis of norm-referenced test scores might at least group the lowest achievers with some average students. This can result in a decrease in the number of levels of a course, perhaps from four or five to two or three, and thus in an amelioration of some of the problems with tracking such as class expectations and discipline. Joe Pius, a middle school principal in Michigan (Hereford, 1993) attributes a 75 percent reduction in discipline referrals to the school's movement away from tracking and toward high-track curriculum for all. Florida is another example of a movement toward the elimination of remedial-level classes and the infusion of enrichment into basic classes.

In the days when materials-driven instruction was the norm, little school-based decision making was necessary. Basals or reading kits dictated the program. With the focus on the role of teachers as decision makers (Stern & Shavelson, 1983) and on students as active participants in the learning process (Ericson & Ellett, 1990), it is imperative that we be knowledgeable about options before making decisions.

An example of a decision maker is seventh-grade teacher Richard Coles (1991), who finds that the choice of instructional strategies influences the organization of the learning experience. Coles allows students to play an important role in the planning and organizing process. They help form groups and offer suggestions about modifying instructional strategies and making the best use of furniture and floor space.

Another example of decision making is one middle school's sixth-grade plan. The reading, social studies, and science teachers work together. Some social studies and science instructional objectives are assigned to the reading teacher, and content materials are provided to the reading teacher so that the instruction is directly relevant. The language arts teacher teaches literary reading. A different, but equally valid plan is one used by a third middle school in which sixth-graders who take reading have a balanced program, with a different focus during each nine-week period. Examples of foci can be reading and computers, content area reading, literary reading, and test-taking strategies.

Following are examples of two organizational models in action. Note the grouping decisions inherent in each. Other program profiles can be found in Condon and Hoffman (1990), Radencich, Beers, and Schumm (1993), and Valencia, McGinley, and Pearson (1990).

1. *Middle school interdisciplinary teams*: A middle school interdisciplinary team typically includes teachers of required subjects who can meet regularly *before* and *after* instruction to plan for the group of students whom they all share (Arhar, Johnston, & Markle, 1988). A second type of team can consist of a similar group of teachers of elective courses. This type can be difficult to schedule because students have different patterns of interests.

Assignment of students to classes and teams is done with care. Two reasons for not grouping students by reading ability are the problems inherent in tracking and the fact that levels of reading might not coincide with levels of performance in other subjects. Students are not grouped randomly, either, because many teachers and parents are uncomfortable with grouping that is completely heterogeneous. Rather, the grouping is done with knowledge of the students involved and regard for overall manageability. Some lessons are individual teacher assignments; others are tied to thematic team projects, often graded by each teacher in the team (Sandweiss, 1990). Cooperative assignments are a regular part of the plan.

2. *Atwell's* In the Middle (1987): Nancie Atwell's (1987) success as an eighth-grade teacher has led middle school teachers and others throughout the country to emulate her reading and writing workshops. In this model, a class is taught by one teacher in a double period (preferably contiguous) of both reading and writing. Students do plentiful reading and writing, with skills introduced as they fit into the reading and writing tasks. Grouping is flexible, with whole class "state-of-the-class" discussions; mini-lessons directed to the whole class, small groups, or individuals; and pairs of students choosing to read the same book or perhaps helping each other in their writing.

Reading Labs

Reading specialists at all levels will typically teach in a special reading lab. This often means a pull-out grouping pattern for low achievers.

Allington (1985) and others have argued convincingly about the typical problems with the more traditional types of labs:

1. The classroom teacher may feel less responsibility for the student's instruction, resulting in lessened efforts when the student is in the regular classroom.

2. There is often little coordination between the classroom teacher and the reading teacher. Thus, the students who can least afford it wind up with a program that is quite fragmented.

3. Lab students are penalized when they are grouped together by being subjected to the problems with ability grouping discussed previously.

4. Students may believe that what they learn in the lab is to be applied there only. They may have difficulty understanding that they are to transfer this learning to their regular classes.

5. A reading teacher who spends the entire day in a lab can serve only a limited number of students. Typically, middle and high achievers will be excluded. In explaining this problem to principals, I often resort to discussing test scores. The only way to raise a school's median percentile

scores is for the middle students to improve, and these are not the students typically served by a lab.

As the earlier section on middle and senior high school grouping indicates, labs do not have to look like this. The point holds for elementary schools as well. An alternative lab model used at one senior high involves regularly rotating all grade 7 English classes through a lab throughout the year, with English teachers accompanying their classes. The reading teacher teaches a strategy first in "reading" materials of limited length and later through complete literary selections. Teachers and students are expected to apply the strategies when regular classes resume. Psychologically, however, there is probably not as much transfer from what is learned in a room other than the regular classroom. Thus, the model whereby a reading resource specialist models lessons in students' classrooms rather than in labs may be preferable. One selling point for this position is that this model frees up a classroom, which can be used for other purposes.

A variation on a reading lab is a computer lab through which students rotate—perhaps taught by a computer teacher with periodic assistance from the reading resource specialist. For pull-in alternatives to labs, see the "Scheduling" section later in this chapter.

Serving Special Needs Students

Organizing to meet the needs of special needs students will go beyond decisions on placement and grouping as described earlier, and beyond issues described in the "Scheduling" section later in this chapter. Organizing to meet the needs of special needs students will also mean a close look at curriculum and instruction. Teachers need a big bag of tricks to serve both regular and special needs students. Students also can help themselves with the growing number of resources directed especially at students with special needs (see "Student Survival Resources" in Appendix E). Some tips that should help with different groups of special needs students follow.

Students for Whom the Textbook Is Too Difficult

This section focuses on content texts that are too difficult. For information specifically on developmental reading instruction for below-level readers when they use a grade-level core selection with the entire class, see the earlier section on student placement and grouping.

When the textook is too difficult, mediated instruction is necessary. Neal and Langer (1992) have developed a Mediated Instruction of Text (MIT) diagram that can serve as a framework. In this structure, the teacher follows different strategies before, during, and after reading. These strategies include:

For activating prior knowledge:

- Questioning
- Brainstorming
- Posing a problem
- Role playing

For predicting content:

- Surveying ideas
- Conducting demonstrations/experiments
- Semantic organizers
- Building word meaning
- Posing purpose questions
- Structured overviews

For constructing meaning:

- Responding to purpose questions
- Verifying predictions
- Responding to study guide

For monitoring understanding:

- Questioning/talking about ideas
- Note taking
- Student-generated quizzes

For processing ideas:

- Summarizing
- Response writing
- Constructing graphic organizers
- Teaching others
- Learning games
- Discussion

For applying knowledge:
• Participating in projects, experiments, and creative work

See Schumm and Strickler (1991) for a second framework that responds to the question, "What do I do when the textbook is too hard for my students?" This framework provides suggestions under the categories of supplementing the textbook (e.g., audiotaping, pairing students), simplifying the textbook (e.g., using abridged versions, outlines, summaries), highlighting key concepts (e.g., previewing, introducing key vocabulary), and helping students retain key ideas (e.g., using postreading activities, memory strategies).

Limited-English-Proficient Students

Limited-English-proficient (LEP) students, sometimes referred to more positively as potentially English-proficient students, are one rapidly growing segment of the U.S. population. These students enrich our classrooms but also present challenges. This is especially true for the increasing influx of older students who have had little schooling. Following are some helpful hints. For additional ideas, see Gunderson (1991) or Nurss and Hough (1992).

Tips: Limited-English-Proficient Students

• Suggest that, to provide plentiful access to language, teachers use cooperative learning and buddy systems. The classroom should be active.

• Facilitate extensive use of media: card readers such as Language Masters, films, tape recorders, filmstrips, computers with clear voice capabilities, and the like.

• Suggest that teachers encourage students to use English outside of school (but teachers should *not* presume to tell parents what language to speak in the home). Students can belong to English-speaking organizations such as scout troops. They can watch television programs that are in English. One third-grade teacher divided students into groups of three who lived close to each other. The students were to learn a television commercial and act it out in class. The technique worked wonderfully!

• Encourage teachers to use the language experience approach with comprehensible input (Moustafa & Penrose, 1985). Comprehensible input is language with an understandable message that is interesting and relevant to the LEP learner, offered in sufficient quantity to allow access to the language, and sequenced for meaning rather than by grammatical forms. Language experience with comprehensible input goes beyond regular language experience primarily in that prewriting is more extensive. During prewriting, teachers develop new referents in addition to those that were previously developed. Furthermore, teachers ensure that oral language is developed before they write it down. Thus, for beginners, considerable time might be spent with the teacher showing different blue and red objects before the students are led to dictate a "story" that repeatedly uses these color words.

- Suggest that, to help students feel free to take risks with language, teachers use masks or puppets. It's O.K. if the *puppet's* English isn't quite right! Students of all ages can identify with masks of faculty members or media stars.

- Help teachers plan lessons that cover both receptive and expressive language skills and focus on language that will be useful to the student.

- Encourage teachers use native foods, music, and so forth to highlight the mainstream and nonmainstream languages and cultures represented in the classroom. Teachers can read from culturally relevant material whenever possible. You can help expand such efforts to make them schoolwide. For example, each room could represent a different country, and students and other guests could have their passports stamped as they traveled from country to country. These efforts should be done not only during a particular week of the year, but on a regular basis. A warm environment can go a long way!

- Help teachers include LEP students in class or group lessons even if the students don't understand a lot. They will learn the language more quickly that way than by sitting alone with an assignment on paper.

- Suggest games with off-the-wall directions, even for high school students. "Simon Says" can yield all kinds of possibilities (Simon Says, "Yell"). Or teachers can try a whisper game in which a child acts out an action whispered by another child and others guess what action is being shown. Teachers should expect answers in complete sentences (Minkoff, 1984).

- Suggest classic games like Hangman for spelling, or Word Lotto or Word Bingo for vocabulary.

- Encourage teachers to use visual aids. For example, older as well as younger students can compose stories for wordless picture books.

- Suggest that teachers teach idioms. Acting out or drawing the literal meaning of idioms (e.g., "raining cats and dogs") is always fun. Trade books that play with idioms include Gwynne's *The King Who Rained* (1970b) and

A Chocolate Moose for Dinner (1970a), and Parish's *Amelia Bedelia* (1986) and its sequels.

- Help teachers of elementary students to obtain and use predictable language books such as Bill Martin's (1967) *Brown Bear, Brown Bear*. Students experience a quick feeling of success with this type of material. They get needed repetition not through drill but through rhyme, rhythm, and fun. Students can then replicate the book's patterns ("María, María, who do you see, I see José looking at me"). (See Appendix D for a sample list of predictable language books.)

- Encourage teachers to read aloud frequently to small groups and to tape-record themselves reading favorite stories so that students can return to them. Books selected should have good text-to-picture match, with pictures that are large enough for the students to see. Teachers should point to pictures, enunciate clearly, and stop as appropriate to allow students to talk about the books.

- Help teachers adapt instruction to include repeated use of key vocabulary and concepts, and to use exaggerated pauses and changes in intonation and volume to focus children's attention on key vocabulary terms. Teachers should use gestures, body motions, facial expressions, or sensory aids to further clarify meaning (Enright, 1986).

- Suggest that teachers use the repetition in raps and songs as the basis for instruction. *Jazz Chants* (Graham, 1978) and *Sound Expressions* (Darquea, 1988) are two sources of this type of material. Choral reading of this and other material can be most effective (McCauley & McCauley, 1992).

- Ensure that reading instruction includes study and test-taking skills as well as strategies for content area reading (Nurss & Hough, 1992).

- Help teachers find someone who can translate both oral and written information as needed when communicating with LEP parents.

- Suggest that teachers encourage parents to read to their children, even in the home language. There is much transfer of story structure, conceptual knowledge, and love of reading.

- Remind teachers that students learn by doing. Help teachers find ways of ensuring that language learning is a joyful experience.

Classrooms for LEP students should include ample opportunities for meaningful oral and written language in a variety of contexts: thematic units, learning centers, social interactions. For instruction to be *"about* something" (Wallace, 1988, p. 13), classrooms should include several types of literacy materials: regulatory (rules or instructions), representational (labels or information), personal (opinions or feelings), and imaginative (make-believe or humorous). LEP students need opportunities to work on the "big" things first—that is, "the strategic capability of keeping your audience interested even if you make mistakes, the discourse competence of getting your main idea across, and the sociolinguistic ability of choosing the right message and format to fit your communication partners" (Nurss & Hough, 1992, p. 282).

Special Education Students

The Individuals with Disabilities Education Act (IDEA) mandates that all children with disabilities in the United States are entitled to a free public education in the "least restrictive environment" possible. In other words, to the degree it is possible, special education students must be placed in the general education classroom, if at all appropriate, for all or part of the day. Following are tips that can help with both mainstreamed and nonmainstreamed students.

Tips: Working with Special Education Students

- Remind general classroom teachers with mainstreamed special education students to read each student's IEP (Individualized Educational Plan). Research indicates that general education teachers (particularly at secondary levels) rarely read IEPs and are thus unaware of the students' special needs (Schumm & Vaughn, 1992).

- Help give special education students a reason for coming to school. When computers were installed in one elementary school, it was the LD students (those with learning disabilities) who learned how to use them first. These children then became tutors for the others. Other ideas include giving the LD student the responsibility to helping a younger child or listening to a child read. As an alternative, pair the child with a grandparent at a neighborhood nursing home!

- If the student is mainstreamed during reading/language arts periods, help the classroom teacher develop activities that are appropriate for the student, are consistent with instruction in the resource room, and will promote inclusion in the regular classroom routine. For example, in the regular classroom, students might reread selections from the resource room to a regular class buddy or to the class during a scheduled class time set aside for this purpose. Students might insert work from the resource room into portfolios housed in the regular classroom. Students might take portable centers from the resource room to practice in the regular classroom—for example, cut-up sentence strips from sentences dictated by students can be brought from the resource room to be sequenced in a manipulatives center in the regular classroom. Cunningham and Allington (1993) describe the use of traveling notebooks which both teachers of pull-out students use to jot down comments about what they are working on and problems or successes students had that day.

- In intermediate, middle, or senior high settings, have a corps of student volunteers tape-record textbook chapters for special education students. These can be listened to in special education or general education settings, or perhaps in the library/media center.

- In middle and senior high settings, use a corps of "study buddies" to help tutor special education students during lunch or after school.

- Be prepared to provide classroom teachers who have mainstreamed students in their classroom with strategies to promote social and academic integration of these students. Bos and Vaughn (1991) have compiled a book of useful strategies for general education teachers.

- Help teachers make accommodations in unobtrusive ways. Some recent research (Vaughn, Schumm, Niarhos, & Gordon, 1993) has suggested that low-achieving students and students with learning disabilities are reluctant to have adaptations made for them when mainstreamed in the general education class because such adaptations may draw attention to their handicaps.

Sometimes special education students are the ones most vulnerable to controversial reading programs. Refer if necessary to the section on "Controversial Instructional Materials" in Chapter 2.

Low-Achieving Students Who Do Not Receive Special Services

Many low-achieving students do not qualify for special education or compensatory education services. These students pose a special challenge for general education teachers who often recognize the learning difficulties of these students but do not have the resources to develop individual instructional programs to meet their needs.

Tips: Low-Achieving Students

- Encourage teachers to employ flexible grouping practices for literacy instruction that discourage student labeling (Radencich et al., in press).

- Work with teachers to identify high-interest, low-vocabulary, age-appropriate trade books that will appeal to low-achieving students.

- Develop a network of volunteers who can help students during and after school.

- Help teachers pinpoint students' strengths and weaknesses in literacy learning and in developing an action plan.

- Help teachers develop a list of practical suggestions for parents to support literacy learning at home.

- Provide workshops for parents who would like to learn more about how to help their children with reading and writing competencies.

- Arrange for in-class or after-school mini-lessons in reading, writing, and study skills strategies that engage diverse student learners.

- Help grade-level or subject area teams to develop strategies, study guides, and audiotapes for content area textbooks.

Unmotivated Students

Students who remain unmotivated even when teachers give their best efforts are among the most frustrating to teachers. One way to attack an individual student's lethargy is with cooperative problem solving. Rather than isolated teachers trying to put a spark under a student, the school counselor can arrange a faculty conference of all teachers who interact with the target student. The conference can include the development of an action plan, which can be structured using the PARS plan suggested by Forgan and Mangrum (1989):

- **Purpose:** What can each teacher do to promote a sense of purpose for learning? Often, unmotivated students simply do not see the relevance of their coursework to their lives. Teachers can make purpose-setting links more easily if they know the students and are aware of student interests and goals. Thus, interest and attitude inventories (Chapter 8) are crucial pieces of information. Adult mentors can serve as role models for unmotivated students and can help students to see the importance of schooling.

- **Attitudes:** What can each teacher do to promote a sense of caring about this student as an individual? What can each teacher do to see that the student has a place to "belong" in the school? At the secondary level, one strategy is assigning students to the same homeroom teacher for the duration of their stay at the school. Similarly, at the elementary level, classes might be assigned to the same teacher for more than one year, or vertical teams of teachers might oversee classes that remain in the "family" for a multiyear period.

- **Results:** What can each teacher do to provide each student with immediate feedback about completed work and to encourage monitoring of individual work (Brozo, 1990)? For example, teachers can provide specific individual feedback about writing strengths and weaknesses, or they can empower students to find the "six" spelling errors in a paper.

- **Success:** What can each teacher do to design opportunities for student social or academic success? One way to help teachers to work collaboratively with students to set realistic goals is the contract approach (Taylor, Harris, & Pearson, 1988). Contracting is based on the notion that students are more likely to complete tasks if they have can participate in selecting and structuring the tasks. Contracts can be made for reading, writing, listening, and speaking goals.

This action plan is simple, but it is not simplistic. Students who understand the purpose for learning have a positive attitude, see results, and have a feeling of success that makes them less likely to become disengaged.

Above-Average Readers

Because of the heavy emphasis on standardized test scores at all levels, even above-average readers can benefit from direct reading and test-taking instruction (Beers, 1986). The needs of above-average readers can be met in different ways.

Beyond the Basal. Above-average readers in elementary school must be challenged in reading. In the past, such students were placed in above-level basals. This strategy is falling into disfavor, however, because even above-level basals are limiting. Selections are often only portions of books and are limited in scope. Thus, teachers often begin with grade-level selections with the whole class but then go beyond these, particularly with above-level readers, with other chapters from the same book, other works by the same author, or additional works on the same subject (Radencich & McKay, in press). Teachers also assign extra projects and expect more and better writing from students who are more capable.

Peer Tutors. Above-average readers can serve as peer tutors. Peer tutoring can be an effective technique at any grade level, providing opportunities for practice and benefiting both tutors and tutees in achievement, self-concept, social relationships, and attitudes toward reading (Cohen, Kulik, & Kulik, 1982; Topping, 1989). As in any strategy, however, moderation is the key. Above-average readers should not be "used" in constant tutoring.

Cooperative Learning. Like peer tutoring, cooperative learning can be beneficial for all learners, but tasks must be carefully structured (Johnson, Johnson, & Holubec, 1990). Above-average readers will resent cooperative learning if they feel that their peers are not cooperating and if their grades suffer as a result (Matthews, 1992). For further details, see the section on cooperative groups earlier in this chapter as well as the Johnson and Johnson (1992) section on using research in Chapter 1.

Homogeneous Groups. Above-average readers need some time to work in homogeneous groups (Johnson & Johnson, 1992). Although these students benefit from heterogeneous instruction, they also benefit from working together.

Reading Rate. Once students read fluently, they should be taught that good readers use a variety of different reading rates. Students must learn to read with flexibility depending on the purpose for reading, the type of material being read, the level of difficulty, and their familiarity with the subject matter. Students should practice finding appropriate reading rates by reading diverse materials at various speeds.

Study Techniques. Although students who read above grade level usually have less trouble than poorer readers in understanding their textbooks, above-average readers can still benefit from specific instruction in study techniques. Some recent research evidence on middle and high school students' perceptions of textbook adaptations suggests that higher achieving students are not receiving the instruction in reading and study strategies they think they need (Schumm, Vaughn, & Saumell, 1992).

Most students develop their study skills by osmosis or by luck. Some of the study skills that may prove most useful to the above-average reader at all grade levels beyond the very early grades include Cornell Notetaking (Pauk, 1983), mnemonic techniques for memory (Bragstadt & Stumpf, 1982), semantic mapping and other visual organizers, time management (Radencich, Beers, & Schumm, 1993), and analytic reading strategies (Whimbey, 1983). All students should be taught to use efficient, effective study strategies.

In summary, don't overlook above-average readers! These students will often use and retain the information shared with them. Efforts with these students may be highly rewarding.

Short- and Long-Term Instructional Planning

A solid instructional program begins with assessment of needs and planning. If planning begins at the district level, subsequent planning will need to take place at the school and classroom level.

Planning for the Year

Planning for the year is important at all levels. At the school level, planning might start with each grade group getting together to discuss pacing and each teacher then submitting his or her own plan. Although the arrival of actual students will force changes and perhaps a revamping of any plan, at least an initial pacing guide lays the foundation for further thinking and organization. Without early thought given to pacing, reading instruction often boils down to "one story a week" regardless of the number of selections that might be included in a reading series, or regardless of student interest or need. Similarly, writing instruction might wind up focusing on narrative writing, with little attention given to other writing modes.

One type of planning that deserves special attention is planning for interdisciplinary units. This might begin with an examination of textbooks to plan for a possible resequencing of chapters to support the units. The planning might begin with scheduling of "large blocks of time for students to explore, extend, or otherwise 'play' around with ideas they've chosen to connect with" (Dalrymple, 1991b, p. 189). One structure for planning an interdisciplinary unit is based on the Smith, Goodman, and Meredith (1976) model of perceiving, ideating, and presenting. Sixth-grade teacher Karen Dalrymple (1991b) has adapted this model, starting with an activity planning form with space for the class to record materials next to each item in a list of activities. She lists activities in the three categories:

- *Activities for perceiving* (gaining new facts, ideas, and impressions): independent reading, read-aloud, independent discussion, presentations, films, photos/posters, and so on

- *Activities for ideating* (responding to new facts, ideas, and impressions): oral, drawing, writing, experimenting, drama, and other

- *Activities for presenting* (sharing facts, ideas, and impressions): oral, drawing, writing, drama, and other

This form serves as the basis for a class web on the theme and for scheduling whole class and small group work.

Multiyear Plans

At the middle and senior high school levels, multiyear plans ensure an overall balanced program. Thus, different years might focus on different genres, literature from different countries, different reading strategies (Simmons-Wolpow, Farrell, & Tonjes, 1991), and different types of writing assignments. Within each year, planning could involve one or more interdisciplinary themes and departmental development of courses of study.

Scheduling

Scheduling is a broad issue to be tackled by administrators and teachers alike. Answers to scheduling dilemmas should be sought with the school philosophy in mind.

Administrators. Elementary administrators face many scheduling headaches—making sure that teachers have uninterrupted times for teaching, that special teachers are scheduled to facilitate rather than obstruct classroom instruction, and that teachers have time for common planning where appropriate. Any cross-grouping can throw one more monkey wrench into the master schedule.

At one elementary school, scheduling took an interested turn when it was decided that cutting class sizes in half for the language arts block would be a priority. The changed schedule was feasible for three grade levels. Half of each class would go to a special area teacher while the other students received their language arts instruction. The groups were then rotated. To accomplish this, each special area teacher took groups from two teachers at a time. Each day of the week, students went to a different "special": counselor, library/media center, career lab, computer lab, and read-alouds.

A scheduling option in some schools involves provision of special education or remedial services through a consulting model, where the special teacher or reading resource specialist teaches *in* the classroom with the teacher present, or even team-teaches. This can eliminate problems typical of pullouts, such as stigmatization, lowered expectations, fragmentation of instruction, and travel time. In this situation, the special teacher need not work exclusively with the remedial students but can work to facilitate a variety of flexible groupings. Indeed, Chapter 1 program regulations now have an "incidental benefits" clause designed to alleviate concerns about Chapter 1 personnel incidentally benefiting non–Chapter 1 eligible children when they work in the classroom (Allington, 1993).

For a consulting model to be successful, the teachers must form a true partnership. Chapter 1 teacher Debra Jacobson (1991) conducts reading/writing workshops in six classrooms, adapting to each teacher. She subtly pays special attention to the Chapter 1 students in the classrooms. The detailed joint planning involved in this collaboration includes contingency plans for schedule mishaps. Thus, Jacobson will pull out one of the Chapter 1 students if the teacher is not ready for her when she arrives. She finds student benefits to the pull-in method—for example, more time for her to conduct individual conferences. She also finds it positive that this method brings teachers together on a regular basis to discuss the developing curriculum.

In the case of special education, there are additional issues to consider. It might be necessary for all special education students to be placed in a limited number of classrooms to enable the special education teacher to schedule assistance to all his or her students. If, instead, students are pulled out, scheduling should ensure that the special education teacher is not fighting a losing battle, with children constantly entering and exiting the special education classroom throughout the school day. Also, if the school is providing integrated reading/language arts instruction, pull-outs should not break up the reading/language arts block.

Schools with more than one special education teacher may have options not available to other schools. For example, at a school with two LD teachers, one may take the lower achieving LD students and the other the higher achievers, rather than necessarily dividing the students strictly by grade placement.

In the case of the middle or senior high school content area classroom, a particular benefit of a pull-in model is that the reading specialist focuses on material from *real* textbooks, something that does not always occur in a reading class (Peters, 1990). Also, students and content area teachers may be more likely to see the relationship between the reading strategies and their subject area if these students are taught in their content classroom rather than in a "reading" room. This model can even be carried out with team teaching over an entire semester. Another variation is for an entire content class (teacher included) to go into a reading lab for instruction, which is to be followed up in the content class. Regardless of the variation used, team teaching involving remedial and special education teachers working with content area teachers already occurs in many middle and high schools (Allington, 1993). Other scheduling quandaries that will arise include those discussed previously in the section on middle/secondary grouping. At all levels, every option should be carefully considered in light of overall goals.

Teachers. For teachers, scheduling can be a problem of trying to fit everything and to put it into a framework that works. The desired balance between structure and flexibility will vary from teacher to teacher. Following are some teachers' comments:

- Fifth-grade teacher Mary Kitagawa keeps an 8:15–10:15 schedule for reading and writing, including any literature study, read-aloud, writing workshop, personal reading, and mini-lessons that are done but are not contained in her thematic unit time (10:15–11:55).

- Fifth-grade teacher Debra Goodman (Goodman & Curry, 1991) finds that her schedule grows more informal and flexible throughout the year, moving to student scheduling of large chunks of the school day.

- Third-grade teacher Karen Dalrymple (1991a) writes no times on her schedule. She prefers to write the activities and then use time as needed to accomplish the work. Children learn that some days may end with plans not having been accomplished. They also learn respect for schedules because those for special classes and lunch are kept inviolate.

- Freeman and Nofziger (1991), teachers of a first–second combination bilingual classroom, write the daily schedule on chart paper covered with clear plastic for easy erasing and changing from day to day without total rewriting.

Lesson Plan Formats[2]

The following section pertains primarily to the elementary level, but administrators looking for middle/senior lesson plan formats will find much that pertains to those levels as well.

With regard to weekly and daily planning at the elementary school, your district will probably have time requirements for at least certain subjects. If you do have flexibility to merge instruction in more than one subject, take advantage of this. Thus, there will be no need, for example, to expect teachers to provide separate scheduled times for spelling, handwriting, reading, and composition, if teachers can teach these areas as a meaningful whole.

Lesson plans have traditionally fit into neat little boxes: boxes for each day of the week, for each subject area, for each reading group. In the words of a teacher in Nacogdoches, Texas, "It forces one's thoughts into tight corners, binding and pinching like ill-fitting shoes" (LaBarbera, 1993, p. 39). But these plan formats just do not work for flexible group instruction. Aside from problems with the traditional lesson plan components (e.g., which objectives to list when you're probably covering quite a few), there are lesson plan questions that relate directly to flexible grouping, decisions on whether and how to distinguish between whole class activities and group activities that are teacher-directed or that students will manage primarily without teacher help.

Lesson plans are so personal that no single alternative works for everyone, but the following are a few possibilities.

[2]Adapted from "Integrated Lesson Plan Formats: How Do You Fit It All In?" by M. C. Radencich, *Florida Reading Quarterly, 29*(2), 1992, pp. 15–17.

1. *Pinellas County Public Schools Model*: Most teachers in Pinellas County, Florida, use a lesson planner designed by a committee and simplified by teachers after the first year of implementation (Radencich & McKay, in press). It has space for each of the four core activities—reading selection instruction, writing, self-selected reading, and skill and strategy instruction—that make up Pinellas County's flexible grouping model. It also has space for planning enrichment activities and the other language arts (Figure 7-1).

2. *Dade County Public Schools Model*: With the implementation of flexible grouping in Dade County, the reading staff developed a repertoire of sample lesson plan formats with varying degrees of structure. They knew that some teachers would want to start with a "cookbook," whereas others would be ready for more open-ended formats. Alternative teacher-made formats were later collected and distributed. Some sample forms are provided in Figure 7-2.

3. *Clusters*: A cluster plan is a web that resembles a wheel and its spokes. Typically, the core selection is written in the center, surrounded by activities grouped as desired by the teacher (e.g., related readings, vocabulary words, content connections, writing, centers). At least one basal publisher suggests a theme cluster format for plans. I have seen kindergarten and first-grade teachers use daily clusters of activities, which they plan around the big book of the day. If administrators allow teachers the flexibility to write plans on posterboard, then theme clusters can work nicely. They can help the whole class see where they are going. They can be easy to fill out because the teacher does not have to spend time figuring out how to condense everything. An alternative to posterboard could be a magnetic board, with movable pieces such as "student" pieces moved around for flexible grouping.

Cluster planning can be intimidating for some teachers. But for those who are interested, questions to ask include the following:

- Will the clustering be for all instruction or only for reading and language arts?

- Will the cluster stand alone, or will it be a skeleton to be accompanied by more detailed plans?

- Will clustering be day by day or for the duration of a theme?

- Will the cluster be organized into subject areas? Or will this still look too much like traditional squares in a plan book?

A graduate class asked to cluster plans for a week all chose to put in the center the theme and/or the selection title(s), some inside an attractive theme-related illustration. One student clustered by day, with five circles around the theme; the procedures were the main circles, with orbiting circles for each day's objectives, materials, and evaluation. A pair of students working to-

DAILY ELEMENTS OF FLEXIBLE GROUPING,
CORE SELECTION MODEL FOR TEACHING READING
K-5

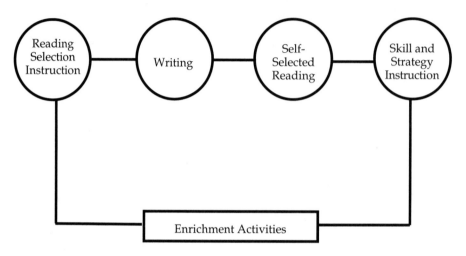

FIGURE 7-1.   Pinellas County's Flexible Grouping Model.

gether chose the following organization around the theme: introduction, applying ideas, skills and strategies, language activities, and theme project. Attached were detailed daily plans in an outline format.

Another student's titles were: purpose, reading, writing projects, spelling/vocabulary, handwriting, content area, home discovery projects. This student had a color-coded key clarifying the days when each activity would take place and the form of evaluation for each. She also had a clever revolving centerpiece that celebrated her instructional philosophy. (See Figure 7-3 for portions of her plan.)

A final pair of students coded each activity as to teacher direction, student participation, day of delivery, and sequence within each day. They used the following structure: student reading time, video/read-aloud, cross-curricular activities, skills and strategies, language activities, evaluations. Most of these sections were accompanied by a speech bubble with a list of objectives.

If clustering can help children with prewriting, maybe it can help teachers in prewriting lesson plans, too.

4. *Use of technology*: Some teachers use word processors to copy or change lesson plan items from one week to the next. I do this for demonstration lessons. The objectives and materials for the entire selection are listed on Day 1. Each day, activities are simply explained and the type of evaluation for each

FIGURE 7-2. Lesson plan forms from Dade County.

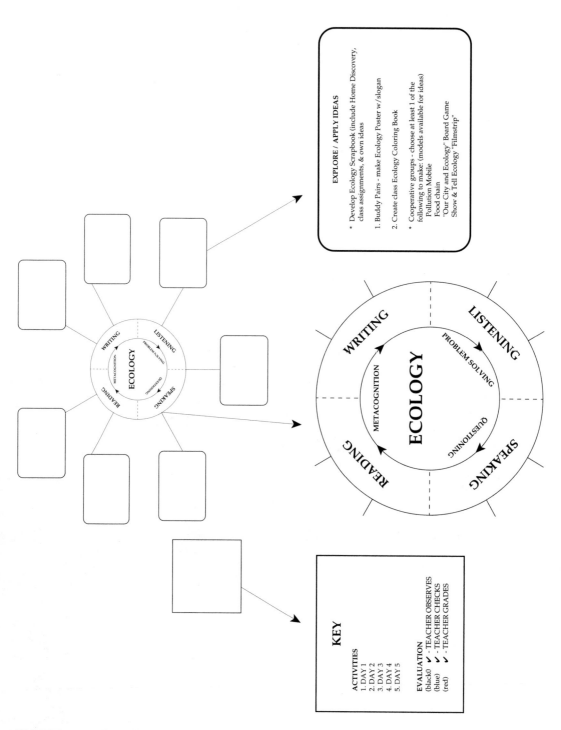

FIGURE 7-3.   Cluster lesson plan.

day is noted. Where flexible grouping occurs, what each group is doing at one time is described in a brief paragraph.

If teachers want to use technology beyond word processing and want to see information organized in more than one way (e.g., by objective, by day of the week, by subject area), a database could be ideal, especially if all teachers and administrators at a school use the same database. One teacher might print the information by day, and the administrator might look at it by day as well as by objective.

Another intriguing option is the use of software specifically designed for lesson planning. Three programs in this category are *Plan to Teach* (Teaching), *Planit* (Amberon), and *Educator Home Card* (Apple Computer), all available for both the IBM and the Macintosh, and all requiring a hard drive.

- *Plan to Teach* allows for the creation of four types of plans: weekly plans, daily plans, individual lesson plans, and a skills checklist. The program includes samples of each. The formats are similar to those found in many lesson plan books. They can be customized.

- *Planit* is a HyperCard program designed to integrate planning, class-room scheduling, and curriculum implementation. Its modules include "Day Book," "Plans," "Calendar," and "Resources." A master schedule is created. Timetables can be set on daily, weekly, or other cyclical schedules. High-quality graphics are an additional enhancement.

- *Education HomeCard* is a set of HyperCard stacks that provides student management tools and lesson management tools (calendar, lesson plans, and presentation stack). The program creates a card for each lesson plan, which has space to enter objectives, additional resources, preparation information, activities, and evaluation. Teachers can elect from a list of keywords to find related lessons. Lesson plan titles can be transferred to a Planner Calendar. Sample lesson plans are included. This product makes use of HyperCard 2.0 capabilities such as animation and sound.

Use of computers for lesson plans is a possibility all teachers might consider, even if only the simpler word-processing and database options are used.

5. *Logs*: Some teachers simply use lesson plan books with several blank lines per day. This simplicity parallels the blank page on which students write in "whole language" classrooms. In one school that uses such a plan, teachers are only required to note what they would do and what the anticipated result would be.

6. *Student involvement*: With completely individualized programs, it is possible for students to do at least some of the recording of their own plans. One teacher empowered her students to take this responsibility once she had

seen that managing the individualized plans herself was not feasible. She found that student involvement helped with student ownership as well as reducing her paperwork.

Changes in teaching may well require changes in lesson plan formats. Time should be spent choosing a possible format, with opportunities for reevaluating and changing this form as needed.

Conclusion

This chapter has focused on organization for instruction. Areas studied include physical design and appearance of classrooms; student placement and grouping; serving special needs students; and yearly, weekly, and daily plans. Organizing for instruction is a fluid process, which will evolve constantly in response to the needs of students and all others in the learning community.

C h a p t e r *8*

Is the Reading/Writing Program Working?

Remember when you received your Scholastic Aptitude Test or Graduate Record Examination scores in the mail? Only a confident few were able to open that envelope without trembling hands. Those scores had an influence on our future. Assessment is much more than test taking; assessment—particularly in the area of literacy education—has an enormous impact on instruction and on individual lives. In this chapter, assessment will be approached as a decision-making process that educators can use in answering the question, "Is the reading/writing program working?"

Assessment is an integral part of instruction and occurs every single school day (Teale, Hiebert, & Chittendon, 1987). Valencia and Pearson (1987) describe optimal assessment as follows:

> . . . the best possible asssessment of reading would seem to occur when teachers observe and interact with students as they read authentic texts for genuine purposes. As teachers interact with students, they evaluate the way(s) in which the students construct meaning, intervening to provide support or suggestions when the students appear to have difficulty (p. 728).

Duffy and Roehler (1989, p. 61) define assessment as "collection of the data used to make decisions." The notion of literacy assessment as a decision-making process can be used to guide the planning of a districtwide or schoolwide assessment program. As with any major program decision, representatives from subgroups in the school community—administrators, classroom teachers, parents, school district personnel, and students—need to be consulted. A Reading Committee (see Chapter 6) can help structure an assessment plan.

Being Test Savvy

Those in charge of structuring assessment plans need to be test savvy. Toward this end, this section will discuss what to assess, why assess, what tools to use, how to manage assessment results, how to cope with high-stakes tests, how to put it all together with portfolio assessment, and what test data won't tell the principal.

What to Assess

The content of literacy assessment can be narrowly viewed as those reading and writing subskills included on standardized tests. This view, however, represents an outmoded definition of literacy. The definition of literacy that sufficed for an earlier generation and a different economy has been replaced by a host of higher literacies: computer, scientific, civic, and cultural. These higher literacies call for students to analyze, think critically, evaluate, synthesize information, communicate more effectively, solve problems, learn how to learn, and in general, learn far more actively than students have traditionally done (Brown, 1989).

Goals for assessment depend on instructional goals (Winograd, Paris, & Bridge, 1991). Paris et al. (1992a) list seven critical dimensions and attributes of literacy that should be considered in assessment plans: engagement with text through reading, engagement with text through writing, knowledge about literacy, orientation to literacy, ownership of literacy, collaboration, and interconnectedness of the curriculum. Duffy and Roehler (1989) have proposed three primary goals that can be used to guide the content of literacy assessment: attitude goals, process goals, and content goals. A comprehensive assessment program should include all three of these goals, and specific assessment tools for each will be offered in this chapter.

- Attitude goals can include not only students' attitudes about reading and writing in general and about themselves as readers and writers, but also attitudes about specific pieces of writing.

- Process goals in the Duffy and Roehler model incorporate the traditional skills we tap in reading and writing tests, as well as metacognitive strategies that empower students to reflect about their own understanding before, during, and after reading.

- Content goals relate to reconstructing the author's intended meaning in textbook, functional, and personal reading. Process goals must be placed within a genuine context or they become isolated subskills that students cannot transfer to similar tasks. Content goals provide this meaningful context.

Why Assess

District reading and language arts supervisors often receive calls from schools asking us what test to order. My first question is always, "Why are you assessing?" Sometimes the answer hasn't been thought out. Yet, the choice of an assessment tool will be contingent on the purpose for testing. Stoodt (1981) suggests five purposes for reading assessment:

1. To assure the teacher that students are grouped appropriately

2. To allow the teacher to meet specific learning needs

3. To evaluate the strengths and weaknesses of the instructional program

4. To assess individual growth and development

5. To account to the community

Purposes for assessment may be set by the state, district, or school. If the assessment program is well defined, test scores will not merely be filed away but will provide data that are an integral part of ongoing instruction.

What Tools to Use

There are no perfect assessment tools. P. David Pearson (1992), in a presentation at the annual conference of the International Reading Association, outlined the advantages and disadvantages of each major form of assessment. He concluded that assessment had to be "messy" to be at all valid. Formal techniques are constraining and often miss some aspects of the human element. More informal techniques often do not offer the comfort of "measurable" gains. Valencia, McGinley, and Pearson (1990) contend that assessment should be multidimensional and that a variety of formal and informal tools should be used in a schoolwide program.

The following series of questions can help in the selection of assessment tools:

Questions for Selecting Assessment Tools: A Baker's Dozen

1. What is my purpose in using this measure?

2. What attitude, process, or content goals does this measure address?

3. Is the type of measure (formal or informal) consistent with our purposes and goals?

4. Are the format and content of the measure consistent with our purposes and goals?

5. Is a commercially prepared assessment or local/teacher-prepared assessment tool most appropriate for our goals and purposes?

6. Are the administration and scoring time reasonable in terms of what we hope to learn?

7. Is the measure biased in any way?

8. Does the measure assume prior knowledge that the student(s) may not possess?

9. In the case of standardized tests, are adequate reliability and validity data available?

10. Are directions for administration, scoring, and interpretation of the measure clear and easy to follow?

11. Is an individual measure necessary, or will a group assessment tool suffice?

12. Are multiple forms and the needed levels of the measure available?

13. Can the results of this measure be communicated easily to parents and the community (depending on the assessment purpose)?

Literally hundreds of commercially produced assessment tools are available to educators. Any listing that this book might offer would certainly not be exhaustive and, at the rate that new measures are being introduced, would become dated immediately. To keep current with newly developed instruments, see test reviews in *The Reading Teacher* and the *Journal of Reading*. For a detailed listing of tests in print up to 1990, see the most recent edition of the classic *How to Increase Reading Ability* (Harris & Sipay, 1990, pp. 697–727). In general, a comprehensive assessment program will include both norm- and criterion-referenced tests as well as informal assessment devices.

Norm-Referenced Tests. Norm-referenced tests compare an individual student's performance with that of his or her peers. The emphasis is not on the mastery of content but, rather, on the relative standing of an individual among students of a "norm" group of the same age or grade level. Norm-referenced tests can be administered either individually or to a group. They are typically recommended both as program evaluation tools and as screening tools (to be followed with measures more appropriate for individual assessment). Norm-referenced tests are also used, sometimes inappropriately, in grouping students. Regardless of the proposed use, norm-referenced tests should be seen as one tool in a multidimensional assessment program, though not necessarily on an annual basis.

The Stanford Achievement Test (1989) and the Iowa Tests of Basic Skills (1990) are typical norm-referenced tests. Although test formats vary, most offer percentile, stanine, and sometimes grade equivalent scores. One instrument, Degrees of Reading Power (DRP) (1984), is a modified cloze test that yields scores in DRP units that can be translated to independent, instructional, and frustration reading levels. Readability data (in DRP units) are available for many textbooks so that teachers can gauge the student–textbook match.

One problem that arises in using norm-referenced tests is in understanding the median. The percentile score that is typically reported for a group is the median or middle score. Educators who wish to boost median scores must realize that the median is not an "average" or mean. The left side of Figure 8-1 shows one student at each of the nine stanine points. The student in the middle of the line has the median score, in this case a 5. On the right is a depiction of "after" scores. Moving the scores of the lowest students to 4's without having any students crossing over the midpoint does not change the median of 5. Similarly, students who started out higher than this midpoint and whose scores were then raised to 9's did not change the median. Median scores are raised only by moving students who are just below the midpoint and getting them to cross this point.

Another point that must be understood is the concept of *regression toward the mean*. This statistical phenomenon is the tendency of extremely low or high scores to revert closer to the mean or average with subsequent test administrations. Parents of high achievers should not be alarmed when extremely high scores drop a bit, nor should a new program be credited with improvement in extremely low scores. With regression toward the mean, both effects are to be expected.

Educators who do not fully understand scores from norm-referenced tests not only have difficulty interpreting scores to parents, they quite often rely on grade-equivalent scores, a practice that was discouraged by the International Reading Association in its 1981 position statement. A grade equivalent is an average point. Thus, in an average fourth grade, half the students will be above the fourth-grade level and half will be below it. Suppose that the test is a measure of knowledge of the alphabet. Virtually all fourth-graders will score 100 percent. So will all twelfth-graders. Thus, a score that places the student at the twelfth-grade level on this test does not mean that the child can identify the alphabet at a twelfth-grade level, only that he or she can do so as well as the average twelfth-grader can, which is also true for the average fourth-grader. Many publishing companies have discontinued the use of grade equivalents in recent years. Baumann and Stevenson's 1982 article in *The Reading Teacher* can help educators interpret standardized test scores.

Also norm-referenced are writing production tests in which students

X	X	X	X	X	X	X	X	X		X	X	X	X	X	X	X	X	X
1	2	3	4	5	6	7	8	9		4	4	4	4	5	9	9	9	9

FIGURE 8-1   Explanation of median score.

respond to a prompt. Norms for these tests are often local ones created on the spot when a team scans through a set of papers to establish "anchors" or typical papers at each scoring level, say 1–4. Once this norming has taken place, other papers are scored to determine where they fall in relation to the anchors.

Criterion-Referenced Tests. Criterion-referenced tests assess student mastery of a specific goal. They are less global than norm-referenced tests and typically more closely linked to a particular curriculum or set of competencies. A student's score on a criterion-referenced test is not compared to a norming population; instead, it is compared to a predetermined criterion. Criteria need not be traditional ones such as correctly completing 7 out of 10 items (70 percent) on a test. For example, a criterion could be using correct punctuation "most of the time," including at least three types of writing in one's portfolio, or reciting a poem following a checklist of desired behaviors.

Criterion-referenced tests typically serve as tools to aid in individualizing instruction, grouping for instruction, and assessing individual progress. Teachers, school systems, and states develop criterion-referenced tests. Publishers also produce both generic criterion-referenced tests and others to accompany many basal reading programs.

Informal Assessment Devices. If we wanted to study the architecture of a building, we would not knock it down and study each brick and board. Something would definitely be missing from such an analysis! Likewise, our aim is to study aspects of reading within the context of real reading, not as isolated components. Therefore, we need assessment devices that use the kind of text students must read in school and at home. Only then can we draw meaningful conclusions about various important reading skills (Gillet & Temple, 1982, p. 82).

Informal assessment devices are the heart of a comprehensive assessment program. They are informal in that administration and interpretation of results are more flexible than with commercially prepared norm- and criterion-referenced materials. Both teacher and student reports of evaluation of student reading and writing are incorporated. Nearly every new issue of professional journals includes new suggestions for informal assessment. The choices are vast, but "We must pick, choose, adapt, and adopt the measures that provide us with the information that fits our vision of reading and writing" (Winograd, Paris, & Bridge, 1991, p. 110).

One strength of informal assessment is its ability to involve students more directly. Students are typically viewed as the object of assessment, but they can also be collaborators in both data collection and data analysis. Students' responsibility for their own learning, though traditionally overlooked (Goodlad, 1984; Gutmann, 1987), is receiving increased attention (Ericson & Ellett, 1990). Students can be involved in identifying components of assessment portfolios. They can be interviewed to help the teacher determine student-identified goals for literacy improvement and the degree to which those goals were met. Finally, students can be taught how to conduct a self-analysis of their own work. Indeed, teachers exploring portfolio assessment are finding that they cannot manage without using students to help with data analysis. Not only does this save time for the teacher, but it offers a richer program for the students as well. Paper-and-pencil assessments are insufficient to identify student needs. The voices of students must be heard.

Another voice that must be heard is that of parents. Parent involvement in assessment can go beyond filling in a parent comment section on the report card. Parents can sit with the teacher to set quarterly goals (Morrissey & Radencich, 1993). Parents also can respond to letters. In response to the letter of a seventh-grade teacher requesting input and suggestions about progress (Curry, 1989), one parent wrote: "Thank you for the opportunity to participate in Carrie's school life. As you know, as children get older opportunities get less frequent. . . ." Parents will see progress from a different angle—and we need that view.

To assist you in selecting informal, multidimensional, authentic assessment tools, an annotated list of informal assessment tools for meeting attitude, process, and content goals is provided here. It is beyond the scope of this book to provide specific details for all assessment tools, but the book will briefly describe various instruments (many of them teacher-constructed) and give you references so you can read more about it. Most of the assessment tools listed here are appropriate for a variety of grade levels and can be used in both reading/writing and content area classrooms. Because some are designed to meet more than one goal, there is some overlap.

Tools for Assessing Attitude Goals

- *Attitude inventories:* Attitude inventories can be helpful in determining student attitudes about reading/writing and about themselves as readers/writers. Some teachers use these inventories at the beginning and end of the year to gauge the impact of personal reading programs. Inventories are available in the form of rating scales and open-ended sentences. Published attitude inventories can be found in the following sources:

Alexander, J. E., & Filler, R. C. (1976). *Attitudes and reading.* Newark, DE: International Reading Association.

Davidson, J. L. (1990). *Holistic reading and writing assessment for adults.* Monroe, NY: Trillium Press.

Kennedy, L. D., & Halenski, R. S. (1975). Measuring attitudes: An extra dimension. *Journal of Reading, 18,* 518–522.

McKenna, M. C., & Kerr, D. J. (1990). Measuring attitude toward reading: A new tool for teachers. *The Reading Teacher, 43,* 626–639.

- *Interest inventories:* At the beginning of the school year, interest inventories are invaluable in helping teachers get to know students' likes and
  dislikes quickly. Sentence completion inventories are probably the most
  useful, but checklists and questionnaires are also available in print and,
  in the case of BookWhiz and Browzer, on diskette:

Dulin, K. L. (1984). Assessing reading interests of elementary and middle school
students. In A. J. Harris & E. Sipay (Eds.), *Readings on reading instruction* (pp.
344–357). New York: Longman.

Eberwein, L. (1973). What do book choices indicate? *Journal of Reading, 17,* 186–191.

Heathington, B. S. (1979). What to do about reading motivation in the middle school?
Journal of Reading, 22, 709–713.

Norris, L., & Shatkin, L. (1987). *BookWhiz* (Grades 6–9). Princeton, NJ: Educational
Testing Service.

Norris, L., & Shatkin, L. (1987). *BookWhiz, Jr.* (Grades 3–6). Princeton, NJ: Educational
Testing Service.

Norris, L., & Shatkin, L. (1987). *BookWhiz Teen* (Grades 9–12). Princeton, NJ: Educational Testing Service.

TASA. *Browzer* (Grades 2–12). Brewster, NY: TASA.

- *Reading logs:* A reading log is one window to student responses to their
  reading. A reading log or journal is a notebook in which students can
  write reflections before, during, and after reading. A format for entering
  log entries should be determined. This format might include the date,
  number of pages read, and title of the passage read. Students then can
  record their personal reactions.

Wollman-Bonilla, J. E. (1989). Reading journals: Invitations to participate in literature. *The Reading Teacher, 43,* 112–120.

- *Dialogue journals:* Like the reading log, a dialogue journal also is a vehicle
  for students to respond to their reading. A dialogue journal, however, is
  specifically intended as a written conversation between individual students and the teacher, or between pairs of students. After reading a book
  or story, a student writes a brief reflection about his or her interest in and
  attitude toward the material. Then the dialogue journal is passed on to
  the "journal partner," who writes a response to the student's entry and
  adds a reflection about his or her own reading. The dialogue format
  encourages communication about reading and is an ongoing record of
  students' interests and attitudes.

Atwell, N. (1984). Writing and reading literature from the inside out. *Language Arts,
61,* 240–252.

Bode, B. A. (1989). Dialogue journal writing. *The Reading Teacher, 42,* 568–571.

Wells, M. C. (1992–1993). At the junction of reading and writing: How dialogue
journals contribute to students' reading development. *Journal of Reading, 36,*
294–302.

- *Teacher-completed checklists:* One way of recording reading/writing attitudes and habits is through checklists completed following teacher observation. These devices can be used at regular intervals to gauge student change.

Au, K. H., Scheu, J. A., Kawakami, A. J., & Herman, P. A. (1990). Assessment of students' ownership of literacy. *The Reading Teacher, 44,* 154–156.

Tompkins, G. E. (1992). Assessing the processes students use as writers. *Journal of Reading, 36,* 244–246.

- *Student interviews:* We would never go to a physician's office and expect a diagnosis before we open our mouths. Yet we determine students' strengths and weaknesses in school without asking them to tell us how they see themselves as readers and writers. We forget to consult the experts—the students themselves. Probably the best way to determine student interests and attitudes is through personal conversations and interviews. During such sessions it is important to *listen* to what the student has to say and to probe for reasons for negative attitudes and for possible areas of interest that may not have been detected with paper-and-pencil instruments. Although such interviews are difficult to arrange, they are imperative in establishing a positive relationship in a community of literacy learners. The teacher takes notes on the interviews and keeps them as brief as possible. Sample questions:

  — What is the best book you ever read? (interest)
  — What is your favorite kind of book? (interest)
  — Do you like to read? (attitude)
  — Do you have a library card? (habits)
  — What would make you a better writer? (knowledge)

- A comprehensive description of various types of semistructured and open-ended interviews is presented in:

Seda, I., & Pearson, P. D. (1991). Interviews to assess learners' outcomes. *Reading Research and Instruction, 31,* 22–32.

- *Learning biographies:* Students can tell (in a personal conversation with the teacher) or write their own "reading and writing history." Histories can include how the students learned to read and write; successes and challenges along the way; and reading/writing habits, interests, and attitudes. These biographies can form the core of a "who I am as a person, as a reader, and as a writer" type of portfolio. For a description of this type of portfolio, see the following.

Hansen, J. (1992). The language of challenge: Readers and writers speak their minds. *Language Arts, 69,* 100–105.

Tools for Assessing Process Goals

- *Metacognitive rating: Metacognition* refers to a reader's ability to monitor his or her comprehension and to use appropriate corrective strategies when comprehension hits a "clunk." Questionnaires have been developed to help students gauge their use of metacognitive strategies.

Davey, B., & Porter, S. M. (1982). Comprehension rating: A procedure to assist poor comprehenders. *Journal of Reading, 26*, 197–201.

Schmitt, M. C. (1990). A questionnaire to measure children's awareness of strategic reading processes. *The Reading Teacher, 43*, 459–460.

- *Think-alouds:* A think-aloud is a structure for promoting students' reflection about their own reading. With a think-aloud, students read a passage orally or silently, ask themselves questions while doing so, reread to clarify, hypothesize, insert bits of prior knowledge, express puzzlement, and engage in other such metacognitive processes. Whenever readers come to a difficult part, they stop, describe the "clunk," and then try to problem-solve about ways to "fix up" the problem. Think-alouds do not come naturally to many students, so the teacher needs to model the process. Think-alouds can provide the teacher and individual students with insight about how students process text. An example:

Yes I know candidates like that.   ←   *The candidates were both lying. Had lying become*
I wonder if "honest Abe" lied ←   *a necessary part of running for office? Had candidates always lied? If so, could the lying be excused*
. . .   *if it was for a greater purpose than simply getting*
Hmm . . . I'm going to need   ←   *elected? These questions needed to be answered.*
to think about that.

Davey, B. (1983). Think-aloud—modeling the cognitive processes of reading comprehension. *Journal of Reading, 27*, 44–47.

Wade, S. E. (1990). Using think alouds to assess comprehension. *The Reading Teacher, 43*, 442–451.

Tools for Assessing Content Goals

- *Informal reading inventories:* In the right hands, informal reading inventories (IRIs) can yield much information about a student's strengths and weaknesses in reading. Henk (1985, p. 284) comments, "An assessment is only as good as the individual who interprets the data." If the information used is limited to quantitative data (independent, instructional, and frustration reading levels), then the potential contribution of the IRI is squandered. Growing numbers of teachers are becoming familiar with the variety of information that an IRI can yield and with the implications of the type of diagnostic thinking that IRI users can carry over to ongoing, informal assessment. For example, teachers may take the suggestions of some IRIs for analysis of graphophonic, syntactic, and semantic miscues, and for analysis of retellings, and then mentally conduct such analyses during routine reading sessions. Many basal readers now include IRIs in their supplementary materials. Commercial inventories other than those included with basals are also available. Here are some examples:

Ekwall, E. (1986). *Ekwall reading inventory,* 2nd ed. Boston: Allyn and Bacon.

Johns, J. (1982). *Advanced reading inventory.* Dubuque, IA: Kendall/Hunt.

Johns, J. (1988). *Basic reading inventory: Pre-primer–Grade eight,* 4th ed. Dubuque, IA: Kendall/Hunt.

Johns, J. (1990). *Computer-based secondary and college reading inventory.* Dubuque, IA: Kendall/Hunt.

Leslie, L., & Caldwell, J. (1990). *Qualitative reading inventory.* Glenview, IL: Scott, Foresman.

- *Interactive teaching/testing assessments:* In recognition of the close relationship between assessment and instruction, a number of tools have been developed to link teaching and testing. The focus is on identification of student needs within genuine reading and writing tasks. Included here are both commercial instruments and teacher-made tools. An example of the latter is the Content IRI, sometimes known as a Group IRI or CIRI, a test prepared by a content area teacher using the text for that class.

Farr, R., & Farr, B. *Integrated assessment system.* (1990). San Antonio, TX: Psychological Corporation.

Raju, N. (1991). *Integrated literature and language arts portfolio program.* Chicago: Riverside.

The Riverside curriculum assessment system. (1991). Chicago: Riverside.

Roswell, F. G., & Chall, J. S. (1991). *Diagnostic assessment of reading with trial teaching strategies (DARTTS).* Chicago: Riverside.

Sammons, R. B., & Davey, B. (1993–1994). Assessing students' skills in using textbooks: The Textbook Awareness and Performance Profile (TAPP). *Journal of Reading, 37,* 280–286.

Sulzby, E. (1991). Assessment of emergent literacy: Storybook reading. *The Reading Teacher, 44,* 498–500.

Tonjes, M. J., & Zintz, M. V. (1992). *Teaching reading thinking study skills,* 3rd ed. Dubuque, IA: William C. Brown.

- *Retellings:* Story retelling is a postreading or postlistening activity in which students tell what they remember orally or in writing. Retelling helps the teacher to assess students' general comprehension of a story, their knowledge of story structure, and their ability to organize their thoughts. Retellings can be unguided or guided with directed questions.

Several evaluation checklists have been devised to assess students' retellings:

Leslie, L., & Caldwell, J. (1990). *Qualitative reading inventory*. Glenview, IL: Scott, Foresman.

Mitchell, J. N., & Irwin, P. A. (1990). The reading retelling profile. In G. G. Duffy (Ed.), *Reading in the middle school* (p. 147). Newark, DE: International Reading Association.

- *Summary writing:* Summaries are a way to assess students' comprehension. One way to diagnose with summaries is to have students read a passage, and then provide them with good and poor summaries of the passage. Another way is to have them write summaries and then conduct a self-peer, or teacher evaluation of the summary.

- *Sentence verification technique:* The Sentence Verification Technique (SVT) is a procedure for assessing reading comprehension of either narrative or expository passages. After reading a passage, students read a list of test sentences and decide if each sentence is an "old" sentence (a quote or paraphrase from the passage) or a "new" sentence (a meaning change of a sentence in the passage or an unrelated sentence). Details for constructing a SVT test are provided in the following article:

Royer, J. M., Greene, B. A., & Sinatra, G. M. (1987). The sentence verification technique: A practical procedure for testing comprehension. *Journal of Reading, 30,* 414–422.

- *Title recognition tasks:* A title recognition task is a quick gauge of the breadth of students' reading and exposure to print. This task involves giving students a list of book titles, including obscure books, moderately familiar books, books that children are likely to encounter, and fake book titles. Each title is followed by spaces for students to check whether or not they have heard of the book. Students are informed that some of the titles are fake and so any guessing will be detected. A title recognition task for fourth- to sixth-graders is now available.

Cunningham, A. E., & Stanovich, K. E. (1991). Tracking the unique effects of print exposure in children: Associations with vocabulary, general knowledge, and spelling. *Journal of Educational Psychology, 83,* 264–274.

- *Anecdotal records:* An anecdotal record is a listing of ongoing observations. Anecdotal records help to show patterns in achievement or behavior. They can take several forms: a sheet in a binder for each student, labels pasted on a folder for each student, or even a card file.

Rhodes, L. K., & Nathenson-Mejia, S. (1992). Anecdotal records: A powerful tool for ongoing literacy assessment. *The Reading Teacher, 45,* 502–509.

How to Manage Assessment Results

At one level, managing assessment results means making the best use of them. When disseminating results of standardized tests to parents, for example, management might mean educating parents in the limitations of standardized testing and the lack of significance in minor score changes from year to year.

When making school use of standardized test results, management involves not only studying scores from each class and each grade but also comparing scores from year to year. Comparisons between years should involve not only examinations of the grade levels themselves (e.g., grade 1 in each year compared) but also tracking of classes of students (e.g., grade 1 in year 1 becoming grade 2 in year 2). Management of standardized test results might also mean looking closely at scores that seem questionable on the basis of everyday performance. Wide discrepancies between standardized test scores and everyday performance can be due to any number of factors—illness on the day of the test, lack of student motivation to perform up to capacity on a daily basis, doctored test scores, error in test administration, test anxiety, or lack of congruence between test and curriculum.

A further dimension of management is that of helping teachers use test results wisely. At the elementary level, because teachers typically have self-contained classes and teach reading and writing, most teachers are aware of students' proficiency in these areas and find little need to use standardized test scores. In middle and senior high departmentalized settings, however, many teachers would like information about students' strengths and weaknesses in order to meet individual needs. A plan for dissemination of data on student reading to those teachers is essential.

On a broader scale, the issue of managing assessment deals not only with standardized test scores, but with the wealth of assessment data that the teacher uses on an ongoing basis: student self-evaluation, observation, questioning of students, and the like. Will any such data go with the student when he or she is promoted or transferred? The contents of cumulative records may be determined by your state department of education or your local school board. However, schools may also make a more informal accumulation of student work for classroom use and/or for presentation to parents and administrators. For example, schools may wish to keep student portfolios with samples of work from every year the students are in attendance. Again, a Reading Committee can be helpful in determining what common information can be kept by all teachers in the school (or at the grade level), how it will be recorded, and who has access to this information.

How to Cope with High-Stakes Tests

It is probably fair to define high-stakes tests operationally as those that are generally reported in the newspaper. We are all concerned with the way high-stakes tests, such as minimum competency tests and standardized tests, are destroying the very learning they are supposed to facilitate. For students, high-stakes tests determine tracking, special programs, promotion, diplomas, and self-concept. For schools, high-stakes tests determine good or bad publicity, administrative jobs, merit school money, and community respect. When test scores are plastered over headlines, the result is virtual elimination from the curriculum of any learning that is not measured on the test.

When students are consulted, the picture becomes even grimmer. Paris, Lawton, and Turner (1992b) found disturbing trends among students in grades 2 through 11 as they get older:

- A growing skepticism about the validity of test scores

- A growing realization that they are not well informed about the purposes and uses of achievement tests

- Increasing apprehension that test scores may become the basis for comparative social judgments

- Decreasing motivation to excel on standardized tests

- The surprising admission among older students that they felt less well prepared to take the tests

Leaders in the fields of reading and writing have called for change in assessment. Sheila Valencia and P. David Pearson (1987, p. 726) write: "The tests used to measure reading achievement do not reflect recent advances in our understanding of the reading process. If we are to foster effective instruction, the discrepancy between what we know and what we measure must be resolved." Both the Association for Supervision and Curriculum Development (ASCD) and the International Reading Association (IRA) have issued position statements in response to the problems with high-stakes tests. In *Becoming a Nation of Readers* (Anderson, Hiebert, Scott, & Wilkinson, 1985, p. 100), the authors state: "If schools are to be held accountable for reading test scores, the tests must be broad-gauged measures that reflect the ultimate goals of instruction as closely as possible. Otherwise, the energies of teachers and students may be misdirected."

At the early childhood level, where children's performance on standardized tests is notoriously unreliable, the movement away from standardized testing is clear (Schultz, 1989). States like North Carolina have chosen to postpone the use of standardized testing. A second strategy is to limit testing to samples of young children, which is enough to give information on overall performance. The National Education Goals Panel (Willis, 1992) has suggested that data for kindergarten children be gathered only on samples of youngsters at different times during the year. These data would be gathered from parents, teachers, and children themselves.

Alternatives to traditional testing that emphasize informal, ongoing assessment are being promoted. Some new basal readers are taking into account this need for informal assessment. School psychologists now have an instrument that can be used to evaluate day-to-day performance (Ysseldyke & Christenson, 1987). However, such informal assessment is generally viewed as a supplement to, not a substitute for, more conventional standardized tests. Despite their many limitations, such tests for accountability are likely to be with us for some time. As we all try to cope, here are some suggestions for surviving high-stakes tests:

Tips: Coping with High-Stakes Tests

- Follow a plan that is agreed on by the district, or at least the school. Everyone wants to "raise test scores," but acceptable methods will vary among districts and schools. For example, the use of commercial materials that practically duplicate the most common standardized tests on the market may or may not be considered ethical in your school or district.

- Keep in mind that any one test is just a fragment of the complete picture of a student's reading/writing profile or of a school's total reading/writing program. The Orange County Public Schools in Florida use a pyramid of blocks to demonstrate this point. The back sides together form the picture of a child. Any one block shows only one piece of the child.

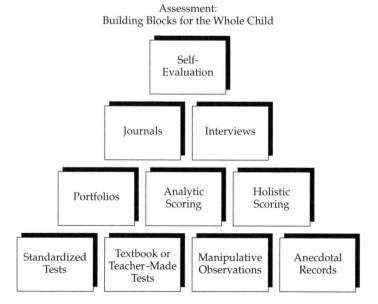

Assessment:
Building Blocks for the Whole Child

- Decide at the beginning of the school year how results from a variety of tests will be communicated to parents and to the community. A plan should be made for disseminating this information.

- Hold an inservice session for teachers so that they are prepared to orient students to the format of the high-stakes test and to general test-taking skills.

- Encourage teachers to prepare for standardized tests all year in informal, contextually appropriate ways that are consistent with the regular instructional program. For example, when reading content area passages in class, students can write and answer questions that are similar to those frequently found on standardized tests (e.g., central thought, detail question, context clue).

- Teachers should avoid the temptation to squander valuable instructional time in teaching to the precise content of tests rather than teaching underlying concepts.

- Provide teachers with practice materials to familiarize students with the test format. In the weeks before the test, students should be oriented to test-taking skills. Many students do not know how to keep their place on an answer sheet, mark answers on a separate answer form, or pace themselves during timed tests.

- Provide teachers with materials to practice reading passages and answering questions under timed conditions. Jamestown Publishers offers *Timed Readings* for grades 4–12, and Teachers College Press publishes the *McCall Crabbs Standard Test Lessons in Reading* for grades 2–12. Flexible reading is more than uniformly fast reading, so the use of timed readings helps only one aspect of reading efficiency.

- Elementary schools can send a letter home to parents before the test with traditional reminders about putting children to bed early, feeding them a good breakfast, and so on. One parent took her child out to breakfast on the first day of testing so that her child would have positive associations with testing! Remind parents that the standardized test is just one facet of a total assessment program.

Remind parents of other assessment results that will be made available to them, and tell them when and how they can expect to see those results. Orange County, Florida, sends elementary report cards home in a pocket in the last page of a student-made book. The book starts with a letter explaining that each page shows a different picture of the child's accomplishments. Pages include such samples as a piece of art, a summary of a scientific experiment, and an "I can do" list.

- Follow the example of Heald-Taylor (1989). She cites what research says about standardized tests in an "overreferenced response," which brings home the point through a letter packed with professional references.

- Prepare a student flyer containing a variety of test-taking tips (see Appendix E).

- Hold an inservice session for teachers so that they know how to interpret the results of the standardized test. (See section on norm-referenced tests in this chapter.)

Putting It All Together with Portfolio Assessment

In recent years, educators have rebelled against the overuse of standardized tests and have advocated individualized, ongoing, dynamic assessment based on a variety of formal and informal tools (Calfee & Hiebert, 1991; Johnston, 1984). Such tools are sometimes gathered in assessment portfolios. Artists, photographers, and models have portfolios to provide representative samples of their work. Student assessment portfolios are similar in that they are compilations of a variety of data about individual students' progress in reading and writing, kept in a special (usually expandable) folder or other personalized container. Teachers can use portfolios to guide further instruction and to provide tangible evidence of literacy development to parents, administrators, and students themselves. Indeed, the National Assessment for Educational Progress (NAEP) and several states, notably California and Vermont, are exploring ways to use work samples for achievement documentation on a statewide basis.

Assessment portfolios are living documents. They are constantly growing, reshaping, and contributing to ongoing decision making about instruction. They are not meant to be secretive and teacher-centered (like a grade book). Rather, they are meant to be a teacher–student collaborative effort to provide evidence of student progress. Parents can also be encouraged to make contributions. Doing this helps them learn more about their child's development as a reader, a writer, and a learner.

Thinking on portfolios is constantly evolving. There is no one right way to create portfolios. They can include a variety of types of entries. Some teachers keep standardized tests and basal reader assessments in the portfolios; others keep such information in a separate "teacher" folder. Still others see portfolios more as scrapbooks (Hansen, 1992). Peters (1991) has suggested, "You can't have authentic assessment without authentic content." He recommends that teachers select material for assessment that reflects themes that are crucial to content learning, and that material be grounded in real-life experiences and reflect students' development as literacy learners.

Options for Inclusion in Portfolios

- Writing samples (all stages of the writing process and representing varied genres)

- Notes on student interviews

- Work samples from literacy assignment and content area assignments

- Personal reading and writing records

- Self-assessments

- Observation checklists

- Interest/attitude inventories

- Audiotapes of reading aloud

- Videotapes or photographs of projects

- Photocopies of passages read fluently

- Sample pages from dialogue journals or reading logs

- "I can do" lists (lists of student accomplishments)

- Diagnostic and achievement tests

- Contributions from parents with parent and/or student comments

- Personal items that are meaningful to the student (e.g., letters to Santa Claus, award ribbons)

- Report cards

Adapted from "Yes, but How Do We Start? Ways of Beginning Portfolio Assessment" by M. C. Radencich, R. Flash, D. Miller, N. Minges, & M. Starrett, unpublished manuscript, 1992.

Detailed guidelines for developing portfolios have been presented elsewhere (Au, Scheu, Kawakami, & Herman, 1990; Flood & Lapp, 1989; Harp, 1991; Tierney, Carter, & Desai, 1991; Valencia, McGinley, & Pearson, 1990; Wolf, 1989). The most immediate reaction from the uninitiated is, "This seems like a lot of work. How can I possibly do this with thirty-five students in my class?" The following tips may help:

Tips for Teachers: Developing Assessment Portfolios

- Develop a portfolio plan that is consistent with your purposes for assessment.

- Clarify what types of entries will go into portfolios and what types of work will go into any other work folders that may be used.

- Start with only a couple of different kinds of entries. Expand as you are ready.

- Work with a buddy or a grade-level team of teachers as a support group as you experiment with portfolios.

- Have as a long-term goal the inclusion of a variety of assessments that address content, process, and attitude goals across the curriculum.

- Place the portfolios in the classroom in a highly accessible spot. Students and teachers should be able to add to the collection quickly and easily.

- Develop summary sheets or graphs that help to collapse a body of information (e.g., "I can do" lists, lists of books read or pieces of writing completed), and let students record these data when possible.

- Don't keep *everything*. Work with the student to choose a few representative measures that will demonstrate literacy progress.

- Review the portfolio with the student periodically, at least four times during the school year. This review should be a time to celebrate progress made and a time to set future goals. Students can review the portfolio with a buddy before reviewing with you. This will prepare them to make decisions about what to keep. Students' and teacher's notes of this review can be kept in the portfolio.

- In preparing for a parent conference, have students develop a table of contents for the portfolio.

- At the end of the school year, evaluate your portfolio experience. Make a list of what you plan to include next year and what you found to be unnecessary.

What Test Data Generally Won't Tell the Principal

As has been pointed out throughout this chapter, test data provide only an incomplete and sometimes distorted picture of achievement. In addition, test data will not tell the principal the reasons behind achievement or lack of it (Barnard & Hetzel, 1986). In terms of school factors, test data will not give information on staff training; staff stability; time apportionment to different subjects; use or misuse of materials; size, quality, and use of classroom and school libraries; preservation of instructional time; use of the reading specialist; the school's affective climate; and the degree of involvement with the community.

In terms of the home, test data will not give information on educational level of parents, the preschool education children will have received, the number of books and magazines in the home, the amount of television watching, or the frequency with which parents read to their children. This chapter provides principals with a variety of means for evaluating the entire literacy picture of their schools. The Program Review form in Appendix C will help here as well.

Models for Monitoring Student Progress

There are endless ways of putting together different assessment components. Following are three models:

Kamehameha Elementary Education Program (KEEP)

Hawaii, like most other states, has used standardized test scores as the basis of its assessment program. To develop an assessment program more compatible with their whole literacy curriculum, Kathryn Au and her colleagues at the Kamehameha Elementary Education Program (KEEP) have developed a portfolio assessment system (Au et al., 1990; Paris et al., 1992a). To guide their portfolios, they determined grade-level benchmarks derived from the state language arts curriculum guide, a standardized achievement test, and their scope-and-sequence charts. Profile sheets were then used to compare students' progress (using data from various assessment tools) with the grade-level benchmarks.

Portfolio Assessment at Blackburn Elementary School

Blackburn Elementary is a primary school in Manatee County, Florida. Blackburn's initiation into portfolio assessment was part of a two-year inservice program focusing on aligning assessment with whole language instruction (Lamme & Hysmith, 1991). Students and teachers collected three different types of information: student work, student reflection and self-evaluation, and teacher anecdotal records (observations, checklists, etc.). Of particular note are the writing, emergent reading, and response to literature developmental scales designed as part of this project. Also noteworthy is the amount of parental and student involvement generated. Teacher reaction to portfolio assessment was generally positive, particularly with teachers who were enthusiastic about whole language in general. Blackburn's assessment devices became the basis for similar assessment throughout the district.

Louisiana State University Laboratory School

A major challenge in high schools is monitoring individual literacy development. We have all heard horror stories of high school graduates who cannot read at a third-grade level. Parents, politicians, and the media ask: "How are these students permitted to graduate from high school?" and "Who is keeping track of whether or not kids can read and write?"

At Louisiana State University Laboratory School, students with low achievement test scores are discussed during an annual grade-level teachers' meeting (Schumm, 1988) where teachers decide if the test score is reflective of the students' ongoing performance in textbook reading assignments. If there seems to be a problem, parents are invited to the school to discuss the possibility of enrolling their child in a credit-bearing reading course. The focus of the course is determined by individual student needs, with a strong emphasis on content area reading and writing competencies. An alternative to the course is an after-school program to assist students with content area reading and writing. Of course, the parent may choose to hire a private tutor or to ignore the options provided by the school. The important point is that students' literacy needs are attended to on a systematic basis and a choice of services is provided.

Conclusion

At the outset of this chapter, an assertion was made that assessment is much more than test taking. The advent of assessment that emphasizes ongoing, informal, and authentic student observation has begun to transform traditional psychometric practices. It is imperative that, as an instructional leader, you keep abreast of developments in this area and communicate to teachers innovations described in the professional literature. Because assessment is a decision-making process with a high impact on student lives, it is necessary that we base our decisions on the best information available.

References

Aaron, E. B. (1990). Inmates captured by literature. *Journal of Reading, 33*, 433–435.

Adams, M. J. (1990). *Beginning to read: Thinking and learning about print.* Cambridge, MA: MIT Press.

Alfonso, R. J., & Firth, G. R. (1990). Supervision: Needed research. A research agenda. *Journal of Curriculum and Supervision, 5*(2), 181–188.

Allen, J. B., Buchanan, J., Edelsky, C., & Norton, G. (1992). Teachers as "they" at NRC: An invitation to enter the dialogue on the ethics of collaborative and non-collaborative classroom research. In C. K. Kinzer & D. J. Leu (Eds.), *Literacy, research, theory, and practice: Views from many perspectives,* Forty-first Yearbook of the National Reading Conference (pp. 357–365). Chicago: National Reading Conference.

Allington, R. (1985). The congruence of classroom and remedial reading instruction. *Elementary School Journal, 85*, 465–477.

Allington, R. L. (1993). Michael doesn't go down the hall anymore. *The Reading Teacher, 46*, 602–604.

Alvermann, D. E., Moore, D. W., & Conley, M. W. (Eds.). (1987). *Research within reach: Secondary school reading.* Newark, DE: International Reading Association.

American Association of School Librarians and Association for Educational Communications and Technology. (1988). *Information power: Guidelines for school library media programs.* Chicago: American Library Association.

Washington, DC: Association for Educational Communications and Technology.

Anders, P. L. (1985). Dream of a secondary reading program? People are the key. In W. J. Harker (Ed.). *Classroom strategies for secondary reading,* 2nd ed. Newark, DE: International Reading Association.

Anders, P. L., & Levine, N. S. (1990). Accomplishing change in reading programs. In G. G. Duffy (Ed.), *Reading in the middle school* (pp. 157–170). Newark, DE: International Reading Association.

Anderson, R. C., Hiebert, E. H., Scott, J. A., & Wilkinson, I. A. G. (1985). *Becoming a nation of readers: A report of the Commission on Reading.* Washington, DC: National Institute of Education.

Arhar, J. M., Johnston, J. H., & Markle, G. C. (1988, July). The effects of teaming and other collaborative arrangements. *Middle School Journal,* 22–25.

Askov, E. N., & Clark, C. J. (1991). Using computers in adult literacy instruction. *Journal of Reading, 34*, 434–448.

Atwell, N. (1987). *In the middle.* Portsmouth, NH: Heinemann.

Atwell, N. (Ed.). (1991). *Workshop 3, the politics of process.* Portsmouth, NH: Heinemann.

Au, K. H. (1993). *Literacy instruction in multicultural settings.* Orlando, FL: Harcourt Brace Jovanovich.

Au, K. H., Scheu, J. A., Kawakami, A. J., & Herman, P. A. (1990). Assessment and accountability in a whole literacy curriculum. *The Reading Teacher, 43,* 574–578.

Bailey, G. (1988, March). Guidelines for improving the textbook/material selections process. *NASSP Bulletin,* 87–92.

Balbi, P. F. (1986). Teaching through a language experience approach in a multilingual setting. *Reading Improvement, 23,* 182–190.

Barchers, S. I. (1990). Creating and managing the literate classroom. Englewood, CO: Teacher Ideas Press.

Barnard, H. (1858). A history of common schools in Connecticut. *American Journal of Education, 5,* 149.

Barnard, D. P., & Hetzel, R. W. (1976). The principal's role in reading instruction. *The Reading Teacher, 29,* 386–388.

Barnard, D. P., & Hetzel, R. W. (1986). *Principal's handbook to improve reading instruction,* 2nd ed. Lexington, MA: Ginn.

Barr, R. (1989). The social organization of literacy instruction. In S. McCormick, & J. Zutell (Eds.), *Cognitive and social perspectives for literacy research and instruction.* Thirty-eighth Yearbook of the National Reading Conference (pp. 19–33). Chicago: National Reading Conference.

Barr, R. (in press). In M. C. Radencich, & L. McKay (Eds.), *Flexible grouping for literacy in the elementary grades.* Boston: Allyn and Bacon.

Bartch, J. (1992). An alternative to spelling: An integrated approach. *Language Arts, 69,* 404–408.

Baumann, J. F., & Johnson, D. D. (Eds.). (1991). *Writing for publication in reading and language arts.* Newark, DE: International Reading Association.

Baumann, J. F., & Stevenson, J. A. (1982). Using scores from standardized tests. *The Reading Teacher, 35,* 528–532.

Beeler, T. (1992). Field trips—Not just for children. *Florida Reading Quarterly, 29,* 19–22.

Beers, P. (1986). Accelerated reading for high school students. *Journal of Reading, 29,* 311–315.

Benne, K. D. (1949). Democratic ethics in social engineering. *Progressive Education, 26*(7), 201–207.

Bereiter, C., & Engelmann, S. (1966). *Teaching disadvantaged children in the preschool.* Englewood Cliffs, NJ: Prentice-Hall.

Bergeron, B. S. (1990). What does the term whole language mean? Constructing a definition from the literature. *Journal of Reading Behavior, 22,* 301–329.

Berghoff, B., & Egawa, K. (1991). No more "rocks": Grouping to give students control of their learning. *The Reading Teacher, 44,* 536–541.

Bird, L. B. (1989). The art of teaching: Evaluation and revision. In K. S. Goodman, Y. M. Goodman, & W. J. Hood (Eds.), *The whole language evaluation book* (pp. 15–24). Portsmouth, NH: Heinemann.

Bird, L. B. (1991). Professional development at Fair Oaks. In Y. M. Goodman, W. J. Hood, & K. S. Goodman (Eds.), *Organizing for whole language* (pp. 323–335). Portsmouth, NH: Heinemann.

Bolin, F. S., & Panaritis, P. (1992). Searching for a common purpose: A perspective on the history of supervision. In C. D. Glickman (Ed.), *Supervision in transition,* Yearbook of the Association of Supervision and Curriculum Development (pp. 30–43). Alexandria, VA: ASCD.

Bos, C. S., & Vaughn, S. S. (1991). *Strategies for teaching students with learning and behavior problems,* 2nd ed. Boston: Allyn and Bacon.

Bragstadt, B. J., & Stumpf, S. M. (1982). *A guidebook for teaching study skills and motivation.* Boston: Allyn and Bacon.

Brandt, R. (1992). Reconsidering our commitments. *Educational Leadership, 5*(2), 5.

Brandt, R. (Ed.). (1991). The reflective educator [Special issue]. *Educational Leadership, 48.*

Brown, E. H. (1911, March). First free school in Queen Anne's County. *Maryland Historical Magazine, 6,* 1–15.

Brown, R. (1989). Testing and thoughtfulness. *Educational Leadership, 46,* 31–33.

Brozo, W. G. (1990). Hiding out in secondary content classrooms: Coping strategies of unsuccessful readers. *Journal of Reading, 33,* 324–328.

Buck, P. S. (1981). *The good earth.* Cutchogue, NY: Buccaneer Books.

Burg, L. A., Kaufman, M., Korngold, B., & Kovner, A. (1978). *The complete reading super-*

visor—Tasks and roles. Columbus, OH: Merrill.

Burgett, R. E. (1976). Increasing the effectiveness of the reading specialist. *Journal of Reading, 20,* 6–8.

Burton, F. R. (1991). Reflections on designing a K–12 whole language curriculum: Implications for administrators and policymakers. Y. M. Goodman, W. J. Hood, & K. S. Goodman (Eds.), *Organizing for whole language* (pp. 364–372). Portsmouth, NH: Heinemann.

Burton, W. H., & Brueckner, L. J. (1955). *Supervision: A social process,* 3rd ed. New York: Appleton-Century-Crofts.

Caine, R. N., & Caine, G. (1991). *Making connections.* Alexandria, VA: Association for Supervision and Curriculum Development.

Calfee, R., & Hiebert, E. (1991). Classroom assessment of reading. In R. Barr, M. L. Kamil, P. Mosenthal, & P. D. Pearson (Eds.), *Handbook of reading research* (Vol. 2, pp. 281–309). White Plains, NY: Longman.

Calkins, L. M., & Harwayne, S. (1991). *Living between the lines.* Portsmouth, NH: Heinemann.

Callahan, R. E., & Button, H. W. (1964). Historical change of the role of the man in the organization: 1865–1950. In D. E. Griffiths (Ed.), *Behavioral Science and Educational Administration,* The Sixty-third Yearbook of the National Society for the Study of Education (pp. 73–92). Chicago: University of Chicago Press.

Cambourne, B. (1988). *The whole story: Natural learning and the acquisition of literacy in the classroom.* Auckland: Scholastic.

Cardarelli, A. F. (1992). Teachers under cover: Promoting the personal reading of teachers. *The Reading Teacher, 45,* 664–668.

Carlson, R. O. (1964). Environmental constraints and organizational consequences: The public school and its clients. In *National Society for Secondary Education Yearbook.* Chicago: University of Chicago Press.

Carnine, D. (1988). How to overcome barriers to student achievement. In S. J. Samuels & P. D. Pearson (Eds.), *Changing school reading programs* (pp. 59–91). Newark, DE: International Reading Association.

Center for the Study of Reading. (1990). *A guide to selecting basal reading programs.* Urbana-Champaign: University of Illinois.

Cheyney, A. (1992). *Teaching reading skills through the newspaper* (3rd ed.). Newark, DE: International Reading Association.

Clark, C., & Peterson, P. (1986). Teachers' thought processes. In M. Witrock (Ed.), *The handbook of research on teaching.* New York: Macmillan.

Cohen, P. A., Kulik, J. A., Kulik, C. C. (1982). Educational outcomes of tutoring: A meta-analysis of findings. *American Educational Research Association, 19,* 237–248.

Coles, R. E. (1991). Adolescents organize: Whole language in the middle grades. In Y. M. Goodman, W. J. Hood, & K. S. Goodman (Eds.), *Organizing for whole language* (pp. 195–202). Portsmouth, NH: Heinemann.

Commission on Supervision, Department of Superintendence, NEA (1930). *The superintendent surveys supervision,* Eighth yearbook of the Department of Superintendence. Washington, DC: National Education Association.

Condon, M. W. F., & Hoffman, J. V. (1990). The influence of classroom management. In G. G. Duffy (Ed.), *Reading in the middle school* (pp. 41–59). Newark, DE: International Reading Association.

Conley, M. W. (1989). Middle school and junior high reading programs. In S. B. Wepner, J. T. Feeley, & D. S. Strickland (Eds.), *The administration and supervision of reading programs* (pp. 76–105). New York: Teachers College Press.

Conn, S. (1988). Textbooks: Defining the new criteria. *Media and Methods, 24,* 30–31, 64.

Conniff, B., Bortle, C., & Joseph, M. F. (1993–1994). Poetry in the adult literacy class. *Journal of Reading, 37,* 304–308.

Cook, G., and others. (1983, November). *Summary of questionnaire results,* Sub-committee on the status of supervision of the CEE Commission on Supervision and Curriculum Development. Conference on English Education, Urbana, IL: Commission on Supervision and Curriculum Development.

Copenhaver, J. (1993, April). Instances of inquiry. *Primary Voices K–6,* 6–12.

Cotton, E. G., Casem, C. B., Kroll, M. A., Langas, E. U., Rhodes, A. W., & Sisson, J. R. (1988). Using a skill trace to solve the basal reader adoption dilemma. *The Reading Teacher, 41,* 550–554.

Courtis, S. A. (1926). Reading between the lines. In G. M. Whipple (Ed.), *Curriculum-making: Past and present*, Twenty-sixth Yearbook of the National Society for the Study of Education, Part 1 (pp. 91–98). Bloomington, IL: Public School Publishing.

Crowell, C. G. (1991). Becoming biliterate in a whole language classroom. In Y. M. Goodman, W. J. Hood, & K. S. Goodman (Eds.), *Organizing for whole language* (pp. 95–111). Portsmouth, NH: Heinemann.

Crowley, P. (1989). "They'll grow into 'em": Evaluation, self-evaluation, and self-esteem in special education. In K. S. Goodman, Y. M. Goodman, & W. J. Hood (Eds.), The whole language evaluation book (pp. 237–247). Portsmouth, NH: Heinemann.

Cullinan, B. E., Greene, E., & Jaggar, A. (1990). Books, babies, and libraries: The librarian's role in literacy development. *Language Arts*, *67*, 750–755.

Cunningham, L. L. (1963). Effecting change through leadership. *Educational Leadership*, *21*(2), 75–79.

Cunningham, P. M. (1991). Research directions: Multimethod, multilevel literacy instruction in first grade. *Language Arts*, *68*, 578–584.

Cunningham, P. M. (1992). What kind of phonics instruction will we have? In C. K. Kinzer & D. J. Leu (Eds.), *Literacy research, theory, and practice: Views from many perspectives*, Forty-first Yearbook of the National Reading Conference (pp. 17–31). Chicago: National Reading Conference.

Cunningham, P. M., & Allington, R. L. (1994). *Classrooms that work—They can all read and write*. New York: HarperCollins.

Curry, T. K. (1989). Everyone's in the act: Evaluation in a seventh-grade classroom. In K. S. Goodman, Y. M. Goodman, & W. J. Hood (Eds.), *The whole language evaluation book* (pp. 131–137). Portsmouth, NH: Heinemann.

Dales, B. (1990). Trusting relations between teachers and librarians. *Language Arts*, *67*, 732–734.

Dalrymple, K. S. (1991a). The chicken study: Third graders prepare for independent study of animals. In Y. M. Goodman, W. J. Hood, & K. S. Goodman (Eds.), *Organizing for whole language* (pp. 118–133). Portsmouth, NH: Heinemann.

Dalrymple, K. S. (1991b). Comprehension: Framework for thematic unit studies. In Y. M. Goodman, W. J. Hood, & K. S. Goodman (Eds.), *Organizing for whole language* (pp. 183–194). Portsmouth, NH: Heinemann.

Danielson, K. E. (1992). Picture books to use with older students. *Journal of Reading*, *35*, 652–654.

D'Annuncio, A. (1990). A nondirective combinatory model in an adult ESL program. *Journal of Reading*, *34*, 198–202.

Darling-Hammond, L., with Sclan, E. (1992). Policy and supervision. In C. D. Glickman (Ed.), *Supervision in transition*, Yearbook of the Association for Supervision and Curriculum Development (pp. 7–29). Alexandria, VA: Association for Supervision and Curriculum Development.

Darquea, D. (1988). *Sound expressions*. Bakersfield, CA: D & D Productions.

de Bono, E. (1986). *Six thinking hats—An essential approach to business management*. Boston: Little, Brown.

Deep, S., & Sussman, L. (1990). *Smart moves*. Reading, MA: Addison-Wesley.

Degrees of Reading Power. (1984). Brewster, NY: The College Entrance Examination Board.

Department of Supervisors and Directors of Instruction. (1943). *Leadership at work*. Washington, DC: Department of Supervisors and Directors of Instruction, National Education Association.

Dombart, P. M. (1992). Will it play in Mayberry? *Educational Leadership*, *50*, 96.

Dooley, C. (1993). The challenge: Meeting the needs of gifted readers. *The Reading Teacher*, *46*, 546–551.

Duffy, G. G., & Roehler, L. R. (1989). *Improving classroom reading instruction: A decision-making approach*. New York: Random House.

Duke, D. L., Showers, B. K., & Imber, M. (1980). Teachers and shared decision-making: The cost and benefits of involvement. *Educational Administration Quarterly*, *16*, 93–106.

Dumaine, B. (1989). What leaders of tomorrow see. *Fortune*, *120*(1): 48–62.

Durkin, D. (1981). Reading comprehension instruction in five basal reader series. *Reading Research Quarterly*, *16*, 515–544.

Edelsky, C. (1992). A talk with Carol Edelsky

about politics and literacy. *Language Arts, 69,* 324–338.

Edmonds, R. (1979). Effective schools for the urban poor. *Educational Leadership, 37*(1), 15–24.

Edwards, P. A. (1990). *Parents as partners in reading.* Chicago: Children's Press.

Elliott, E. C. (1914). *City school supervision.* New York: World Book.

Elsbree, W. S., & Reutter, E. E. (1954). *Staff personnel in the public schools.* Englewood Cliffs, NJ: Prentice-Hall.

Enright, D. S. (1986). "Use everything you have to teach English": Providing useful input to young language learners. In P. Rigg & D. S. Enright (Eds.), *Children and ESL: Integrating perspectives* (pp. 115–162). Alexandria, VA: Teachers of English to Speakers of Other Languages.

Ericson, D. P., & Ellett, F. J. (1990). Taking student responsibility seriously. *Educational Researcher, 19,* 3–10.

Evertson, C., & Emmer, E. (1982). Preventive classroom management. In D. Duke (Ed.), *Helping teachers manage classrooms* (pp. 2–31). Alexandria, VA: Association for Supervision and Curriculum Development.

Fairfax County Public Schools. (1988, July). *Writing to Read Program Evaluation Report.* Fairfax, VA: Fairfax County Public Schools.

Faulkner, W. (1975). *Requiem for a nun,* Act 1, Scene 3, p. 80.

Fields, S. (1993, March 1). Personal communication.

Flood, J., & Lapp, D. (1989). Reporting reading progress: A comparison portfolio for parents. *The Reading Teacher, 42,* 508–512.

Florida Reading Association. (1990). *Teachers on the cutting edge: Textbook Adoption.* Orlando, FL: Author.

Ford, P. (1992). Storytelling for adults. *Journal of Reading, 35,* 484–485.

Forgan, H. W., & Mangrum, C. T. (1989). *Teaching content area reading skills,* 4th ed. Columbus, OH: Merrill.

Fox, S. M., & Singletary, T. J. (1986). Deductions about supportive induction. *Journal of Teacher Education, 37*(1), 12–15.

Fraatz, J. M. B. (1987). *The politics of reading.* New York: Teachers College Press.

Franseth, J. (1955). *Supervision in rural schools.* Bulletin 1955 No. 11. Washington, DC: U.S. Department of Health, Education, and Welfare, Office of Education.

Freeman, Y. S., & Freeman, D. E. (1989). Evaluation of second-language junior and senior high school students. In K. S. Goodman, Y. M. Goodman, & W. J. Hood (Eds.), *The whole language evaluation book* (pp. 141–150). Portsmouth, NH: Heinemann.

Freeman, Y. S., & Nofziger, S. D. (1991). WAlk to RnM33: Vien Vinidos al cualTo 33. In Y. M. Goodman, W. J. Hood, & K. S. Goodman (Eds.), *Organizing for whole language,* pp. 65–83. Portsmouth, NH: Heinemann.

Freyd, P., & Lytle, J. H. (1990a). A corporate approach to the two R's: A critique of IBM's Writing to Read program. *Educational Leadership, 47*(6), 83–89.

Freyd, P., & Lytle, J. H. (1990b). Let the readers decide: A response to Nelms. *Educational Leadership, 47,* 91–92.

Fry, E. (1977). Fry's readability graph: Clarifications, validity, and extension to level 17. *Journal of Reading, 21,* 242–252.

Gallagher, M. C., Goudvis, A., & Pearson, P. D. (1988). Principles of organizational change. In S. J. Samuels & P. D. Pearson (Eds.), *Changing school reading programs* (pp. 11–39). Newark, DE: International Reading Association.

Gilbert, T. F. (1978). *Human competence.* New York: McGraw-Hill.

Gillet, J. W., & Temple, C. (1982). *Understanding reading problems: Assessment and instruction.* Boston: Little, Brown.

Glickman, C. D. (1992). Introduction: Postmodernism and supervision. In C. D. Glickman (Ed.), *Supervision in transition,* Yearbook of the Association for Supervision and Curriculum Development. Alexandria, VA: Association for Supervision and Curriculum Development, 1–3.

Goldstein, S. (1992). *Creative training techniques.* Minneapolis: Lakewood.

Good, T. (1981). Teacher expectations and student perceptions: A decade of research. *Educational Leadership, 39,* 415–422.

Goodlad, J. (1984). *A place called school.* New York: McGraw Hill.

Goodman, D., & Curry, T. K. (1991). Teaching in

the real world. In Y. M. Goodman, W. J. Hood, & K. S. Goodman (Eds.), *Organizing for whole language* (pp. 137–169). Portsmouth, NH: Heinemann.

Goodman, Y. (1991). Kidwatching as well. In K. S. Goodman, L. B. Bird, & Y. M. Goodman (Eds.), *Whole language catalog*. Santa Rosa, CA: American Book Publishers.

Gordon, C. (1985). Modeling inference awareness across the curriculum. *Journal of Reading, 28,* 444–447.

Gove, A. (1891, October). City school supervision. *Educational Review, 2,* 260.

Graham, C. (1978). *Jazz chants.* New York: Oxford University Press.

Graves, D. (1990). *Discover your own literacy.* Portsmouth, NH: Heinemann.

Green, J. L. (1987). Course materials, The Ohio State University.

Greenwood, J. (1888). Efficient school supervision. *Proceedings of the Annual Convention of the National Education Association* (pp. 519–523). San Francisco: National Education Association.

Grimmett, P. P., Rostad, O. P., & Ford, B. (1992). The transformation of supervision. In C. D. Glickman (Ed.), *Supervision in transition,* Yearbook of the Association for Supervision and Curriculum Development (pp. 185–202). Alexandria, VA: Association for Supervision and Curriculum Development.

Gueulette, D. G. (Ed.) (1986). *Using technology in adult education.* Glenview, IL: Scott, Foresman. Washington, DC: American Association for Adult and Continuing Education.

Gunderson, L. (1991). *ESL literacy instruction: A guidebook to theory and practice.* Englewood Cliffs, NJ: Regents/Prentice-Hall.

Gwynne, F. (1970a). *A chocolate moose for dinner.* Englewood Cliffs, NJ: Messner.

Gwynne, F. (1970b). *The king who rained.* Englewood Cliffs, NJ: Messner.

Gutmann, A. (1987). *Democratic education.* Princeton, NJ: Princeton University Press.

Hagerty, P. J. (1990). How supervisors can help select reading teachers. *Journal of Reading, 34,* 226–227.

Hall, G. E., & Hord, S. M. (1987). *Change in schools: Facilitating the process.* New York: State University of New York Press.

Hansen, J. (1992). The language of challenge: Readers and writers speak their minds. *Language Arts, 69,* 100–105.

Harp, B. (Ed.). (1991). *Assessment and evaluation in whole language programs.* Norwood, MA: Christopher-Gordon.

Harris, A. J., & Sipay, E. R. (1990). *How to increase reading: A guide to developmental and remedial methods,* 9th ed. New York: Longman.

Harris, B. M. (1986, March). *Leadership for quality instruction: Looking toward the twenty-first century.* Paper presented at the Annual Meeting of the Association for Supervision and Curriculum Development, San Francisco.

Harste, J. C. (1990). Forward. In M. W. Olson (Ed.), *Opening the door to classroom research* (pp. v–viii). Newark, DE: International Reading Association.

Harste, J. C. (1993, April). Inquiry-based instruction. *Primary Voices K-6,* pp. 2–5.

Haycock, K. (1992). *What works—Research about teaching and learning through the school's library resource center.* Seattle: Rockland Press.

Heald-Taylor, G. (1989). *The administrator's guide to whole language.* Katonah, NY: Richard Owen.

Heffernan, H., & Bishop, L. J. (1965). The supervisor and curriculum director at work. In R. R. Leeper (Ed.), *Role of supervisor and curriculum director in a climate of change,* Yearbook of the Association for Supervision and Curriculum Development. Washington, DC: Association for Supervision and Curriculum Development.

Helwig, C. (1968). *Democratic supervision and creative supervision: Are they misnomers?* (Report No. EA-003-661). U.S. Department of Health, Education, and Welfare, Office of Education. ERIC Document No. ED 055 324.

Henk, W. A. (1985). Assessing children's reading abilities. In L. W. Searfoss & J. E. Readence (Eds.), *Helping children learn to read* (pp. 280–320). Englewood Cliffs, NJ: Prentice-Hall.

Hereford, N. (1993, April). The case against tracking. *Middle Years,* pp. 22–27.

Hergert, L., Mundry, S., Kolb, F., Rose, R., & Corro, J. (1988). *Making change for school improvement: A simulation game.* Andover, MA: The Network.

Herndon, J. (1985). *Notes from a school teacher.* New York: Simon & Schuster.

Hill, D. (1992, November–December). Christian soldier. *Teacher Magazine*, 18–21.

Hill, P. T., & Bonan, J. (1991). *Decentralization and accountability in public education*. Santa Monica, CA: Rand.

Hood, W. J. (1989). If the teacher comes over, pretend it's a telescope. In K. S. Goodman, Y. M. Goodman, & W. J. Hood (Eds.), *The whole language evaluation book* (pp. 27–44). Portsmouth, NH: Heinemann.

Hord, S. M., Rutherford, W. L., Huling-Austin, L., & Hall, G. E. (1987). *Taking charge of change*. Alexandria, VA: ASCD. Austin, TX: SEDL.

Hostrop, R. W. (1973). *Managing education for results*. Homewood, IL: ETC.

Howie, S. H. (1990). Adult literacy in a multiliterate society. *Journal of Reading, 33*, 260–263.

Hubbard, R. S., & Power, B. M. (1993). *The art of classroom inquiry—A handbook for teacher-researchers*. Portsmouth, NH: Heinemann.

Hysmith, C., Lamme, L. L., Mason, A., & Willis, C. (1990, August). *Blackburn teachers' involvement in school improvement—whole language*. Paper presented at the Whole Language Umbrella Conference, St. Louis, MO.

International Reading Association. (1991a, November–December). Advertising group questions "Hooked on Phonics." *Reading Today* (p. 6). Newark, DE: International Reading Association.

International Reading Association. (1991b, June–July). Reading educators question advertising of "Hooked on Phonics" reading program. *Reading Today* (pp. 1, 22). Newark, DE: International Reading Association.

International Reading Association (1992). *Teens' favorite books*. Newark, DE: International Reading Association.

International Reading Association (1992). *Standards for reading professionals*. Newark, DE: International Reading Association.

International Reading Association/Children's Book Council. (1991). *Kids' favorite books*. Newark, DE: International Reading Association.

Iowa tests of basic skills. (1990). Chicago: Riverside.

Irvin, J. L. (1990). *Reading and the middle school student*. Boston: Allyn and Bacon.

Irwin, J. W., & Davis, C. J. (1980). Assessing readability: The checklist approach. *Journal of Reading, 24*, 124–130.

Jachym, N. K., Allington, R. L., & Broikou, K. A. (1989). Estimating the cost of seatwork. *The Reading Teacher. 43*, 30–35.

Jacobson, D. (1991). The Chapter 1 reading teacher enters the classroom. In Y. M. Goodman, W. J. Hood, & K. S. Goodman (Eds.), *Organizing for whole language* (pp. 316–322). Portsmouth, NH: Heinemann.

Johnson, D. E., Meiller, L. R., Miller, L. C., & Summers, G. F. (1987). *Needs assessment: Theory and methods*. Ames: Iowa State University Press.

Johnson, D. W., & Johnson, R. T. (1992). What to say to advocates of the gifted. *Educational Leadership, 50*(2), 44–47.

Johnson, D. W., & Johnson, R. T., & Holubec, E. (1990). *Circles of learning: Cooperation in the classroom*, 3rd ed. Edina, MN: Interaction Book Company.

Johnson-Weber, M. (1989). Picture books for junior high. *Journal of Reading, 33*, 219–220.

Johnston, J. S., & Wilder, S. L. (1992). Changing reading and writing programs through staff development. *The Reading Teacher, 45*, 626–631.

Johnston, P. H. (1984). Assessment in reading. In P. D. Pearson, R. Barr, M. L. Kamil, & P. Mosenthal (Eds.), *Handbook of reading research* (Vol. 1, pp. 147–182). White Plains, NY: Longman.

Jongsma, K. S. (1993). What students' written reflections reveal about literacy. In L. Patterson, C. M. Santa, K. G. Short, & K. Smith (Eds.), *Teachers are researchers: Reflection and action*. Newark, DE: International Reading Association.

Joyce, B., Hersh, R., & McKibbon, M. (1983). *The structure of school improvement*. New York: Longman.

Joyce, B., & Showers, B. (1982). The coaching of teaching. *Educational Leadership, 40*, 4–10.

Judson, H. F. (1980). *The search for solutions*. New York: Holt, Rinehart & Winston.

Kanter, R. M. (1989). Paper presented at the Association for Supervision and Curriculum Development Annual Conference, Orlando, FL.

Kantrowitz, B. (1991, May 20). The profits of reading. *Newsweek*, p. 67.

Kast, S. E., & Rosenzweig, J. E. (1974). *Organization: A systems approach*, 2nd ed. New York: McGraw-Hill.

Keegan, S., & Shrake, K. (1991). Literature study groups: An alternative to ability grouping. *The Reading Teacher, 44*, 542–547.

Keenan, J. W., Willett, & Solsken, J. (1993). Focus on research: Constructing an urban village: School/home collaboration in a multicultural classroom. *Language Arts, 70*, 204–214.

Kelly, P. R., & Farnan, N. (1990). Practicing what we teach in reading education programs. *Journal of Reading, 33*, 264–269.

Kindsvatter, R., Wilen, W., & Ishler, M. (1988). *Dynamics of teaching*. New York: Longman.

King, J. A., & Ericson, C. J. (1992). School renewal in Chaska, Minnesota, Independent District #112. In C. D. Glickman (Ed.), *Supervision in transition*, Yearbook of the Association for Supervision and Curriculum Development. Alexandria, VA: Association for Supervision and Curriculum Development, 113–125.

Kinsella, B. W., Klopf, G. J., Shafer, H. T., & Young, W. T. (1969). *The supervisor's role in negotiation*. Washington, DC: Association for Supervision and Curriculum Development.

Klassen, C., & Short, K. G. (1992). Collaborative research on teacher study groups: Embracing the complexities. In C. K. Kinzer & D. J. Leu (Eds.), *Literacy research, theory, and practice: Views from many perspectives*, Forty-first Yearbook of The National Reading Conference (pp. 341–348). Chicago: National Reading Conference.

Kliebard, H. M. (1987). *The struggle for the American curriculum: 1893–1958*. New York: Routledge & Kegan Paul.

Kohn, A. (1991, February). Group grade grubbing versus cooperative learning. *Educational Leadership, 48*, 83–87.

Korinek, L., Schmid, R., & McAdams, M. (1985). Inservice types and best practices. *Journal of Research and Development in Education, 18*, 33–38.

Kuhn, T. S. (1970). *The structure of scientific revolutions*. Chicago: University of Chicago Press.

Kulik, J. A., & Kulik, C. C. (1992). Meta-analytic findings on grouping programs. *Gifted Child Quarterly, 36*, 73–77.

Kutz, E. (1992). Teacher research: Myths and realities. *Language Arts, 69*, 193–197.

LaBarbera, D. (1993, April). No more lesson plans. *Teacher Magazine*, p. 39.

Lambert, L. (1989). The end of an era of staff development. *Educational Leadership, 47*(1), 78–81.

Lamme, L. L., & Hysmith, C. (1991). One school's adventure into portfolio assessment. *Language Arts, 68*, 629–640.

Lamme, L. D., & Ledbetter, L. (1990). Libraries: The heart of whole language. *Language Arts, 67*, 735–741.

Lapp, D., & Flood, J. (1983). *Teaching reading to every child*, 2nd ed. New York: Macmillan.

Linek, W. M. (1991). Grading and evaluation techniques for whole language teachers. *Language Arts, 68*, 125–132.

Littky, D., & Fried, R. (1988). The challenge to make good schools great. *National Education Association*, 4–8.

Lubell, D. (1991). Spartan Lotto-Read. *Phi Delta Kappan, 73*(3), 257–258.

Lucio, W. H. (1967). The supervisory function: Overview, analysis, propositions. In W. H. Lucio (Ed.), *Supervision: Perspectives and Propositions* (pp. 1–11). Washington, DC: Association for Supervision and Curriculum Development.

Lucio, W. H., & McNeil, J. D. (1969). *Supervision: A synthesis of thought and action*, 2nd ed. New York: McGraw-Hill.

Mack, K. (1991). Actual and desired roles of reading supervisors. *Journal of Reading, 34*, 568–570.

Manning, G., & Curtis, K. (1988). *Groupstrength: Quality circles at work*. Cincinnati: South-Western.

Manning, G. L., & Manning, J. (1981). What is the role of the principal in the excellent reading program? Principals give their views. *Reading World, 21*, 130–133.

Martin, B. (1967). *Brown bear, brown bear*. New York: Holt.

Martin, B., & Brogan, P. (1971). *Instant Readers teacher's guide, level 1*. New York: Holt.

Marzano, R. (1987, fall). Staff development for teaching thinking: A matter of restructuring. *Journal of Staff Development*, pp. 6–10.

Mathews, J. (1992, July 2). Here's why words were misspelled in kids' letters. *The Orlando Sentinel*, p. A-19.

Matthews, M. (1992). Gifted students talk about cooperative learning. *Educational Leadership, 50*(2), 48–50.

McCabe, P. P. (1992). Teaching adult beginning readers to read through creative plays. *Reading Research and Instruction, 32*(1), 97–103.

McCauley, J. K., & McCauley, D. S. (1992). Using choral reading to promote language learning for ESL students. *The Reading Teacher, 45,* 526–533.

McCoy, R. F. (1961). *American school administration.* New York: McGraw-Hill.

McDonnell, G., Frey, J., & Smith, T. (Eds.). (1991). *Teaching and researching.* Falls Church, VA: IRA Special Interest Group's Newsletter.

McTighe, J., & Lyman, F. T. (1988, April). Cueing thinking in the classroom: The promise of theory-embedded tools. *Educational Leadership,* pp. 18–24.

Messerli, J. (1977). Foreward in H. A. Robinson (Ed.), *Reading and writing instruction in the United States: Historical trends.* Newark, DE: International Reading Association.

Meyer, J. W., Scott, W. R., & Deal, T. E. (1979). *Institutional and technical sources of organizational structure explaining the structure of educational organizations.* Paper prepared for a conference on human service organizations, Center for Advanced Study in the Behavior Sciences. Stanford, CA.

Meyer, L. A., Gersten, R. M., & Gutkin, J. (1984). Direct Instruction: A Project Follow Through success story in an inner-city school. *Elementary School Journal, 84,* 241–252.

Miller, P. (1988). *Nonverbal communication.* West Haven, CT: National Education Association.

Michigan Reading Association. (1990). *Secondary reading: A new direction for the future.* Grand Rapids, MI: Author.

Minkoff, D. (1984). Game activities for practicing English as a second language. *Journal of Reading, 28,* 40–42.

Mocker, D. W. (1975). Cooperative learning process: Shared learning experience in teaching adults to read. *Journal of Reading, 18,* 440–444.

Morgenthaler, S. (1993). Adult new readers get "A feel for books." *Journal of Reading, 36,* 570–571.

Morris, D., & Nelson, L. (1992). Supported oral reading with low-achieving second graders. *Reading Research and Instruction, 32*(1), 49–63.

Morrissey, T., & Radencich, M. C. (1993). *Kidwatching instead of grades.* Unpublished manuscript.

Morrow, L. M. (1993). *Literacy development in the early years.* Boston: Allyn and Bacon.

Mosher, R. L., & Purpel, D. E. (1972). *Supervision: The reluctant profession.* Boston: Houghton Mifflin.

Moustafa, M., & Penrose, J. (1985). Comprehensible input plus the language experience approach: Reading instruction for limited English speaking students. *The Reading Teacher, 38,* 640–647.

Murphy, J. (1989). Is there equity in educational reform? *Educational Leadership, 46*(5), 32–33.

Muther, C. (1985a, January). How to evaluate a basal textbook: The skills trace. *Educational Leadership,* 79–80.

Muther, C. (1985b, February). Reviewing research when choosing materials. *Educational Leadership,* 86–87.

Muther, C. (1985c, April). What every textbook evaluator should know. *Educational Leadership, 42,* 4–8.

Muther, C. (1987, October). Evaluating reading textbooks with the story-sort comparison. *Educational Leadership,* 87–90.

Muther, C. (1988). *Textbook adoption: A process for decision-making.* Manchester, CT: Textbook Adoption Advisory Services.

Neal, J. C., & Langer, M. A. (1992). A framework of teaching options for content area instruction: Mediated instruction of text. *Journal of Reading, 36,* 227–230.

Neilsen, L. (1991). Professional conversations: How to open the staffroom door. *The Reading Teacher, 44,* 676–678.

Neilsen, L. (1992). Eternity's sunrise and other multiple choice questions. *The Reading Teacher, 45,* 642–643.

Nelms, V. (1990). Not a balanced assessment: A response to Freyd and Lytle. *Educational Leadership, 47,* 89–91.

Newman, J. M., & Church, S. M. (1991). Myths of whole language. *The Reading Teacher, 44,* 20–26.

Nolan, J., & Francis, P. (1992). Changing perspectives in curriculum and instruction. In C. D.

Glickman (Ed.), *Supervision in transition*, Yearbook of the Association for Supervision and Curriculum Development (pp. 44–60). Alexandria, VA: Association for Supervision and Curriculum Development.

Nurss, J. R., & Hough, R. A. (1992). Reading and the ESL student. In S. J. Samuels & A. E. Farstrup (Eds.), *What research has to say about reading instruction* (pp. 277–313). Newark, DE: International Reading Association.

O'Brien, D. G., & Stewart, R. A. (1990). Preservice teachers' perspectives on why every teacher is not a teacher of reading. *Journal of Reading Behavior, 22,* 101–129.

O'Connor, K. (1990, October). Anatomy of a winning grant proposal. *Instructor,* 32–34.

Oestreicher, S. (1992). *The Clay County language arts assessment project.* Unpublished manuscript.

O'Flahavan, J. F., & Blassberg, R. (1992). Toward an embedded model of spelling instruction for emergent literates. *Language Arts, 69,* 409–417.

Ogle, D. (1986). KWL: A teaching model that develops active reading of expository text. *The Reading Teacher, 39,* 364–370.

Ogletree, J. R. (1972). Changing supervision in a changing era. *Educational Leadership, 29*(6), 507–510.

Olson, M. W. (1990). The teacher as researcher: A historical perspective. In M. W. Olson (Ed.), *Opening the door to classroom research* (pp. 1–20). Newark, DE: International Reading Association.

O'Neal, S. (1990). Leadership in the Language Arts—Controversial books in the classroom. *Language Arts, 67,* 771–775.

Onore, C., & Lester, N. B. (1985). Immersion and distancing: The ins and outs of inservice education. *English Education, 17,* 7–13.

Opitz, M. F., & Cooper, D. (1993). Adapting the spelling basal for spelling workshop. *The Reading Teacher, 47,* 106–113.

Osborn, J. (1984). Purposes, uses, and content of workbooks. In R. C. Anderson, J. Osborn, & R. J. Tierney (Eds.). *Learning to read in American schools: Basal readers and content texts* (pp. 110–111). Hillsdale, NJ: Erlbaum.

Padak, N. D., & Padak, G. M. (1991). What works: Adult literacy program evaluation. *Journal of Reading, 34,* 374–379.

Pajak, E. (1992). A view from the central office. In C. D. Glickman (Ed.), *Supervision in transition,* Yearbook of the Association for Supervision and Curriculum Development (pp. 126–138). Alexandria, VA: Association for Supervision and Curriculum Development.

Pajak, E. (1993). Change and continuity in supervision and leadership. In G. Cawelti (Ed.), *Challenges and achievements of American education,* Yearbook of the Association for Supervision and Curriculum Development (pp. 158–186). Alexandria, VA: Association for Supervision and Curriculum Development.

Palincsar, A. S., & Brown, A. L. (1984). Reciprocal teaching of comprehension-fostering and comprehension-monitoring activities. *Cognition and Instruction, 1,* 117–175.

Palincsar, A. S., Brown, A. L., & Martin, S. M. (1987). Peer interaction in reading comprehension instruction. *Educational Psychologist, 22,* 231–253.

Palmer, D. M., & Associates. (1988). *Staff development: Guidelines from the literature.* Regina, SK: Monograph prepared for the Saskatchewan Professional Development Unit and the Saskatchewan School Trustees Association Research Centre.

Paratore, J. R. (1991). Flexible grouping: Why and how. In *The Leadership letters—Issues and trends in reading and language arts.* Columbus, OH: Silver Burdett & Ginn.

Pardo, L. S., & Raphael, T. E. (1991). Classroom organization for instruction in content areas. *The Reading Teacher, 44,* 556–565.

Paris, S. G., Calfee, R. C., Filby, N., Hiebert, E. H., Pearson, P. D., Valencia, S. W., & Wolf, K. P. (1992a). A framework for authentic literacy assessment. *The Reading Teacher, 46,* 88–98.

Paris, S. G., Lawton, T. A., & Turner, J. C. (1992b). Reforming achievement testing to promote students' learning. In C. Collins & J. N. Mangieri (Eds.), *Teaching thinking: An agenda for the twenty-first century.* Hillsdale, NJ: Erlbaum.

Parish, P. (1986). *Amelia Bedelia.* New York: Harper & Row.

Pates, A., & Evans, M. (1990). Writing workshops: An experience from British adult literacy. *Journal of Reading, 34,* 244–248.

Patterson, L., & Shannon, P. (1993). In L. Patterson, C. M. Santa, K. G. Short, & K. Smith (Eds.), *Teachers are researchers: Reflection and action*. Newark, DE: International Reading Association.

Pauk, W. (1983). *How to study in college*. Boston: Houghton Mifflin.

Pavan, B. N. (1992). The benefits of nongraded schools. *Educational Leadership, 50,* 22–23.

Pearson, P. D. (1974–1975). The effects of grammatical complexity on children's comprehension, recall, and conception of certain semantic relations. *Reading Research Quarterly, 10,* 155–192.

Pearson, P. D. (1992, May). *Effective literacy assessment: Practices and possibilities*. Chair of Preconvention Institute of the Thirty-seventh Annual Convention of the International Reading Association, Orlando, FL.

Peck, R. N. (1979). *The day no pigs would die*. New York: Dell.

Peters, C. W. (1990). Content knowledge in reading: Creating a new framework. In G. G. Duffy (Ed.), *Reading in the middle school* (pp. 62–80). Newark, DE: International Reading Association.

Peters, C. W. (1991). You can't have authentic assessment without authentic content. *The Reading Teacher, 44,* 590–591.

Pickles-Thomas, P. (1992). A motivational program to empower high-risk students: What principals can do. *The Reading Teacher, 46,* 268–271.

Pierson-Hubeny, D., & Archambault, F. X. (1985). Role stress and perceived intensity of burnout among reading specialists. *Reading World, 24,* 41–52.

Pikulski, J. J. (1988). Questions and answers. *The Reading Teacher, 42,* 76.

Pikulski, J. J. (1989). Questions and answers. *The Reading Teacher, 42,* 725.

Pincus, J. (1974). Incentives for innovation in the public schools. *Review of Educational Research,* 113–144.

Pinnell, G. S., DeFord, D. E., & Lyons, C. A. (1988). *Reading Recovery: Early intervention for at-risk first graders*. Arlington, VA: Educational Research Service.

Pinnell, G. S., & Matlin, M. L. (Eds.). (1989). *Teachers and research: Language learning in the classroom*. Newark, DE: International Reading Association.

Polette, K. (1989). Using ABC books for vocabulary development in the secondary school. *English Journal, 78,* 78–80.

Power, J. (1988). What is your body language telling your students? *NEA Today, 6*(8), 5.

Radencich, M. C. (1991). Publishing computer software. In J. F. Baumann & D. D. Johnson (Eds.), *Writing for publication in reading and language arts* (pp. 169–191). Newark, DE: International Reading Association.

Radencich, M. C. (1992a). Integrated lesson plan formats: How do you fit it all in? *Florida Reading Quarterly, 29*(2), 15–17.

Radencich, M. C. (1992b). *Reading Recovery our way: Miami's Reading Reentry program*. Unpublished manuscript.

Radencich, M. C. (1993). *Curiouser and curiouser . . . The Reading Teacher, 47,* 173–175.

Radencich, M. C. (1994). *Adult literacy: A compendium of articles from the Journal of Reading*. Newark, DE: International Reading Association.

Radencich, M. C., Beers, P. G., & Schumm, J. S. (1993). *A handbook for the K–12 reading resource specialist*. Boston: Allyn and Bacon.

Radencich, M. C., Flash, R., Miller, D., Minges, N., & Starrett, M. (1992). *Yes, but how do we start? Ways of beginning portfolio assessment*. Unpublished manuscript.

Radencich, M. C., & McKay, L., Eds. (in press). *Flexible grouping for literacy in the elementary grades*. Boston: Allyn and Bacon.

Radencich, M. C., McKay, L., Paratore, J. R., Nelms, P., Moore, P., Plaza, G. L., & Lustgarten, K. (in press). Keeping flexible groups flexible—Grouping options and grouping models. In M. C. Radencich, & L. McKay (Eds.), *Flexible grouping for literacy in the elementary grades*. Boston: Allyn and Bacon.

Radencich, M. C., & Schumm, J. S. (1988). *How to help your child with homework*. Minneapolis, MN: Free Spirit.

Rankin, J. L. (1992). Connecting literacy learners: A pen pal project. *The Reading Teacher, 46,* 204–214.

Raygor, A. (1977). The Raygor readability estimate: A quick and easy way to determine difficulty. In P. D. Pearson (Ed.), *Reading: Theory, research and practice*, Twenty-sixth Yearbook of the National Reading Conference.

Readence, J. E., Bean, T. W., & Baldwin, R. S. (1992). *Content area reading: An integrated approach*, 4th ed. Dubuque, IA: Kendall/Hunt.

Renzulli, J. S. (1977). *The enrichment triad model: A guide for developing defensible programs for the gifted.* Mansfield, CT: Creative Learning Press.

Reutzel, D. R., & Cooter, R. B. (1991). Organizing for effective instruction: The reading workshop. *The Reading Teacher, 44,* 548–554.

Reutzel, D. R., & Cooter, R. B. (1992). *Teaching children to read.* New York: Macmillan.

Rice, R. (1987). Clearly defined staff roles: A key to effective programs. *AARSIC Abstracts, 11*(3), 4.

Rogers, E. (1971). *Diffusion on innovations.* New York: Free Press.

Rosow, L. (1990). Consumer advocacy, empowerment, and adult literacy. *Journal of Reading, 34,* 258–262.

Routman, R. (1991). *Invitations: Changing as teachers and learners K–12.* Portsmouth, NH: Heinemann.

Rowan, B. (1977). Bureaucratization in the institutional environment: The case of California Public Schools, 1930–1970. In M. R. Davis, T. E. Deal, J. W. Merey, B. Rowan, W. R. Scott, & E. A. Stackhouse (Eds.), *The structure of educational systems: Explorations in the theory of loosely coupled organization.* Stanford, CA: Stanford Center for Research and Development in Teaching.

Rugg, H. O. (1926). Curriculum-making: Points of emphasis. In G. M. Whipple (Ed.), *Curriculum-making: Past and present,* Twenty-sixth Yearbook of the National Society for the Study of Education, Part 1 (pp. 147–162). Bloomington, IL: Public School Publishing.

Ryder, R. J., Graves, B. B., & Graves, M. F. (1989). *Easy reading: Book series and periodicals for less able readers,* 2nd ed. Newark, DE: International Reading Association.

Samuels, S. J. (1981). Characteristics of exemplary reading programs. In J. T. Guthrie (Ed.), *Comprehension and teaching: Research reviews* (pp. 255–273). Newark, DE: International Reading Association.

Samuels, S. J., & Edwall, G. (1976). An overview of the research literature on educational innovation. In J. T. Guthrie (Ed.), *A study of the locus and nature of reading problems in elementary schools.* Washington, DC: National Institute of Education.

Samuels, S. J., & Pearson, P. D. (1988). *Changing school reading programs.* Newark, DE: International Reading Association.

Samuels, S. J., Schermer, N., & Reinking, D. (1992). Reading fluency: Techniques for making decoding automatic. In S. J. Samuels & A. E. Farstrup (Eds.), *What research has to say about reading instruction* (pp. 124–144). Newark, DE: International Reading Association.

Sandweiss, K. (1990). A middle school program evolves. In J. L. Irvin (Ed.), *Reading and the middle school student* (pp. 214–218). Boston: Allyn and Bacon.

Santa, C., Danner, M., Havens, L., Scalf, J., & Scalf, L. (1985). *CRISS—Content Reading in Secondary schools.* Kalispell, MT: School District No. 5.

Santa, C., Isaacson, L., & Manning, G. (1987). Changing content instruction through action research. *The Reading Teacher, 40,* 434–438.

Schierloh, J. M. (1992). Using classic novels with adult new readers. *Journal of Reading, 35,* 618–622.

Schlissel, L. (1987). *Women's diaries of the westward journey.* New York: Schocken.

Schon, D. A. (1988). Coaching reflective teaching. In P. P. Grimmett & G. L. Erickson (Eds.), *Reflection in teacher education* (pp. 19–29). New York: Teachers College Press.

Schultz, T. (1989). Testing and retention of young children: Moving from controversy to reform. *Phi Delta Kappan, 71,* 125–129.

Schumm, J. S. (1988, February). *A strategy for planning comprehensive secondary reading programs.* Paper presented at the International Reading Association Southwest Regional Reading Conference, Oklahoma City, OK.

Schumm, J. S., Konopak, J. P., Readence, J. E., & Baldwin, R. S. (1989). Considerate text: Do we practice what we preach? In S. McCormick & J. Zutell (Eds.), *Cognitive and social perspectives for literacy research and instruction,* Thirty-eighth Yearbook of the National Reading Conference (pp. 205–211). Chicago: National Reading Conference.

Schumm, J. S., & Mangrum, C. T. (1991). FLIP: A framework for fostering textbook thinking. *Journal of Reading, 35,* 120–125.

Schumm, J. S., & Strickler, K. (1991). Guidelines for adapting content area textbooks: Keeping teachers and students content. *Intervention*, 27, 79–84.

Schumm, J. S., & Vaughn, S. (1991). Making adaptations for mainstreamed students: General classroom teachers' perceptions. *RASE—Remedial and Special Education*, 12(4), 18–27.

Schumm, J. S., & Vaughn, S. (1992). Planning for mainstreamed special education students: Perceptions of general classroom teachers. *Exceptionality*, 3, 81–98.

Schumm, J. S., Vaughn, S., & Saumell, L. (1992). What teachers do when the textbook is tough: Students speak out. *Journal of Reading Behavior*, 24, 481–503.

Schutz, W. (1961). Interpersonal underworld. In W. G. Bennis, K. D. Benne, & R. Chin (Eds.), *The planning of change* (p. 305). New York: Holt, Rinehart and Winston.

Schweinhart, L. J. (1988). *A school administrator's guide to early childhood programs*. Ypsilanti, MI: High/Scope.

Senge, P. M. (1990a). *The fifth discipline: The art and practice of the learning organization*. New York: Doubleday/Currency.

Senge, P. M. (1990b, Fall). The leader's new work: Building new organizations. *Sloan Management Review*, 7–23.

Sergiovanni, T. J. (1992). Moral authority and the regeneration of supervision. In C. D. Glickman (Ed.), *Supervision in transition*, Yearbook of the Association of Supervision and Curriculum Development (pp. 203–214). Alexandria, VA: ASCD.

Sergiovanni, T. J., & Starratt, R. J. (1979). *Supervision, human perspectives*, 2nd ed. New York: McGraw-Hill.

Shannon, P. (1987). Commercial reading materials: A technological ideology, and the deskilling of teachers. *Elementary School Journal*, 87, 311–313.

Shannon, P. (1991). Talking back to critics. *Teachers Networking—The Whole Language Newsletter*, 10(3), 1, 12–14.

Shannon, P. (1993). Foreward. In P. Shannon (Ed.), *Becoming political*. Portsmouth, NH: Heinemann.

Sharp, P. A. (1993). *Sharing your good ideas—A workshop facilitator's handbook*. Portsmouth, NH: Heinemann.

Short, K. G., Crawford, K., Kahn, L., Kaser, S., Klassen, C., & Sherman, P. (1992). Teacher study groups: Exploring literacy issues through collaborative dialogue. In C. K. Kinzer & D. J. Leu (Eds.), *Literacy research, theory, and practice: Views from many perspectives*, Forty-first Yearbook of the National Reading Conference (pp. 367–377). Chicago: National Reading Conference.

Showers, B., Joyce, B., & Bennett, B. (1987). Synthesis of research on staff development: A framework for future study and state of the art analysis. *Educational Leadership*, 45(3), 77–88.

Simmons-Wolpow, R., Farrell, D. P., & Tonjes, M. J. (1991). Implementing a secondary reading/study skills program across disciplines. *Journal of Reading*, 34, 590–594.

Singer, H. (1986). Friendly texts: Description and criteria. In E. K. Dishner, T. W. Bean, J. E. Readence, & D. W. Moore (Eds.), *Reading in the content areas: Improving classroom instruction* (pp. 112–118). Dubuque, IA: Kendall/Hunt.

Slavin, R. E. (1991). Are cooperative learning and "untracking" harmful to the gifted? *Educational Leadership*, 48(6), 68–71.

Slavin, R. E. (1992). The nongraded elementary school: Great potential, but keep it simple. *Educational Leadership*, 50, 24.

Smith, E. B., Goodman, K., & Meredith, R. (1976). *Language and thinking in schools*, 2nd ed. New York: Holt, Rinehart and Winston.

Smith, N. B. (1965). *American reading instruction*. Newark, DE: International Reading Association.

Solé, D. (1990). Using student journals in the workplace ESL classroom. *Journal of Reading*, 34, 301.

Solity, J. L. (1985). *Working class women's literacy and publishing*. Master's dissertation, University of London Institute of Education.

Sommerville, J. C. (1971). Leadership that "rocks the boat," a boat that needs rocking! *Educational Leadership*, 29(1), 45–49.

Sparks-Langer, G. M., & Colton, A. B. (1991). Synthesis of research on teachers' reflective thinking. *Educational Leadership*, 48(6), 37–44.

Stanford Achievement Test, 8th ed. (1989). San Antonio, TX: Psychological Corporation.

Stasz, B. B., Schwartz, R. G., & Weeden, J. C. (1991). Writing our lives: An adult basic skills program. *Journal of Reading, 35*, 30–33.

Stern, P., & Shavelson, R. J. (1983). Reading teachers' judgments, plans, and decision making. *The Reading Teacher, 35*, 884–889.

Stoll, D. R. (Ed.). (1990). *Magazines for children.* Glassboro, NJ: Educational Press Association of America. Newark, DE: International Reading Association.

Stoodt, I. (1981). *Reading instruction.* Boston: Houghton Mifflin.

Strickland, D. S. (1988). The teacher as researcher: Toward the extended professional. *Language Arts, 65*, 754–764.

Strickland, D. S. (1992). Organizing a literature-based reading program. In B. E. Cullinan (Ed.), *Invitation to read*: *More children's literature in the reading program* (pp. 110–121). Newark, DE: International Reading Association.

Tanner, D., & Tanner, L. (1987). *Supervision in education.* New York: Macmillan.

Taylor, B., Harris, L. A., & Pearson, P. D. (1988). *Reading difficulties: Instruction and assessment.* New York: Random House.

Teale, B. (Ed.). (1992). But what about spelling? [Special issue]. *Language Arts, 69*.

Teale, W. H., Hiebert, E. F., & Chittendon, E. A. (1987). Assessing young children's literacy development. *The Reading Teacher, 40*, 772–777.

Templeton, S. (1992). New trends in an historical perspective: Old story, new resolution—Sound and meaning in spelling. *Language Arts, 69*, 454–463.

Tierney, R. J., Carter, M. A., & Desai, L. E. (1991). *Portfolio assessment in the reading–writing classroom.* Norwood, MA: Christopher-Gordon.

Toepfer, C. F. (1973). The supervisor's responsibility for innovation. *Educational Leadership, 30*(8), 740–743.

Tracy, S. J., & MacNaughton, R. H. (1989). Clinical supervision and the emerging conflict between the neo-traditionalists and the neo-progressives, *Journal of Curriculum and Supervision, 4*(3), 246–256.

Topping, K. (1989). Peer tutoring and paired reading: Combining two powerful techniques. *The Reading Teacher, 42*, 488–494.

Trelease, J. (1989). *The new read-aloud handbook.* New York: Viking Penguin.

Tsuchiya, Y. (1988). *Faithful elephants.* Boston: Houghton Mifflin.

Valencia, S. (1990, January). A portfolio approach to classroom reading assessment: The whys, whats, and hows. *The Reading Teacher, 43*, 338–340.

Valencia, S. W., McGinley, W., & Pearson, P. D. (1990). Assessing reading and writing. In G. G. Duffy (Ed.), *Reading in the middle school* (pp. 124–153). Newark, DE: International Reading Association.

Valencia, S. W., & Pearson, P. D. (1987). Reading assessment: Time for a change. *The Reading Teacher, 40*, 726–732.

Vaughn, S., Schumm, J. S., Niarhos, F., & Gordon, J. (1993). Students' perceptions of two hypothetical teachers' instructional adaptations for low achievers. *Elementary School Journal, 94*(1), 87–102.

Vogt, L. A., Jordan, C., & Tharp, R. G. (1987). Explaining school failure, producing school success: Two cases. *Anthropology and Education Quarterly, 18*(4), 276–286.

Vogt, M. E. (1991). An observation guide for supervisors and administrators: Moving toward integrated reading/language arts instruction. *The Reading Teacher, 45*, 206–210.

Vygotsky, L. S. (1978). *Mind in society.* Cambridge, MA: Harvard University Press.

Wallace, C. (1988). *Learning to read in a multicultural society*: *The social context of second language literacy.* Englewood Cliffs, NJ: Prentice-Hall.

Walmsley, S. A., & Adams, E. L. (1993). Realities of "whole language." *Language Arts, 70*, 272–280.

Warger, C., & Moffett, C. (1988). *Human resource development handbook.* Washington, DC: Association for Supervision and Curriculum Development.

Weaver, C. (1990). *Understanding whole language— From principles to practice.* Portsmouth, NH: Heinemann.

Weed, J. (1991). Living daily in a whole language classroom. In Y. M. Goodman, W. J. Hood, & K. S. Goodman (Eds.), *Organizing for whole language* (pp. 84–94). Portsmouth, NH: Heinemann.

Weick, K. E. (1982). Administering education in loosely coupled schools. *Phi Delta Kappan, 27*(2), 673–676.

Wepner, S. B. (1989). Roles and responsibilities of reading personnel. In S. B. Wepner, J. T. Feeley, & D. S. Strickland (Eds.), *The administration and supervision of reading programs* (pp. 22–44). New York: Teachers College Press.

Wepner, S. B., Feeley, J. T., & Strickland, D. S. (Eds.). (1989). *The administration and supervision of reading programs.* New York: Teachers College Press.

Whimbey, A. (1983). *Analytic reading and reasoning.* Stamford, CT: Innovative Sciences.

Wilde, S. (1990). A proposal for a new spelling curriculum. *Elementary School Journal, 90,* 275–289.

Wilhelms, F. (1946). Tomorrow's assignment. In T. J. Sergiovanni (Ed.), *Leadership through supervision.* Washington, DC: Association for Supervision and Curriculum Development.

Willis, S. (1992a, December). Ready to learn. *ASCD Update, 34,* 1, 6, 8.

Willis, S. (1992b, September). Restructuring under fire. *ASCD Update, 34,* 1, 4–5.

Wilson, R. M., & Becker, H. L. (1984). An educational audit of a district's reading personnel. *Reading World, 24,* 69–72.

Windsor, S., et al. (1991). Parents supporting whole language. In Y. M. Goodman, W. J. Hood, & K. S. Goodman (Eds.), *Organizing for whole language* (pp. 284–299). Portsmouth, NH: Heinemann.

Winograd, P., Paris, S. G., & Bridge, C. (1991). Improving the assessment of literacy. *The Reading Teacher, 45,* 108–116.

Wolf, D. P. (1989). Portfolio assessment: Sampling student work. *Educational Leadership, 46,* 35–39.

Wollman-Bonilla, J. E. (1991, February). Shouting from the tops of buildings: Teachers as learners and change in schools. *Language Arts, 68,* 114–120.

Wood, F., Killian, J., McQuarrie, F., & Thompson, S. (1993). *How to organize a school-based staff development program.* Alexandria, VA: Association for Supervision and Curriculum Development.

Wood, K. D. (1987). Fostering cooperative learning in middle and secondary level classrooms. *Journal of Reading, 31,* 10–18.

Woodley, J., & Woodley, C. (1989). Whole language, Texas style. In K. Goodman, Y. Goodman, & W. Hood (Eds.), *The whole language evaluation book* (pp. 69–75). Portsmouth, NH: Heinemann.

Worcester, S. (1857). *Report, School Committee,* 9–10.

Yatvin, J. (1992). *Developing a whole language program for a whole school.* Newark, DE: International Reading Association.

Young, M. J., & Riegeluth, C. (1988). *Improving the textbook selection process.* Bloomington, IN: Phi Delta Kappa Educational Foundation.

Young, W. F. (1969). Influencing professional negotiation. In W. H. Lucio (Ed.), *The supervisor: New demands, new dimensions.* Washington, DC: Association for Supervision and Curriculum Development.

Ysseldyke, J. E., & Christenson, S. L. (1987). *TIES—The Instructional Environment Scale.* Austin, TX: Pro-Ed.

Zimpher, N. L., & Grossman, J. E. (1992). Collegial support by teacher mentors and peer consultants. In C. D. Glickman (Ed.), *Supervision in transition,* Yearbook of the Association for Supervision and Curriculum Development (pp. 141–154). Alexandria, VA: Association for Supervision and Curriculum Development.

Appendix A

The Preschool Program

In the twenty-five years prior to 1988, the percentage of preschool attendance quadrupled (Sava, in Schweinhart, 1988). Elementary administrators are increasingly responsible for these programs. The information that follows can help with the instruction and assessment of preschool youngsters. Although instruction and assessment must be intertwined, these elements are separated here according to the major purpose of each item.

Instruction

One document that can be especially helpful in guiding preschool instructional programs is the "Appropriate Education in the Primary Grades" Position Statement of the National Association for the Education of Young Children (NAEYC, 1834 Connecticut Avenue, N.W., Washington, DC 20009). Another is "Literacy Development and Prefirst Grade, a Joint Statement of Concerns about Present Practices in Prefirst Grade Reading Instruction and Recommendations for Improvement" (distributed by the International Reading Association, P.O. Box 8139, Newark, DE 19714–8139). Both position statements are similar in philosophy. Tenets of the latter are as shown in the box on page 228.

Administrators responsible for guiding emergent literacy in preschool programs may wish to write for information from the following sources:

- *ALERTA*: A multicultural, bilingual approach. P.O. Box 9, Teachers College, Columbia University, New York, NY 10027 (212-678-3970).

- *American Montessori Society*: Information on Montessori programs in the United States. Paul Koenigstein, American Montessori Society, 150 Fifth Avenue, New York, NY 10011.

- *Collaboration with the Community*: Annual workshops and Preschool

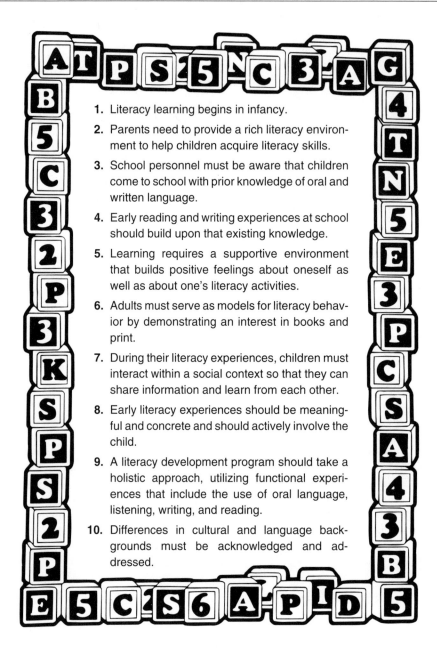

1. Literacy learning begins in infancy.

2. Parents need to provide a rich literacy environment to help children acquire literacy skills.

3. School personnel must be aware that children come to school with prior knowledge of oral and written language.

4. Early reading and writing experiences at school should build upon that existing knowledge.

5. Learning requires a supportive environment that builds positive feelings about oneself as well as about one's literacy activities.

6. Adults must serve as models for literacy behavior by demonstrating an interest in books and print.

7. During their literacy experiences, children must interact within a social context so that they can share information and learn from each other.

8. Early literacy experiences should be meaningful and concrete and should actively involve the child.

9. A literacy development program should take a holistic approach, utilizing functional experiences that include the use of oral language, listening, writing, and reading.

10. Differences in cultural and language backgrounds must be acknowledged and addressed.

Liaison Program. Bebe Fearnside, Alachua County School District, 620 East University Avenue, Gainesville, FL 32601 (904-336-3616).

- *Cooperative Preschools*: Parents of all participating preschoolers donate a number of days in the classroom. Burton Arnold, Dade County Public Schools, 1410 N.E. 2 Avenue, Miami, FL 33132 (305-995-1000).

- *High/Scope Training of Teacher-Trainers System*: Training for implementing the High/Scope curriculum. David Weikart, 600 North River Street, Ypsilanti, MI 48198 (313-485-2000).

- *Kentucky Parent and Child Education Program*: Family support and education program. PACE Coordinator, Division of Community Education, Kentucky Department of Education, 19th floor, Capital Plaza Tower, Frankfort, KY 40601 (502-564-2117).

- *The Maryland Certification-Accredited Project*: The main goal of this program to insure that state-funded prekindergartens put into practice those elements that are crucial to high-quality childhood programs. Maryland State Department of Education, Division of Instruction, 200 West Baltimore Street, Baltimore, MD 21201.

- *Schools of the 21st Century*: Use of public schools for on-site and outreach services. Edward Zigler, P.O. Box 11A, Yale Station, New Haven, CT 06520 (203-432-4576).

See also the section on family literacy in Appendix B.

Assessment

Early childhood evaluation should assess both program quality and children's development (Schweinhart, 1988). For an evaluation of program quality, see Schweinhart's (1988) questionnaire, which addresses the issues of adult/child ratios, educational background of staff, parent involvement, supervisory support and inservice training, meeting of noneducational needs of children and families, and child development curriculum. For example, questions regarding the child development curriculum include the following (p. 33):

- Are the early childhood classrooms arranged in interest areas?

- Do the early childhood classrooms have a balance of materials, commercial and noncommercial, that are accessible to the children and that have a variety of uses?

- Do children in early childhood classrooms spend a substantial portion of time each day engaged in activities that they initiate themselves with teacher support?

- Does your early childhood teaching staff spend substantial time talking to children as individuals and in small groups?

Assessment of children's development should be a part of instruction. Following are some sources that can help guide assessment of young children.

- *Documentation of Children's Learning*: Alternatives to conventional testing practices. Edward Chittenden or Rosalea Courtney, Educational Testing Service, Princeton, NJ 08541 (609-921-9000).

- *Literacy Development in the Early Years* (Morrow, 1993): Development of student portfolios.

Adult Education

Senior high administrators who are responsible for adult education as well know that the possible range of adult education courses is broad. The focus here will be on courses for beginning and developing literacy. The curriculum for such courses overlaps with that for K–12, but strategies and materials need to be carefully thought out, as do forms of assessment. Although instruction and assessment must be intertwined, the following lists of tested instructional possibilities and of assessment tools are separated according to the major purpose of each item. For more detail on instruction and assessment of adult learners, see Radencich (1994).

Instruction

- *Writing workshops*: Pates and Evans (1990) have surveyed adult writing workshops followed by writing weekends and regular writing groups for the writing of books and magazines. Solity (1985) reports on workshops where "the writing is conversational in style, writing from the personal, the personal being the political in that they gained control over their own lives and independence, whilst at the same time inspiring each other." Conniff, Bortle, and Joseph (1993–1994) tell a success story about the use of poetry writing by female Adult Basic Education (ABE) students.

- *Language experience*: D'Annunzio (1990) reports the success of the language experience approach (LEA) when working with an adult English as a Second Language (ESL) program. He points out (p. 199) that LEA makes use of the adults' experience and promotes reading as a by-product of their thinking and oral expression. Also, LEA allows for one-on-one, personalized learning situations.

- *Creative plays*: McCabe (1992) describes success with an extension of language experience, having adult beginning readers enact individual or group generated stories. McCabe cites three reasons that this can be effective: (1) the stories are personalized in theme as well as language structure; (2) students find pleasure in seeing their own words and ideas in print and performance; and (3) when the play emanates from group discussion, it may provide alternative strategies for negotiating life's daily frustrations.

• *Cooperative learning*: It is often assumed that adults in literacy programs prefer to work alone. Yet, Howie (1990, p. 263) points out that "grouping can fulfill adult longing for social interactions with other adults. Such grouping counters a sense of isolation and anxiety regarding formal learning. Furthermore, grouping deals with necessary aspects of adult learning outlined by Mocker (1975) that differ from children's learning: (1) providing for student-to-student communication that recognizes the experience and knowledge of each; (2) placing responsibility for learning on the students to foster independence; and (3) having the teacher assume the role of co-learner rather than controller of all knowledge."

• *Print materials*: Materials for adult basic education classes can range from picture books (Danielson, 1992) to carefully selected adaptations of classic novels (Schierloh, 1992) to materials related to consumer advocacy. Danielson recommends that picture books be selected for their dialect and character development, jargon and lingo, parts of speech, and writing possibilities (e.g., journal entries from different points of view following Tsuchiya's *Faithful Elephants* [1988], or alphabet books following the reading of a few of this genre). Schierloh found that, in using excerpts from adapted classic novels, (1) passages of dialogue are easier for students than passages of description, (2) excerpts of scenes involving exciting action are effective, (3) excerpts yielding deep insights into a major character can bring life to flat characters, and (4) excerpts should be brief and be read with as few explanations as possible. See Danielson and Schierloh's recommendations in "Readings for Less Proficient Senior High and Adult Readers" in the suggested readings for students in Appendix D. For activities using picture books, see Johnson-Weber (1989) or Polette (1989).

• *Multimedia materials*: Rosow (1990) describes her success using consumer advocacy teaching with television programming and print advertising as core materials. Rosow's group, which included multilingual, multicultural adults at different levels in learning English, learned their lessons well.

As noted in Chapter 3, for many at-risk learners, computers can be especially attractive in that they can provide privacy, individualization, demonstrated achievement gains, cost-effectiveness, control of learning, flexibility in scheduling, open entry and exit, and a modern way to learn (Askov & Clark, 1991; Howie, 1990). See journal reviews of software as well as specialized lists such as Howie (1990) and Askov and Clark (1991). Gueulette (1986) provides further information on using technology in adult education.

- *Journals in the workplace ESL classroom*: Solé (1990) reports moving workplace English as a Second Language (ESL) students from "You know I can't write" to emotionally charged, coherent personal accounts when students write from a well-defined springboard.

- *Conversations about books*: Morgenthaler (1993) writes of a group of adults at grade 2–6 reading levels who, as discussion facilitators, read and discuss humanities-based stories and their relationship to life.

- *Storytelling*: Ford (1992) sparks the interest of adult students through her storytelling. Students emerge from the spell with an interest in reading a particular book, or they remember a book they have enjoyed that they would like to share. Ford's suggested titles include those from children's, young adult, and adult literature. Examples include Buck's *The Good Earth* (1981), Peck's *A Day No Pigs Would Die* (1979), and Schlissel's *Women's Diaries of the Westward Journey* (1987).

- *Volunteers*: In 1988 the board of directors of the International Reading Association approved a position statement on adult literacy volunteer tutors, the background of which reads in part:

Volunteer tutors make a contribution in the eradication of illiteracy and need to be actively recruited. However, they need to first participate in well designed preparation programs. Unfortunately, in some of the existing volunteer literacy programs as little as 10 hours or less of training are provided for the tutors. This training does not prepare them to identify or work with learning disabled adults or adults who are not native speakers of their native language.

The resolution goes on to make a plea for greater support to training programs.

- *Family literacy*: Family literacy refers to programs that serve both adults and their young children. Projects may involve both adult and child, or the adult alone. In the latter case, the adult is helped with his or her own literacy as well as with techniques on developing literacy with young children. Projects often occur in partnerships and may be spearheaded by public schools, adult literacy programs, community-based groups, and/or government agencies (Morrow, 1993).

Stasz, Schwartz, and Weeden (1991) describe a Head Start program in conjunction with a Student Literacy Corps grant where the atmosphere is like that of a painting studio or a craft workshop. The mothers and the students formed a writing community that resulted in four books: stories about their grandmothers, a book of family histories and recipes, a children's play, and a history of Head Start in the community.

For further information, contact ASCD's Intergenerational/Family Literacy Professional Network (1250 North Pitt Street, Alexandria, VA 22314-1403).

Assessment

In addition to the assessment tools described in Chapter 8, the following sources, which specifically address adult learners, should be considered:

Literacy Volunteers of America. (1993). *Literacy assessment tool* (LAT). Syracuse, NY: Author.

One unique area represented by this test is the assessment of goals, which should be a prime element in the assessment of adult students.

Padak, N. D., Davidson, J. L., & Padak, G. M. (1990). Exploring reading with adult beginning readers. *Journal of Reading, 34,* 26–29.

This article addresses dictations. Dictations by an adult beginning reader can help explore his or her ability as a reader, including knowledge of words. One advantage of dictation over other means of diagnosis is that understanding is ensured, and meaning is inherent in the learner's dictated accounts of experiences or ideas. Moreover, because dictations are recorded verbatim, vocabulary and language patterns will also be familiar to the adult. Following the dictation, the adult can be asked to read the dictation silently, then to underline words he or she knows, and finally to read these words orally.

This article also explains why standardized tests are also a problem with Adult Basic Education programs and with adult beginning readers. These students are reminded of unpleasant prior experiences. Their test-taking fear can counteract attempts to create the positive initial experiences so important to retention in programs. In addition, standardized tests often give only percentiles or the like and do not provide details regarding student needs.

For program evaluation of adult education, see Padak and Padak (1991). See also the list of professional resources in Appendix D.

Whatever the instruction and assessment used with adult students, special care must be given to the learning environment. For students who may not remember their school days fondly, it is particularly important to have an attractive setting. An "office" environment, with plants, computers, and the like, will be more appealing than a "classroom" atmosphere.

Appendix C

Tools of the Trade

Glossary of Curriculum Terms

Clustering: Brainstorming words or phrases related to a given word and writing these in rays surrounding the word; generally used as a prereading or prewriting activity. For example, clustering for *celebrations* might yield words like *Christmas, Kwanzaa, eating,* and *firecrackers.*

Conferencing: Discussing one's literacy, particularly one's writing; can be teacher–student or student–student; can occur at any stage of the writing process.

Drafting: See *Writing process.*

Editing: See *Writing process.*

Emergent literacy: A reconceptualization of reading readiness, with *emergent* suggesting something that is dynamic and becoming, not a specific point in time, and *literacy* stressing not just reading but the interrelatedness of the language arts, with a host of activities (shared reading, celebrations of beginning stages of writing, etc.) used to make reading and writing come alive and to help young children acquire important skills for later success (Pikulski, 1988).

Expository: Pertaining to content area reading and writing from subjects such as science and social studies.

Flexible grouping: Grouping students on an ad hoc rather than a fixed basis, with instruction given to the whole class, to various kinds of needs-based groups, and to individuals (Radencich & McKay, in press).

Holistic: Sometimes used interchangeably with *whole language* and *literature-based*; a philosophy in which instruction moves from the whole to its parts.

Invented spelling: The understanding that children go through a set of predictable levels in learning to spell, just as they do in learning to walk or to talk (Radencich, Beers, & Schumm, 1993). A more appropriate term than *invented* is *temporary* because the spelling follows developmental stages rather than being creatively invented. Moreover, the term *temporary* helps to relieve parents and others who otherwise may be concerned at the initial lack of accuracy.

Journal: A notebook in which students record personal thoughts, notes about their learning, or other ideas, and later sometimes use for sharing; can be used in a variety of ways—for example, as a diary or a learning log.

Literature-based: Often contrasted with skill-based; refers to a curriculum that starts with the literature and pulls skills from the literature, at its best without overdoing the skill work and without neglecting expository reading.

Metacognition: A reader's ability to monitor his or her comprehension and to use appropriate corrective strategies when necessary.

Portfolio: Definitions vary widely. Generally, a compilation of a variety of meaningful data about an individual student kept in a special folder or other personalized container. Sheila Valencia (1990, p. 340) notes:

The real value of a portfolio . . . [lies] . . . in the mindset that it instills in students and teachers. Portfolios represent a philosophy that demands that we view assessment as an integral part of our instruction, providing a process for teachers and students to use to guide learning. It is an expanded definition of assessment in which a wide variety of indicators of learning are gathered across many situations before, during, and after instruction. It is a philosophy that honors both the process and the products of learning as well as the active participation of the teacher and the students in their own evaluation and growth.

Prewriting: See *Writing process.*

Publishing: See *Writing process.*

Revising: See *Writing process.*

Strategy: A conscious knowledge of how, when, and where to apply a thinking process (e.g., knowing three ways to attack a word). *Strategy* is distinguished from *skill,* which is a less conscious application—that is, simply being or not being able to say the word correctly.

Structural analysis: The study of the structure of a word to note its root, prefixes, suffixes, inflected endings, and syllabication so that the word may be decoded.

Trade books: In common parlance, "library books."

Whole language: Definitions vary widely. A philosophy of education at all grade levels in which listening, speaking, reading, and writing across the curriculum are integrated and are taught with a whole-to-part rather than a part-to-whole skills-based perspective; a political movement of empowering teachers and students to make decisions based on ongoing observation; a child-centered perspective that bases learning on authentic reading and writing experiences (Radencich, Beers, & Schumm, 1993).

Writing process: Although there is really no universal process of writing, the field refers to writing as a recursive, not linear, process in which writers go through the following stages, with teacher and peer conferencing anywhere along the way:

- *Prewriting: Thinking about what to write, perhaps based on material found in experiences or in books, perhaps with help from activities such as free writing and clustering.*
- *Drafting: Getting something down on paper.*
- *Revising: Improving the content (not yet the mechanics!) of the draft*—perhaps a better beginning sentence, an improved sequence, or an increased use of truly descriptive language.
- Editing: Correcting spelling and mechanics.

- Publishing: Sharing one's writing through reading it aloud, mailing it to someone, posting it on a bulletin board, and the like. See "Publishers of Student Writing" later in Appendix C.

Common Questions and Answers

There are some typical questions pertaining to literacy that you might expect to hear as a supervisor/administrator. Although there is no substitute for in-depth knowledge, the following set of questions and answers will give you

a head start. The focus here is not on the "Why can't our children read today?" variety of question, for which answers abound, but rather on questions for which you may need ammunition beyond what is provided elsewhere in this book.

Why didn't the teacher correct the spelling? Orange County, Florida, program specialist Jackie Mathews (1992), in responding to a newspaper column complaining of children's misspellings in second-graders' letters to a pizza restaurant, eloquently explained the developmental nature of spelling. After graciously thanking the author for her interest, she went on as follows:

> *Current research in literacy education reports that children can learn to read and write very easily if the same conditions are present as when they learned to talk. When children first say "Da Da," everyone celebrates their attempt at language. Children feel secure enough to keep trying. The result is, most children can speak the language of their culture with few mistakes by the time they enter school.*
>
> *Although everyone readily accepts children's attempts while they are learning to talk, many of us expect adult competence from children almost immediately upon their entering school at age 5.*
>
> *Children are learning to read and write the same way they learned to talk. Teachers are celebrating early attempts at writing so that children have the confidence to keep on writing, just as they had the confidence to learn to talk. The teacher encourages the child to take risks and spell by writing the letters they hear in words.*
>
> *By concentrating on the message the child is trying to convey rather than the correctness of the spelling, children astound us with their knowledge and understanding of the world as well as with their creativity.*
>
> *As children gain confidence as writers, they are taught that correct spelling and the conventions of language are important. While teachers let children know that they don't need to be concerned about correctness in their rough drafts, writers should strive to make their published pieces error-free.*

Teachers build independence and responsibility in their students by encouraging them to edit their own work as much as possible. The teacher may need to assist in fixing up anything the child might have missed. Even though it is important for writing to be error-free when it is published, the teacher who sent the children's rough-draft letters to the pizza restaurant may have done so because many adults enjoy seeing the children's approximated spelling since it reveals so much about their development and thinking. . . .

Mistakes are part of the human condition. It is critical that we help children understand that everyone makes mistakes and that worse than making a mistake is being afraid to try.

But how do you teach spelling? Spelling is a thorny question. Teachers who abandon spellers in favor of integrating spelling with their other instruction are often left unsure about how to select words for instruction. Often they will select vocabulary words from their reading, words that may be too difficult to spell and unlikely to appear in student writing. These words are generally forgotten as soon as the spelling test is over. The spelling question remains unresolved; *Language Arts* dedicated the entire October 1992 issue to this topic. In summarizing the special issue, Teale (1992, pp. 401–402) states:

Traditional approaches to spelling (the list of 15 words given on Monday and tested on Friday) and the idea that spelling will take care of itself if children are allowed to write a lot are both dismissed as fundamentally wrong. The field is struggling with finding a coherent approach to spelling. Such an approach would emphasize integrated, functional, holistic language arts instruction, while at the same time it would draw children's attention to the orthographic patterns of words in ways that help them learn principles and strategies they use in writing and reading. Memorizing spellings is not useful; learning how words work and seeing the application of these insights for reading and writing is.

In the October 1992 *Language Arts* issue, second-grade teacher Judie Bartch describes her elimination of a weekly spelling test in favor of a multifaceted spelling strategy, which she taught for about forty-five minutes once a week. Her strategy includes word banks, picture dictionaries and thesauruses, printed resources such as maps, a word wall, environmental print in the classroom, spelling rules, attempts to write the words in three different ways to see which appears to be correct, slow articulation ("stretch") of some words, diagnostic observation of student writing, and modeling.

O'Flahavan and Blassberg (1992) go on to discuss an embedded model of spelling instruction for emergent literates. They propose that words or spelling patterns chosen for instruction from students' writing need to conform to four conditions: (1) that the word or pattern be an approximation of the conventional spelling, (2) that the student be confident that the word is not spelled conventionally, (3) that all phonemes be represented sufficiently through symbol use (e.g., *OHVORE* for *over*), and (4) that the student play a role in choosing words or patterns for further study.

In another article in the special issue, Templeton (1992, p. 455) reminds us that "throughout our history, perhaps more so than in any other English-speaking society, Americans have perceived spelling to be the very soul and fiber of education, and at times, it seemed, of society as well." It behooves us to avoid overemphasis on spelling, yet to use sound instructional practices to give it its rightful place in our curriculum.

Should I buy handwriting, grammar, and spelling books? As teachers move toward meaningfully integrating the language arts, the need for separate books for handwriting, grammar, and spelling will decrease. But a school should have a few copies available, samples at least, to serve as reference tools. Beginning teachers might not know how to teach handwriting strokes. Teachers needing reassurance that no skills are being left out may find individual copies of the books to be a necessary security blanket. In general, however, schools are moving toward spending the dollars that typically go into the purchase of these materials on classroom libraries, manipulatives, and other resources.

But how do I grade? Crowley (1989, p. 240) points out that "grading is a political issue, not a pedagogical one." For that reason, letter grades, at least at the upper grade levels, are undoubtedly here to stay. Yet letter grading on traditional report cards is ill matched to the developmental, child-centered learning in so many of today's classrooms. Teachers who celebrate children's progress through the stages of writing are loath to send a different message when forced to assign a "D" to a child who has progressed but who still performs below grade level. Teachers who integrate instruction find it hard to isolate grades for each area of the language arts. Teachers who emphasize process reject requirements for paper products to attach to each grade. Teachers who keep a grid of the conditions under which tasks are completed (alone, in a cooperative group, etc.) find it difficult to assign grades accordingly. Where report cards do not match instruction, schools must find ways of putting round pegs into square holes. For example, from one final writing product teachers can draw several grades, such as handwriting, composition, response to literature, mechanics, and spelling.

Linek (1991) suggests that philosophy guide grading with a comparison process based on individual, group, and/or criteria comparisons. Linek suggests gradual implementation of alternative grading options: first, portfolios, surveys, and simple checklists, followed by tally lists, journals, and anecdotal records. He also provides suggestions for times of the year when different types of data will be most useful. For example, questionnaires, surveys, and miscue analyses might be especially helpful at the beginning, middle, and end of the year; observations, anecdotal records, checklists, tally sheets, and taping could be used selectively and intermittently throughout the year; dialogue journals and portfolios could be used on an ongoing basis.

If letter grades are to be administered, Woodley and Woodley (1989) suggest holistic scores ranging from 5 to 1, based on the degree to which students have completed the task, their effectiveness in expressing themselves, and any growth or development that the writing or reading demonstrates. These numbers can be converted to letter grades or percentages.

Freeman and Freeman (1989), in discussing grading for secondary and adult education, provide guidelines that have some relevance for all grade levels:

- The system should be easy for both the teacher and the students to understand.

- At least as much weight should be given to work in progress as to final products.

- The students should be involved in negotiating the system.

- Awarding or taking away credit should never become part of the discipline system.

- The focus of the class should be on the content, not on the evaluation.

Teachers, schools, and districts must work together to ensure that report cards match their instruction. Schools or districts looking for change should become familiar with the many changing report card formats in use across the nation. Newer report cards are likely to replace letter grades with behavioral statements such as "takes risks when reading" ("frequently," "sometimes," or "rarely"). Changing grading systems must actively involve all interested parties, such as parents and teachers' unions. To help with the transition, some districts begin with two or three grade levels and then work their way up. Some districts use transitional report cards before making all desired changes.

My first-grade teachers say the kindergarten teachers aren't doing their job. What should I do? There has traditionally been some friction between kindergarten and first-grade teachers. Often, kindergarten teachers focus on social and language skills and on developmentally appropriate instruction, whereas first-grade teachers are concerned about their instructional responsibilities. The tension between them is sometimes exacerbated in schools making a transition to more holistic instruction. It is important to understand that pushing the first-grade curriculum into kindergarten may not help children's literacy as much as will providing an environment in which confident children explore and take risks and learn.

In my experience, however, first-grade teachers who do not find their students to be adequately prepared often have a point. When I visit the kindergarten and first-grade classrooms in question, I sometimes find that the kindergarten experience does not provide enough of an opportunity for children to experiment with temporary spellings. I tell teachers that ten minutes of journal writing is just not enough! Sometimes I find all centers but the writing center devoid of paper and writing implements. Sometimes I find that shared reading does not progress beyond memorization, so that students lack opportunities to work with phonemic awareness and sight vocabulary. Of course, these problems often occur in the first-grade classroom as well.

First-grade teachers sometimes need to rethink their priorities. Maybe it's not so bad if the children don't know the sounds of a couple of letters if, instead, they do know how to work in groups, they choose to read and write in and out of school, and they show progress in the stages of developmental writing.

Where tension occurs, kindergarten and first-grade teachers should get together with someone whose expertise they both respect to discuss their goals and their instructional procedures.

What is the readability of this? Pikulski (1989) said in his last Questions and Answers column for *The Reading Teacher* that, among his fifty columns, the question that had evoked the strongest response was readability. He had warned of the enormous limitations of all readability formulas but then suggested one rough, easy-to-calculate estimate.

My experience is that requests for readability levels are generally made by people who do not understand the limits of readability formulas. I estimate difficulty levels by looking at the material under question and taking into account all aspects of readability, both reader-based (e.g., prior knowledge and interest) and text-based (e.g., concept density, layout, sentence length and complexity, vocabulary, clarity of the writing, text considerateness). (See the section on difficulty level in Chapter 2.) I avoid using formulas, because the seductiveness of an exact number is generally so strong that any cautions surrounding this number are too easily ignored.

Along with my estimate, I explain that readability formulas were meant to *predict* but not to *estimate* the difficulty of text. A lack of understanding on this point has led to texts being written to fit a given readability level. The resulting short words and sentences appear to be "easy" according to a formula but, in effect, can be difficult because of the increased inferential load (Pearson, 1974–1975). Thus, in one passage, a reader may be forced to use an illustration to realize that *man* refers to *lifeguard.* In another, the reader may need to infer the causal connection in "Mary ate too much. Mary got sick."

If my questioner insists on a figure, I will use more than one formula and thus show the variability inherent in this process.

ACTION PLAN

COMMITTEE _____

CHAIRPERSON _____

WHAT NEEDS TO BE DONE	WHAT STEPS NEED TO BE TAKEN?	WHEN WILL IT BE DONE?	WHO WILL DO IT?	COST	HOW WILL YOU KNOW YOU'VE REACHED YOUR GOAL?

Contract

Student _____

READING CONTRACT

Today's Date _____   Due Date _____

I, _____, agree to read _____
            STUDENTS NAME
books. I agree to complete the books on time. I also agree to indicate
how I will share what I read by doing the following:

_____

_____

_____

_____   _____
STUDENT'S   TEACHER'S
SIGNATURE   SIGNATURE

_____
PARENT'S
SIGNATURE

READ-ALOUD CONTRACT

_____

Today's Date _____   Due Date _____

I, _____, agree to read _____
                     READER'S NAME

books out loud to _____. I agree to
                              LISTENER'S NAME

complete the books on time.

_____   _____
      STUDENT'S   TEACHER'S
      SIGNATURE   SIGNATURE

Today's Date: _____   Due Date:
_____

I, _____, agree to listen to _____

books that _____ will read out loud
                     READER'S NAME

to me. I agree to complete the books on time.

_____   _____
      STUDENT'S   TEACHER'S
      SIGNATURE   SIGNATURE

ɛɑɛɑɛɑɛɑ

WRITING CONTRACT

_____

Today's Date _____   Due Date _____

I, _____, agree to write _____
           STUDENT'S NAME

_____. I agree to

TITLE OF WORK

complete the written assignment on time.

_____   _____

STUDENT'S   TEACHER'S
SIGNATURE   SIGNATURE

_____

PARENT'S
SIGNATURE

ɛɑɛɑɛɑɛɑ

PROGRAM REVIEW

REVIEWER _____ DATE _____

| | STATUS (check one) | | | COMMENTS |
INDICATORS	1	2	3	RECOMMENDATIONS

I. Program organization
   A. Grade/department/team leadership facilitates achievement of goals.
   B. Each teacher has relevant district and state materials.
   C. There is evidence of appropriate pacing.
   D. Lesson plans, grade books, and classroom activities correlate with each other and reflect instructional objectives that correlate to student's assessed needs.
   E. Appropriate texts and support materials are available.
   F. All teachers are properly certified in their field.

II. General program delivery strategies:
   A. Students are aware of specific course objectives and expectations.
   B. Both direct instruction and flexible group activities (e.g., cooperative learning, buddy reading, peer editing) are used.
   C. Teachers use strategies to meet different learning styles.

1 = Appropriate   2 = Needs Improvement   3 = Not Applicable

INDICATORS	STATUS (check one) 1 2 3	COMMENTS RECOMMENDATIONS

D. Support materials
   (i.e., books, audio-
   visual) and/or person-
   nel are used in a
   planned way to meet
   individual needs.

E. Homework is varied,
   correlates with course
   objectives, and is
   checked promptly

F. Students are engaged.

G. The climate is condu-
   cive to interaction
   (student–teacher,
   student–student).

H. Parent/community
   support is active.

III. Specific language
arts strategies:

A. Teaching of read-
   ing/writing strategies
   extends across the
   curriculum.

B. Compositions give evi-
   dence that students
   are engaged in the writing process.

C. Opportunities are pro-
   vided for writing in
   several modes and for
   authentic audiences.

D. A continuous program
   for the improvement of
   spelling, punctuation,
   and standard American
   usage is integrated
   into the total lan-
   guage arts program.

E. Recently dated stu-
   dent writing is readily
   visible. This writing in-

1 = Appropriate   2 = Needs Improvement   3 = Not Applicable

continued

PROGRAM REVIEW continued

	STATUS (check one)	COMMENTS
INDICATORS	1 2 3	RECOMMENDA-TIONS

      cludes individual work, not just "carbon copies," for all students.

F. Students are encouraged to see the language arts as parts of an integrated whole.

G. Techniques, materials, and the like that have been recommended in workshops, program reviews, and elsewhere are in use (if applicable).

H. Strategic instruction includes teaching *what* is to be learned *why* it is to be learned, and *when* to use it.

I. The study of literature is planned to provide for students' growth.

J. The use of the library and reference resources is taught in relation to needs.

K. Media specialists support overall program (e.g., organizing materials by themes, supporting ongoing schoolwide motivational reading programs).

L. Students are encouraged in a variety of ways to do voluntary reading and report their individual reading experiences.

M. Instruction in listening, speaking, and viewing

	STATUS (check one)			COMMENTS
INDICATORS	1	2	3	RECOMMENDA-TIONS

is an integral part of the program.

N. Student-directed prob-
lem solving is evident
in discussions, projects,
and written work.

O. Study skills instruction
is ongoing within
each subject area.

P. Class activities place
emphasis on the
growth of each child
toward higher cogni-
tive levels.

Q. Learning centers, in-
cluding library corners,
are attractive and well
stocked with varied and
appropriate materials.

IV. Student records:

A. Records adhere to
school policies.

B. Student folders con-
tain work in creative and
expository composition,
all major tests and/or assessment items, and
only representative
samples of practice
exercises of grammar,
vocabulary, and spelling.

C. Portfolios are kept.
These can include read-
ing logs, informal as-
sessment, writing sam-
ples from different
stages of the writing
process, "can do" lists,
and the like.

D. A variety of formal
and informal eval-
uative techniques is
used (e.g., objective

1 = Appropriate   2 = Needs Improvement   3 = Not Applicable

continued

PROGRAM REVIEW continued

	STATUS (check one)			COMMENTS
INDICATORS	1	2	3	RECOMMENDA-TIONS

and essay tests,
self- and peer eval-
uations, projects).
V. Professional growth:
  A. Schoolwide profes-
    sional activities are
    available.
  B. Teachers participate
    in professional
    growth activities
    (attending profes-
    sional meetings,
    reading journals).
VI. Program articulation:
  A. Program continuity
    is maintained through
    communication within
    grade levels/teams/
    departments, and
    among all teachers
    and administrators.
  B. Program continuity
    exists for all students,
    including those in spe-
    cial programs.
  C. Program continuity is
    maintained through
    communication
    among feeder elemen-
    tary and secondary
    schools.
VII. Facilities
  A. Instructional equip-
    ment is adequate and
    in good working order
  B. Storage facilities for
    instructional materials
    are adequate.

Adapted with permission from Program Review forms used by Dade

County (Miami, Florida) Public Schools

Using Research: Key Studies and Reference Literature

Curriculum leaders on the cutting edge often have favorite references to fall back on when speaking with fellow educators or parents. Following are some key studies that have served me well.

Adams, M. J. (1990). *Beginning to read: Thinking and learning about print.* Cambridge, MA: MIT Press.

This book was written in response to the U.S. Department of Education's request for some answers on the issue of phonics. A summary of the original book is available from the Center for the Study of Reading at the University of Illinois, Champaign-Urbana. Both versions are very well written, but they are difficult reading. An oversimplified summary is that phonics is important, but not at the expense of meaning. A few quotes:

Somehow phonics and comprehension had come to be seen as mutually incompatible . . . and highly political. (p. 5)

It is obvious that print is essential to reading—no gas, no driving. But print alone is not enough to make the reading system go. Just as cars will not start without spark plugs, reading cannot begin without the spark of recognition. (p. 19)

Anderson, R. C., Hiebert, E. H., Scott, J. A., & Wilkinson, I. A. G. (1985). *Becoming a nation of readers: A report of the Commission on Reading.* Washington, DC: National Institute of Education.

This readable summary of research on reading, distributed by the International Reading Association, is made even more user-friendly with its glosses and summaries. It is a must for every professional library. Here are a few quotes:

Based on what we now know, it is incorrect to suppose that there is a simple or single step which, if taken correctly, will immediately allow a child to read. Becoming a skilled reader is a journey that involves many steps. Strengthening any one element yields small gains. For large gains, many elements must be in place. (p. 4)

The single most important activity for building the knowledge required for eventual success in reading is reading aloud to children. (p. 23)

What the child who is least ready for systematic reading instruction needs most is ample experience with oral and printed language, and early opportunities to begin to write. (p. 29)

The amount of time children spend reading in the average classroom is small.

*An estimate of silent reading time in the typical primary school class is 7 or 8
minutes per day. (p. 76)*

Cambourne, B. (1988). *The whole story: Natural learning and the acquisition of literacy in
the classroom.* Auckland: Scholastic.

*Cambourne's seven conditions for literacy learning apply to staff development as well as
to student learning. Following are early childhood examples of the seven conditions:*

1. *Immersion:* Children need many and varied opportunities for reading
   and writing. Classrooms should contain a large variety of print.

2. *Demonstration:* Teacher reads aloud and models comprehension strategies. Teacher models writing through notes, messages on the board,
   journals, language experience stories, and so on.

3. *Expectation:* The teacher assumes that everyone will read and write.
   Everyone's work is celebrated.

4. *Responsibility:* Children decide what to write about, how long their story
   is going to be, whether they need pictures or words to tell their story,
   and so forth. Children learn the conventions when they need them.

5. *Approximation:* Encourage and celebrate children's inventive spelling.
   Encourage and celebrate children's strategies for reading (picture reading, memorized retelling, or making it up using their prior knowledge).

6. *Employment:* Opportunities for authentic reading and writing take place
   all day.

7. *Feedback:* Stories shared in the author's chair are retold. Teachers help
   children edit their writing for publication.

Johnson, D. W., & Johnson, R. T. (1992). What to say to advocates of the gifted.
Educational Leadership, 50(2), 44–47.

*The use of cooperative learning with gifted students is a subject of some controversy.
The following quotes from Johnson and Johnson help put the issue in perspective.*

*Consistently, the mastery and retention of assigned material by high-ability
students has been found to be higher in cooperative than in competitive or
individual learning situations. What they learned within the group discussion
they demonstrated and used in subsequent situations when working alone. (p.
44)*

*In an explanation of why heterogeneous cooperative learning benefits high-ability stu-
dents:*

*First, learning material with the expectation of teaching it to others results in
learning it at a higher cognitive level than does learning material to pass a test.
Second, explaining the material to others increases the level of one's achieve-*

ment and of one's cognitive reasoning; it also increases retention. Third, check-ing the explanations of others for accuracy tends to increase the high-ability student's achievement. Fourth, cognitive growth requires social interaction and the exchange of varied opinion. (p. 45)

Martin, B., & Brogan, P. (1971). *Instant Readers teacher's guide, level 1.* New York: Holt.
Bill Martin (Martin & Brogan, 1971), in discussing the value of predictable language books, urges that teachers honor children's expectations of being able to read a book from cover to cover on the very first day of school since this "wholebooksuccess" aids in the child's desire to become a lifelong reader.

Trelease, J. (1989). *The new read-aloud handbook.* New York: Viking Penguin.
This source is invaluable not only for its annotated list of titles, but also for Trelease's poignant comments. Here is one quote:

Would you estimate that you've taken your child to the shopping mall ten times more often than the library or one hundred times more often? (p. 84)

Publishers of Student Writing

(Send self-addressed stamped envelope with each submission. Note that submissions may not be returned.)

Magazines for Young Children through Age 12 or 13

Boys' Life. 1325 Walnut Hill Lane, Irving, TX 75038-3096. Short stories or articles for boys (around 15,000 words). Age 8–18.

Child Life. 1100 Waterway Boulevard, Indianapolis, IN 46206. Short stories (1,000 words) and poetry. Age 10–12.

Children's Album. EGW Publishing Company, Box 6080, Concord, CA 94524. Short stories (adventure, humorous, religious, romance, science fiction, fantasy, hor-ror), 50–1,000 words. Fillers—short humor, crossword puzzles, sayings, car-toons. Age 8–14.

Children's Digest. P.O. Box 567, Indianapolis, IN 46206. Drawings and poems, jokes and riddles.

Clubhouse. Family Clubhouse Editor, Pomona, CA 91799. Focus on the family. Poems (4–24 lines), cartoons, short stories (adventure, historical, humorous, but not science fiction, romance, or mystery), responses to editor's questions (e.g., "What's the funniest thing that ever happened to you?"), and some drawings. Submissions should depict positive family values such as bravery, kindness, and the like.

Cobblestone Magazine. 20 Grove Street, Peterborough, NH 03458. History magazine. Drawings, letters, and projects to "Ebenezer" with name, age, and address. Ebenezer also asks questions and publishes student answers.

Cricket. Cricket League, P.O. Box 300, Peru, IL 61354. Poetry, story-writing, and art contests. Submissions must be accompanied by a statement signed by a teacher or parent assuring originality and that no help was given.

Highlights for Children. Honesdale, PA 18431. Poems, stories, black-and-white drawings to Our Own Pages with name, age, address.

Jack and Jill Magazine. 1100 Waterway Boulevard, P.O. Box 547, Indianapolis, IN 76206. Drawings and poems with name, age, school, and address.

Kids Magazine. P.O. Box 3041, Grand Central Station, New York, NY 10017. Short stories, poetry, nonfiction, black-and-white art, puzzles, games—400-word limit. Small honorary payments for published work. Age 5–15.

National Geographic World. 17th and M Streets, N.W., Washington, DC 20036. Short writings about hobby or special collection for Focus on Collections Column.

Ranger Rick. 1412 16th Street, N.W., Washington, DC 20036. Fiction, nonfiction, puzzles on nature themes.

Reflections. Dean Harper, Editor, Box 368, Duncan Falls, OH 43734. Attractive poetry magazine published by Duncan Falls Junior High students. Accepts poems by students from nursery school to high school. Authors include name, age, school, address, and teacher's name in upper right-hand corner. Include statement signed by author and teacher or parent attesting to the originality of the poetry. Payment is a copy of *Reflections.*

Shoe Tree: The Literary Magazine by and for Children. 215 Valle Del Sol Drive, Santa Fe, NM 87501. A quarterly published by the National Association for Young Writers, "Helping Children Write to the Top." All stories, poems, and artwork are done by children. Holds annual competition for young writers in fiction, poetry, and nonfiction. Age 5–14.

Skipping Stones. P.O. Box 3939, Eugene, OR 97403. A multiethnic magazine that encourages an understanding of different cultures and languages, with an emphasis on ecology and human relationships. Artwork, writings, riddles, book reviews, news items, and a pen pal section. Work by children around the world. English and Spanish/English editions.

Stone Soup. P.O. Box 83, Santa Cruz, CA 95063. A literary magazine written by children. Published by the Children's Art Foundation, a nonprofit organization devoted to encouraging children's creativity. Stories of any length, poems, book reviews, and art (in any size and any color), and photographs.

Storyworks. Scholastic, 730 Broadway, New York, NY 10003. A literature-based magazine for grades 3–5. Includes book reviews by students.

Tyketoon Young Author Publishing Company, 7414 Douglas Lane, Fort Worth, TX 76180. Approximately one book per grade level 1-8 published yearly. Authors and illustrators receive cash scholarships paid as a royalty on each book sold.

Magazines that Publish Teenagers' Writings

Boys' Life. 1325 Walnut Hill Lange, Irving, TX 75038-3096. Short stories or articles (around 15,000 words) for boys. Age 8–18.

Clubhouse. Family Clubhouse Editor, Pomona, CA 91799. Focus on the family. Poems (4–24 lines), cartoons, short stories (adventure, historical, humorous, but not science fiction, romance, or mystery), responses to editor's questions (e.g., "What's the funniest thing that ever happened to you?"), and some drawings. Submissions should depict positive family values such as bravery, kindness, and so on.

Co-Ed Magazine. Your Space, Co-Ed Magazine, 50 West 44th Street, New York, NY 10036. Poetry page (poems require written statement from author as well as his or her English teacher attesting to its originality—teacher's statement on school stationery. Poets must include name, address, home phone number, age, grade, and school.

Dark Starr. Drawer 4127, Oceanside, CA 92054. Science fiction to 5,000 words, poetry 1–40 lines (must be horror, science fiction, mystery).

English Journal. 1111 Kenyon Road, Urbana, IL 61801. Annual "Spring Poetry Festival."

Kids Magazine. P.O. Box 3041, Grand Central Station, New York, NY 10017. Short stories, poetry, nonfiction, black-and-white art, puzzles, games—400-word limit. Small honorary payments for published work. Age 5–15.

Merlyn's Pen (grades 7–10) and *Merlyn's Senior Edition* (grades 9–12). P.O. Box 1058, East Greenwich, RI 02818. Dedicated to student writing and drawing. Short stories, science fiction, reviews, essays, scripts up to 2,500 words, poems up to 100 lines. Submissions should include author's name, grade, age, school and home address and phone numbers, county, and name of supervising teacher. Typed work preferred, two-inch margins and double-spaced.

National Council of Teachers of English Promising Young Writers Program. NCTE, 1111 Kenyon Road, Urbana, IL 61801. Open to eighth-graders nominated by February. Write NCTE for applications.

Penworks. P.O. Box 452, Belvedere, NJ 07823. A literary magazine by and for teens.

Purple Cow. Suite 320, 3423 Piedmont Road, N.E., Atlanta, GA 30305. General interest articles, 1,000 words maximum and cartoons.

Read Magazine. Xerox Education Publications, 245 Long Hill Road, Middletown, CT 06467. Once a year features a special student issue devoted to students' poetry, short stories, plays, and feature articles. Regularly includes students' jokes and poetry. Grades 7–9.

Reflections. Dean Harper, Editor, Box 368, Duncan Falls, OH 43734. Attractive poetry magazine published by Duncan Falls Junior High students. Accepts poems by students from nursery school to high school. Authors include name, age, school, address, and teacher's name in upper right-hand corner. Include statement signed by author and teacher or parent attesting to the originality of the poetry. Payment is a copy of *Reflections.*

Scholastic Scope Magazine. 50 West 44th Street, New York, NY 10036. Grades 7–12. Poems, plays, stories, "mini-mysteries." Entries should be typed or neatly printed and accompanied by a note certifying originality and signed by the student and teacher or parent. Send entries in care of "Student Writing" or "Mini-Mysteries." Written for adolescents who read at the fourth- to sixth-grade level.

Scholastic Voice Magazine. 50 West 44th Street, New York, NY 10036. Poems and stories of under 500 words. Frequent writing contests on specific themes. Entries should be typed or neatly printed and accompanied by a note certifying originality and signed by the student and teacher or parent. Grades 7–12, especially grades 8–10.

Scholastic Writing Awards Program. 50 West 44th Street, New York, NY 10036. Junior Division contest features essays, poetry, short stories, and dramatic scripts. Entries must be accompanied by an official entry blank. Deadline is January. Cash awards. Grades 7–9.

Seventeen Magazine. 850 Third Avenue, New York, NY 10022. Fiction, nonfiction, poetry, and a Free for All column.

Skipping Stones. P.O. Box 3939, Eugene, OR 97403. A multiethnic magazine that encourages an understanding of different cultures and languages, with an emphasis on ecology and human relationships. Artwork, writings, riddles, book reviews, news items, and a pen pal section. Work by children around the world. English and Spanish/English editions.

Tyketoon Young Author Publishing Company, 7414 Douglas Lane, Fort Worth, TX 76180. Approximately one book per grade level 1–8 published yearly. Authors and illustrators receive cash scholarships paid as a royalty on each book sold.

Voices of Youth, P.O. Box JJ, Sonoma, CA 95476. A magazine by, about, and for high school students, which publishes art and writing on varied topics ranging from personal concerns to social and political issues.

Writing! General Learning Corporation, P.O. Box 310, Highwood, IL 60040. Writing magazine ordered through schools. Student writing and articles on tips for writers.

Young American, America's Newspaper for Kids. Box 12409, Portland, OR 97212. Short stories (adventure, fantasy, humorous, mystery, science fiction, suspense—no stories relating to drugs, religion, or sex) (500–1,000 words). Poetry (4 lines to 500 words). Fillers—facts and short humor (30–300 words). Articles—general interest, crafts, humor, interview/profile, and newsworthy kids (350 words maximum).

Young Author's Magazine (YAM). 3015 Woodsdale Boulevard, Lincoln, NE 68502. All writing done by students. Personal experience articles, 1,000–2,500 words. Short stories (adventure, fantasy, humorous, mystery, or science fiction—preferred four-page maximum). Poetry (preferred 10 lines maximum).

Young Miss Magazine. "Through Your Eyes . . .," 685 Third Avenue, New York, NY 10017. Poetry page. Authors accompany submissions with a statement attesting to originality. Also "Youth Beat," where readers speak their own minds.

For a more extensive list of markets for young writers, see *Market Guide for Young Writers* by Kathy Henderson. Check your library or write P.O. Box 228, Sandusky, MI 48471. In addition to its lists of more than 100 markets and contests, it has many helpful tips, and it profiles young published authors. Also, keep your eyes open for local and state writing contests sponsored by local newspapers, civic organizations, teachers' organizations, and professional organizations.

List of Publishers

Allyn and Bacon
160 Gould Street
Needham Heights,
MA 02194

Apple Computer, Inc.
20525 Mariani
Cupertino, CA 95014

Berrent Publications, Inc.
1025 Northern Boulevard
Roslyn, NY 11576

Broderbund Software—Direct
P.O. Box 12947
San Rafael, CA 94913-2947

Childrens Press
5440 North Cumberland Avenue
Chicago, IL 60656

Christopher-Gordon Publishers, Inc.
480 Washington Street
Norwood, MA 02062

Continental Press, Inc.
520 East Bainbridge Street
Elizabethtown, PA 17022

Coronet
108 Wilmot Road
Dearfield, IL 60015

Curriculum Associates, Inc.
5 Esquire Road
North Billerica, MA 01862

Discis Knowledge Research
P.O. Box 45099
5150 Yonge Street
Toronto, ON M2N 6N2

Educational Testing Service/"BOOKWHIZ"
Library and Reference Services
Princeton, NJ 08541

Educators Publishing Service
75 Moulton Street
Cambridge, MA 02138

Free Spirit Publishing
400 First Avenue North,
Suite 616
Minneapolis, MN 55401

Globe/Fearon
500 Harbor Boulevard
Belmont, CA 94002

Harcourt Brace School Department
6277 Sea Harbor Drive
Orlando, FL 32887

HarperCollins
10 East 53rd Street
New York, NY 10022

DC Heath and Company
125 Spring Street
Lexington, MA 02173

Heinemann Educational Books,
Inc.
361 Hanover Street
Portsmouth, NH 03801

Houghton Mifflin Company
School Division
One Beacon Street
Boston, MA 02108

IBM Corporation
360 Hamilton Avenue
White Plains, NY 10601

Ideal School Supply
11000 South Lavergne
Oak Lawn, IL 60453

Jamestown Publishers
P.O. Box 9168
Providence, RI 02940

Jostens Learning
6170 Cornerstone Court East
San Diego, CA 92121-3710

Just Us Books, Inc.—Afro-Bets
301 Main Street, Suite 22-24
Orange, NJ 07050

Kendall/Hunt Publishing Company
4050 Westmark Drive
Dubuque, IA 52002

Lawrence Productions
1800 South 35th Street
Galesburg, MI 49053

Learning Links, Inc.
2300 Marcus Avenue
New Hyde Park, NY 11042

Macmillan/McGraw-Hill
School Publishing Company
866 Third Avenue
New York, NY 10022

MECC
6160 Summit Drive North
Minneapolis, MN 55430

Midwest Publications
P.O. Box 448
Pacific Grove, CA 93950-0448

Modern Curriculum Press,
Inc.
13900 Prospect Road
Cleveland, OH 44136

Newsweek Education
444 Madison Avenue
New York, NY 10022

Open Court Publishing Company
407 South Dearborn Street,
Suite 1300
Chicago, IL 60605

Richard C. Owen Publishers,
Inc.
135 Katonah Avenue
Katonah, NY 10536

Perfection Form Company
1000 North 2nd Avenue
Logan, IA 51546

Prentice-Hall School Division
113 Sylvan Avenue
Englewood Cliffs, NJ 07632

The Psychological Corporation
555 Academic Court
San Antonio, TX 78204

Random House
225 Park Avenue South
New York, NY 10003

Reading Is Fundamental, Inc.
600 Maryland Avenue, S.W., Suite
500
Washington, DC 20024

Rigby Education
P.O. Box 797
Crystal Lake, IL 60039-0797

Silver Burdett Ginn
250 James Street
Morristown, NJ 07960

Sports Illustrated for Kids
1271 Avenue of the Americas
New York, NY 10020

SRA School Group
250 Old Wilson Bridge Road, Suite
310
Worthington, OH 43085

Steck-Vaughn Company
P.O. Box 26015
Austin, TX 78755

Sunburst Communications
101 Castleton Street
Pleasantville, NY 10570

Sundance Publishers and Distributors
P.O. Box 1326—
Newtown Road
Littleton, MA 01460

TASA
Fields Lane, Box 382
Brewster, NY 10509

Teacher Support Software, Inc.
1035 N.W. 57th Street
Gainesville, FL 32605

Teachers College Press
1234 Amsterdam Avenue
New York, NY 10027

U.S. Department of Education
400 Maryland Avenue SW
Room 2089—FOB #6
Washington, DC 20202

Weekly Reader Corporation
245 Long Hill Road
Middletown, CT 06457

The Wright Group
19201 120th Avenue NE
Bothell, WA 98011

Write Source Educational Publishing House
P.O. Box 460
Burlington, WI 53105

Zaner-Bloser
P.O. Box 16764
Columbus, OH 43216-6764

Staff Development Needs Assessment

Please check areas of staff development in which you would like to participate. Then rank those in priority order.

___ ___ Classroom organization options

___ ___ Meeting the needs of hard-to-reach students

___ ___ Challenging accelerated students

___ ___ Cooperative learning

___ ___ Alternatives to seatwork

___ ___ Computers and reading/writing

___ ___ Word recognition strategies

___ ___ Vocabulary strategies

___ ___ Reading comprehension strategies

___ ___ Thinking skills/strategies

___ ___ Study skills/strategies

___ ___ Teaching the limited English proficient

___ ___ Teaching special education students

___ ___ Newspaper in Education

___ ___ Children's/young adult literature

___ ___ Multicultural teaching strategies

___ ___   Integrating reading and writing

___ ___   Spelling

___ ___   Reading and writing across the curriculum

___ ___   Writing process

___ ___   Journal writing

___ ___   Book reports

___ ___   Alternate means of assessment

___ ___   Update on research on reading/writing

___ ___   Teacher as researcher

___ ___   Understanding test scores

___ ___   Increasing parental involvement

___ ___   Grant writing

___ ___   Other: _____

_____

Please indicate the modes by which you would like to receive this staff development—for example, guest speaker, opportunities to visit fellow teacher, discussion of videotapes, discussion of professional readings, demonstration, hands-on experience, visits to my classroom, etc.

_____

_____

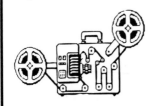

Audiovisual Tips

Follow these tips (Deep & Sussman, 1990, Warger & Moffett, 1988) for effective use of audiovisual materials.

When to Use Visual Aids

- Use visuals to get the audience's attention. Kick off the session with an attention-grabber such as a cartoon or quotation.

- Use visuals to emphasize key points. Ask yourself: What are the three to five issues participants should remember when they leave? One visual for each key concept is a good rule of thumb.

- Use visuals to present statistical data in an easy-to-read format, like a bar graph or pie chart.

How to Choose the Most Effective Media

- Consider your style, your message, and the size of your audience.
- Slides work well when they are high quality. They require a darkened room and should not involve note taking. They generally involve little, if any, audience participation and may be used with large groups.
- Video provides full motion visuals with integrated sound. Large-screen projection generally requires a darkened room and works well with large groups. Viewing video with television monitors works well with smaller groups and may not require a darkened room.
- Electronic media add interactivity to live presentations. They allow the presenter to include animation and special effects with slides and video. Large-screen projection may not require a darkened room.

How to Use Audiovisual Equipment

- Use your own equipment when you can. You know how to operate your equipment, how well it works, and that it will be there on time.

- Expect trouble. Have a back-up activity planned in case the equipment does not work.

- Be certain people throughout the room can see your visuals. Preview them from the same distance your audience will see them. Be sure they are not blocked by you, the lectern, or anything else.

- Speak to the audience, not the visual aid.

If you use films or videos, follow some of these pointers for before, during, and after viewing.

Position monitors where all can see them without annoying reflections on the screen. Close drapes or blinds if necessary.

If you use 35mm slides, follow this pointer:

Before

Preview programs to be sure they are not obviously dated. You do not want the audience to snicker and be distracted by clothing style.

Position monitorswhere all can see them without annoying reflections on the screen. Close drapes or blinds if necessary.

Ask small groups to brainstorm ideas on topics to be shown in the video. Discuss the predictions after the video is shown.

Ask participants to jot down a definition pertinent to the topic to be viewed, record some of the definitions on a chart, discuss them briefly, run the video segment, and then add to or alter the original definitions.

Use open-ended or directed vierwing work-sheets to channel observation and thinking about the content.

Use a "fishbowl" technique to foster response. For example, give half the group an assignment to discuss based on the video. The other viewers surround this group and watchsilently. After ten minutes, the groups trade places. The new group "in the fishbowl" responds to the first group's conclusions and develops the topic further.

Viewers pair off and react to the video's content.

If triads are used, one viewer can serve as recorder. A group representative then shares one idea with the larger group.

Use the "jigsaw" technique to allow viewers to become experts in particular aspects of the video and teach that topic to others in their group. First, participants are divided into "home groups." Then each member of each home group is assigned a different topic from the video. Viewers with like topics form an "expert group" to discuss what they've seen, highlight major points, and cite examples. When homegroups reconvene, these experts will teach the material they worked on in their expert groups.

During   *After*

If you use overheads, follow these pointers.

Making the Transparency

Use a horizontal format.

Put ten words or fewer and no more than six lines on an overhead.

Use both upper- and lower-case letters of at least one-half inch in height.

Leave space between lines.

Use no more than two typefaces. Add variety by changing the size and style of the text

If you use a computer that provides different typefaces, from traditional to frivolous, choose one that conveys the tone of your message.

Use color if possible.

Use charts and illustrations.

Use cartoons and humor.

Put captions on top and use the top two-thirds of the visual for images.

Use only clean transparencies. Use several simple overheads rather than one complex one.

Using the Transparency

Clean the lens and glass—especially underneath.

Focus and position the transparency so it is not under an overhead light.

Keep the lights on, except perhaps those closest to the screen.

Position the projector so image fills up most of the screen.

Point to items on the transparency.

Cover the projector's bulb between transparencies rather than providing a distraction by repeatedly turning it on and off.

Uncover information as you discuss it.

Figure on 15 to 20 seconds per transparency.

Use and write notes on the edge of the transparency rather than referring to pages of notes.

If you use 35 mm slides, follow this pointer:

- Make a duplicate of your best slide and insert it at the end of the tray to accompany closing remarks. This will reinforce the message.

Handout Tips

Follow these tips for effective use of handouts.

Types and Uses

- *A complete text of presentation:* For further in-depth study

- *A working outline—key spaces with blank spaces for notes:* To keep audience organized

- *Key ideas only:* As a refresher of the big picture

- *Supplemental readings:* For further study by interested participants

- *Charts/graphs:* For clarity and recall

- *"AH-HA" sheets:* To catch fleeting ideas; encourages audiences to write down ideas and to get involved

- *No handouts:* No use—leaves audience with a feeling of something missing

Helpful Hints

- Use people's names or the organization's name in the copy.

- Use colored paper, colored ink, and/or illustrations. Use one main color and, if needed, only two or three others. Too many can be confusing. Use light colors on a dark background for highlighting. Be consistent—always choose the same color for the same element.

- Use large type for easier reading and leave white space.

- Use a different computer typeface or a headline-making machine for key points and titles.

- Always have materials that look professional, with careful proofreading, clear printing, and the like.

- Keep handouts current if you want them to be effective.
- Run off a few extra copies of your handout—promising to send copies just isn't the same as having them on hand.

- If you will not be working with your handouts, distribute them at the end of the session to encourage listening rather than reading during your presentation.

- Honor copyrights—always obtain permission to reprint.

- Customize handouts for your audience.

- Give people permission to copy your handouts for responsible use.

Grant Writing

You may be interested in writing a grant to initiate a new instructional program, fund a motivational reading effort, or support a research project. Grants are available though federal, state, and local governments, as well as businesses, philanthropic foundations, and professional organizations. Some university faculty members interested in educational research will co-author grants with district or school personnel. Money for good ideas is available, but securing grant funds does take some effort. Here are some suggestions for writing grants. Included in this list are a number of secrets of successful grantwriters (O'Connor, 1990):

1. Activate your grant radar! Start looking for funding sources at your public library. Call the appropriate office at your local school district and your state department of education. You may have to dig to find the right funding source for your project.

2. Start with a small grant to get exposure to the grant-writing process.

3. After you find a call for proposals that seems to fit your needs, read the proposal carefully. Once your idea is fleshed out, call the funding source. They will usually tell you whether your idea fits with what they had in mind. Also, you may win an advocate.

4. Make a list of all required grant components, and set a timeline for completion of each. If possible, give yourself twice as much time as you think you'll need. This will allow for collective brainstorming and for drafting and extending ideas after completion of a first draft, as well as for having colleagues help with revising and editing. Be sure to include among your helpers someone who has successful grant-writing experience. Building in time for collaboration throughout the process not only enhances the grant but also helps to extend its ownership.

5. If the grant requires paperwork from other persons (e.g., resumés or letters of support), request it early.

6. Format your proposal according to the structure suggested in the call for proposals. Reviewers may deduct points if you organize your proposal in a different way or if the proposal does not conform to length requirements.

7. Make sure all parts of the grant are consistent—the plan itself, the budget, the evaluation, and the abstract.

8. Make your proposal easy to read by using simple English and making use of an outline format where appropriate.

9. Be positive and enthusiastic. Don't bemoan budget cuts.

10. Put all important information in the proposal itself, not in an appendix.

11. Make certain that the proposal contains all components requested in the call for proposals. Incomplete proposals may be rejected automatically.

12. If an abstract of project summary is required, spend a great deal of time polishing this piece. The abstract may be your best opportunity to "sell" your project to hurried reviewers. Generally, it should be no more than one page long. It should (1) state simply and clearly what your project is about, (2) tell how you'll achieve your aim, and (3) describe any relevant philosophies.

13. Include explicit statements explaining how your project's objectives are consistent with those delineated by the funding agency. For example, if the agency is seeking literacy projects that are replicable and sustainable, then explain in detail how your project plans to meet those objectives.

14. Include a resumé that is up to date and complete. Provide a biographical sketch that highlights your training and experiences that relate to the management of the proposed project.

15. When you prepare your budget, do your homework. Make calls rather than estimating. Enlist the help of a colleague to double-check your budget calculations.

16. Accompany your budget with a narrative that identifies each item with a couple of lines, so that a hurried reviewer who looks only at the abstract and the budget will see that you have thought out your plan.

17. Allow enough time to polish your final draft. Laser printing and graphics help. Use plenty of headings and subheadings, and boldface key ideas.

18. Before mailing, do a thorough final check for each of the proposal elements.

19. Funding agencies often have stringent deadlines for proposals. Keep a post office receipt to verify that you mailed the proposal on time.

20. Keep trying. Proposals, even those written by experienced grant writers, often are not funded on the first submission. Use reviewers' comments to revise your proposal. Then, try another agency or enter the same agency's next competition.

21. Acknowledge your donors. Write thank-you letters, mention donors in your program, and send them project souvenirs.

For further information, see:

Locke, L. F., Spirduso, W. W., & Silverman, S. J. (1987). *Proposals that work,* 2nd ed. Newbury Park, CA: Sage Publications.

Text Friendliness Checklist

Reader Tools

Table of Contents	Yes	No
Comprehensive Glossary	Yes	No
Comprehensive Index	Yes	No
Useful Appendix	Yes	No

Background

1. Are the assumptions about students' vocabulary, prior knowledge about the content, and experiential background appropriate? — Yes — Sometimes — No
2. Are students reminded about the information they already know about a topic? — Yes — Sometimes — No

Organization

1. Does the author provide questions or statements that help guide the student in reading the chapter? — Yes — Sometimes — No
2. Do new units or chapters begin with a general introduction of the content, with chapter contents then following logically? — Yes — Sometimes — No
3. Do the topics and subtopics specify the main ideas of the chapters? — Yes — Sometimes — No
4. Is the number of visual aids sufficient? — Yes — Sometimes — No
5. Are visual aids placed on the same page as the written information related to the aid? — Yes — Sometimes — No
6. Do consumable materials interrelate well with the textbook? — Yes — Sometimes — No

Motivation

1. In introducing a new concept, does the author use motivational devices (practical examples, cartoons, etc.) to make the reading interesting? — Yes — Sometimes — No
2. Are topic presentations likely to make students want to pursue the topic further? — Yes — Sometimes — No

3. Are the cover, format, print size, and pictures appealing?	Yes	Sometimes	No
4. Are there positive and motivating models for both sexes and for different racial and ethnic groups?	Yes	Sometimes	No

Readability

1. Are key concepts highlighted with underlining, boldface, or italics?	Yes	Sometimes	No
2. Are sentences generally of an appropriate length—not too long?	Yes	Sometimes	No
3. Are most verbs in the active voice?	Yes	Sometimes	No
4. Are abstract concepts introduced with sufficient examples to make the concepts comprehensible?	Yes	Sometimes	No
5. Are there explicit signals for examples (e.g., *for example, such as*)?	Yes	Sometimes	No
6. Are explicit signals used to indicate sequencing of ideas (*first, second, next*)?	Yes	Sometimes	No
7. Are emphasis words used to indicate important concepts (*most of all, a key feature, a significant factor*)?	Yes	Sometimes	No
8. Are explicit signals used to indicate comparisons (*but, however, on the other hand*)?	Yes	Sometimes	No
9. Are explicit signals used for conclusions (*therefore, as a result*)?	Yes	Sometimes	No
10. Are there fewer than 5 new vocabulary words in 100-word passages?	Yes	Sometimes	No
11. Are new vocabulary words introduced with sufficient context (definitions, examples, contrasts, support for inferences)?	Yes	Sometimes	No
12. Does the writing flow in a simple to more complex progression?	Yes	Some times	No
13. Are there a sufficient number of details without the inclusion of superfluous details?	Yes	Sometimes	No

Review

1. Is there a summary of essential concepts at the end of chapters?	Yes	Sometimes	No

2. Are review sections keyed to specific book
   sections to allow for easy review?   Yes   Sometimes   No
3. Are questions clearly worded?   Yes   Sometimes   No
4. Do questions and activities draw attention
   to the organizational pattern of the material
   (e.g., chronological, cause–effect, spatial,
   topical)?   Yes   Sometimes   No
5. Do discussion questions help students eval-
   uate the information in the text? Analyze it?
   Generate their own ideas?   Yes   Sometimes   No

Teacher Friendliness

1. Are there useful suggestions for special
   needs students?   Yes   Sometimes   No
2. Are there useful enrichment activities
   suggested?   Yes   Sometimes   No
3. Are there lists of accessible resources with
   alternative readings for very poor or very
   advanced students?   Yes   Sometimes   No

A p p e n d i x D

Lists of Books and Nonprint Media

Resources for Parents

Books

Barron, M. (1990). *I learn to read and write the way I learn to talk.* Katonah, NJ: Owen.

Binkley, M. R. (1988). *Becoming a nation of readers: What parents can do.* Washington, DC: U.S. Department of Education.

Butler, D., & Clay, M. (1987). *Reading begins at home,* rev. ed. Portsmouth, NH: Heinemann.

Graves, R. (Ed.). (1987). *Reading is fundamental: Guide to encouraging young readers.* New York: Doubleday.

Kimmel, M. M., & Segal, E. (1988). *For reading out loud! A guide to sharing books with children.* New York: Delacorte.

Lipson, E. R. (1991). *The New York Times parent's guide to the best books for children.* New York: Random House.

Radencich, M. C., & Schumm, J. S. (1988). *How to help your child with homework.* Minneapolis, MN: Free Spirit Publishing.

Russell, W. (1992). *Classics to read aloud to your children.* Knob Noster, MO: Crown.

Taylor, D., & Strickland, D. (1986). *Family storybook reading.* Portsmouth, NH: Heinemann.

Trelease, J. (1989). *The new read-aloud handbook.* New York: Penguin.

Resources from Professional Organizations

International Reading Association, 800 Barksdale Road, P.O. Box 8139, Newark, DE 19714.

Baghban, M. *How can I help my child learn to read English as a second language?* (This publication as also been translated into Spanish by R. L. García and R. M. Deyoe.)

Baghban, M. *You can help your young child with writing.*
Beverstock, C. *Your child's vision is important.*
Chan, J. *Why read aloud to children?*
Eberly, D. W. *How does my child's vision affect his reading?*
Glazer, S. M. *Creating readers and writers.*
Glazer, S. M. *How can I help my child build positive attitudes toward reading?*
Grinnel, P. C. *How can I prepare my young child for reading?*
Idaho Literacy Project. *Read to me.* (a videotape for parents)
Myers, J. *You can encourage your high school student to read.*
Ransbury, M. K. *How you can encourage your primary grade child to read.*
Reed, A. *Comics to classics: A parent's guide to books for teens and preteens.*
Roser, N. L. *Helping your child become a reader.*
Shefelbine, J. *Encouraging your junior high student to read.*
Silvern, S. B., & Silvern, L. R. *Beginning literacy and your child.*
Winebrenner, R. *How can I get my teenager to read?*

> Note: *IRA also offers single copies of brochures for parents at no charge. When request-ing copies, please enclose a self-addressed, stamped envelope:*

- "Good Books Make Reading Fun for Your Child"

- "Summer Reading Is Important"

- "You Can Encourage Your Child to Read"

- "Your Home Is Your Child's First School"

American Library Association, 50 East Huron Street, Chicago, IL 60611.
> *The ALA develops book lists for a variety of age groups.*

National Council for Teachers of English, 1111 Kenyon Road, Urbana, IL 61801.
> *NCTE offers brochures for parents.*

- "How to Help Your Child Become a Better Writer"

- "How to Help Your Child Become a Better Reader"

Reading is Fundamental, Inc. (RIF), 600 Maryland Avenue, S.W., Washington, DC 20024.
> *RIF offers brochures for parents.*

- "Children Who Can Read, but Don't"

- "Choosing Good Books for Children"

- "TV and Reading"

- "Upbeat and Offbeat Activities to Encourage Reading"

Professional Resources

P = Preschool   E = Elementary   S = Secondary (Middle/Senior)   A = Adult

Books

Atwell, N. (1987). *In the middle*. Portsmouth, NH: Heinemann. (S)

Bos, C. S., & Vaughn, S. (1991). *Strategies for teaching students with learning and behavior problems*, 2nd ed. Boston: Allyn and Bacon. (E/S)

Calkins, L. (1986). *The art of teaching writing*. Portsmouth, NH: Heinemann. (E)

Calkins, L., & Harwayne, S. (1991). *Living between the lines*. Portsmouth, NH: Heinemann. (E)

Cunningham, P. M. (1991). *Phonics they use: Words for reading and writing*. New York: HarperCollins. (E)

Cunningham, P. M., & Allington, R. L. (1993). *Classrooms that work—They can all read and write*. New York: HarperCollins. (E)

Duffy, G. G. (Ed.). (1991). *Reading in the middle school*. Newark, DE: International Reading Association. (S)

Fry, E. B., Polk, J. K., & Fountoukidis, D. (1984). *The reading teacher's book of lists*. Englewood Cliffs, NJ: Prentice-Hall. (E/S/A)

Goodman, K. S., Bird, L. B., & Goodman, Y. M. (1991). *The whole language catalog*. Santa Rosa, CA: American School Publishers. (E/S)

Graves, D. (1983). *Writing: Teachers and children at work*. Portsmouth, NH: Heinemann. (E/S)

Gueulette, D. G. (Ed.). (1986). *Using technology in adult education*. Glenview, IL: Scott, Foresman. Washington, DC: American Association for Adult and Continuing Education. (A)

Gunderson, L. (1991). *ESL literacy instruction: A guidebook to theory and practice*. Englewood Cliffs, NJ: Regents/Prentice-Hall. (E/S)

Heald-Taylor, G. (1990). *The administrator's guide to whole language*. Katonah, NY: Owen. (E)

Irwin, J. W., & Baker, I. (1990). *Promoting active reading comprehension strategies*. Englewood Cliffs, NJ: Prentice-Hall. (E/S)

Kasten, W. C., & Clarke, B. K. (1993). *The multi-age classroom—A family of learners*. Katonah, NY: Owen. (E)

Merriam, S. B. (Ed.) (1986). *Being responsive to adult learners*. Glenview, IL: Scott, Foresman. Washington, DC: American Association for Adult and Continuing Education. (A)

Miller-Lachmann, L. (1992). *Our family, our friends, our world*. New Providence, NJ: Bowker. (E/S)

Mocker, D. W. (Ed.) (1986). *Teaching reading to adults*. Glenview, IL: Scott, Foresman. Washington, DC: American Association for Adult and Continuing Education. (A)

Monahan, J. N., & Hinson, B. (1988). *New directions in reading instruction.* Newark, DE: International Reading Association. (E/S/A)

Morrow, L. M. (1993). *Literacy development in the early years.* Boston: Allyn and Bacon. (P/E)

National Council of Teachers of English. (1984–). *Ideas Plus series.* Urbana, IL: Author. (S)

Radencich, M. C., Beers, P. G., & Schumm, J. S. (1993). *Handbook for the K–12 Reading Resource Specialist.* Boston: Allyn and Bacon. (E/S)

Radencich, M. C., & McKay, L. (Eds.). (in press). *Grouping for literacy in the elementary grades.* Newark, DE: International Reading Association. (E)

Readence, J. E., Bean, T. W., & Baldwin, R. S. (1992). *Content area reading: An integrated approach,* 4th ed. Dubuque, IA: Kendall/Hunt. (S)

Rosenthal, N. (1987). *Teach someone to read—A step-by-step guide for literacy tutors.* Belmont, CA: Fearon. (A)

Routman, R. (1991). *Invitations: Changing as teacher and learner.* Portsmouth, NH: Heinemann. (E/S)

Taylor, S. E., Frackenpohl, H., & White, C. E. (1979). *EDL core vocabularies in reading, mathematics, science, and social studies.* New York: McGraw-Hill. (E/S)

Tierney, R. J., Readence, J. E., & Dishner, E. K. (1990). *Reading strategies and practices: A compendium,* 3rd ed. Boston: Allyn and Bacon. (E/S/A)

Yatvin, J. (1992). *Developing a whole language program for a whole school.* Newark, DE: International Reading Association. (E)

Other Resources

American Library Association. *Book Links: Connecting Books Libraries and Classrooms.* A thematic publication issued six times a year (*Book Links* Subscriptions, P.O. Box 1347, Elmhurst, IL 60126-1420). (E)

Association for Supervision and Curriculum Development (ASCD). *Educational Leadership.* A monthly journal (1250 North Pitt Street, Alexandria, VA 22314-1403). (P/E/S/A)

Calkins, L. *The writing workshop—A world of difference.* Videotape with staff development guide (Heinemann, 361 Hanover Street, Portsmouth, NH 03801-3959). (E)

Center for the Study of Reading. (1991). *The reading/writing connection.* Videotape in "Teaching Reading: Strategies from Successful Classrooms," six-part series (University of Illinois at Urbana-Champaign, 51 Gerty Drive, Champaign, IL 61820). (E)

Christopher-Gordon Publishers. *The New Advocate.* A quarterly journal (Christopher-Gordon Publishers, 480 Washington Street, Norwood, MA 02062). (E)

International Reading Association. *Journal of Reading.* A monthly journal (P.O. Box 8139, Newark, DE, 19714). (S/A)

International Reading Association. *The Reading Teacher.* A monthly journal (P.O. Box 8139, Newark, DE, 19714). (E)

International Reading Association. *Reading Today.* A bimonthly newspaper (P.O. Box 8139, Newark, DE, 19714). (E/S/A)

International Reading Association. *Secondary School Reading.* A position statement (P.O. Box 8139, Newark, DE, 19714). (S)

National Association for the Education of Young Children (NAEYC). *Young Children.* A monthly journal (1834 Connecticut Avenue, N.W., Washington, DC 20009). (P)

National Council of Teachers of English. *English Journal.* A monthly journal (1111 Kenyon Road, Urbana, IL 61801). (S)

National Council of Teachers of English. *Language Arts.* A monthly journal (1111 Kenyon Road, Urbana, IL 61801) (E)

National Council of Teachers of English. *Primary Voices K–6.* A quarterly journal (1111 Kenyon Road, urbana, IL 61801). (E)

Phi Delta Kappa (PDK). *Phi Delta Kappan.* A monthly journal (P.O. Box 789, Bloomington, IN 47402). (P/E/S/A)

Predictable Language Books

Levels refer to average kindergarten and less proficient first-grade children being able to remember most of the text as follows:

> Level I—following one or two read-alouds
> Level II—following two or three read-alouds
> Level III—following three or four read-alouds

Predictable Language Trade Books

Level I

Brown, R. (1981). *A dark dark tale.* New York: Dial Press.
Ginsburg, M. (1972). *The chick and the duckling.* New York: Macmillan.
Krauss, R. (1948). *Bears.* New York: Scholastic.
Langstaff, J. (1974). *Oh, a-hunting we will go.* New York: Atheneum.
Mack, S. (1974). *10 bears in my bed.* New York: Pantheon.
Martin, B. (1983). *Brown bear, brown bear, what do you see?* New York: Holt, Rinehart & Winston.
Peek, M. (1985). *Mary wore her red dress and Henry wore his green sneakers.* New York: Clarion.
Robart, R. (1986). *The cake that Mack ate.* Glenview, IL: Scott Foresman.

Level II

Becker, J. (1973). *Seven little rabbits.* New York: Scholastic.
Brown, M. W. (1952). *Where have you been?* New York: Scholastic.
Hutchins, P. (1972). *Goodnight owl.* New York: Macmillan.
Kalin, R. (1981). *Jump, frog, jump.* New York: Scholastic.
Quackenbush, R. (1973). *She'll be comin' 'round the mountain.* Philadelphia: Lippincott.
Westcott, N. B. (1987). *Peanut butter and jelly.* New York: Dutton.
Zolotow, C. (1969). *Some things go together.* New York: Crowell.

Level III

Aliki. (1974). *Go tell Aunt Rhody.* New York: Macmillan.
Galdone, P. (1984). *The teeny tiny woman.* Boston: Houghton Mifflin.
Guarino, D. (1989). *Is your mama a llama?* New York: Scholastic.
Langstaff, J. (1957). *Over in the meadow.* New York: Harcourt Brace Jovanovich.
Westcott, N. B. (1988). *The lady with the alligator purse.* Boston: Little, Brown.

Predictable Language Books from Commercial Series (One Sample per Series)

Level I

Allen, R. V. (1985). *I love ladybugs.* Allen, TX: DLM. Predictable Storybooks, Set 1.
Cairns, S. (1986). *Oh no!.* Crystal Lake, IL: Rigby. More Traditional Tales and Con-
temporary Stories.
Cowley, J. (1980). *Mrs. Wishy-Washy.* San Diego: The Wright Group. The Story Box
Read-Together.
Nellie Edge Big Books. (1988). *Teddy bear, Teddy bear.* Salem, OR: Resources for Crea-
tive Teaching. Nellie Edge Big Books.
Nelson, J. (1989). *There's a dragon in my wagon.* Cleveland: Modern Curriculum Press.
Reading Friends.
Robinson, E. (1987). *If I had a dragon.* Allen, TX: DLM. Read-aloud Predictable Story-
books.
Skelly, A. (1989). *If you're happy.* Crystal Lake, IL: Rigby. Literacy 2000, Stage 4, Set A.

Level II

Allen, C. (1986). *Beautiful breezy blue and white day.* Allen, TX: DLM. Predictable
Storybooks, Set 2.
Allen, R. V. (1987). *Eating peanuts.* Allen, TX: DLM. Read-Aloud Predictable Story-
books.
Blocksma, M. (1984). *Rub-a-dub-dub, What's in the tub?* Chicago: Children's Press. Just
One More.
Greenes, C. (1989). *Rebecca's party.* Allen, TX: DLM. Math Predictable Storybooks.
Martin, B., & Archambault, J. (1987). *Here are my hands.* Allen, TX: DLM. Bobber
Books.
Parkes, B. (1986). *Who's in the shed?* Melbourne: Rigby. Traditional Tales, Rhymes,
and Contemporary Stories.

Level III

Lucky, S. (1989). *There's a moose and a goose in the caboose.* Allen, TX: DLM. The Bill
Martin Jr. Library.
Robinson, E. (1987). *The dinosaur ball.* Allen, TX: DLM. Predictable Storybooks, Set 3.

Robinson, E. (1989). *The garden walked away.* Allen, TX: DLM. Science Predictable Storybooks.

Source: Adapted from M. C. Radencich & A. G. McKinney, "Brown Bear, Brown Bear, What Do You See?—Levels for Predictables: 1, 2, 3, " Florida Reading Quarterly, 29 (1993), 5–14.

Read-Aloud Lists

Following is a listing of favorite read-aloud books for primary, intermediate, and secondary (middle/senior high) students. For additional books, refer to *Kids' Favorite Books* (International Reading Association/Children's Book Council, 1991) or *The New Read-Aloud Handbook* (Trelease, 1989).

Primary Read-Aloud List

Allard, H. (1978). *Miss Nelson is missing.* New York: Scholastic.
Allard, H. (1974, 1977). *The Stupids step out.* Boston: Houghton Mifflin.
Allsburg, C. V. (1989). *The polar express.* Boston: Houghton Mifflin.
Bemelmans, L. (1939). *Madeline.* New York: Viking.
Bonne, R. (1987). *I know an old lady.* New York: Scholastic.
Brown, M. (1988). *The three billy goats gruff.* New York: Harcourt Brace Jovanovich.
Brown, M. (1989). *Once a mouse.* New York: Scribner.
Brown, M. W. (1984). *Goodnight moon.* New York: Harper.
Buffet, J., & Buffet, S. (1988). *The jolly mon.* New York: Crowell.
Carle, E. (1986). *The very hungry caterpillar.* New York: Putnam.
Cohen, M. (1977). *When will I read?* New York: Greenwillow.
Delacre, L. (1989). *Arroz con leche: Popular songs and rhymes from Latin America.* New York: Scholastic.
de Paola, T. (1978). *Pancakes for breakfast.* New York: Harcourt Brace Jovanovich.
Flournoy, V. (1985). *The patchwork quilt.* New York: Dial.
Gag, W. (1928, 1977). *Millions of cats.* New York: Coward, McCann.
Guy, R. (1980). *Mother crocodile.* New York: Delacorte.
Hamilton, V. (1985). *American black folktales.* New York: Knopf.
Keats, J. (1964). *Whistle for Willie.* New York: Viking.
McCloskey, R. (1976). *Make way for ducklings.* New York: Viking.
Martin, B. (1983). *Brown bear, brown bear, what do you see?* New York: Holt, Rinehart & Winston.
Parish, P. (1970). *Amelia Bedelia.* New York: Scholastic.
Prelutsky, J. (1983). *The Random House book of poetry.* New York: Random House.
Rey, H. A. (1973). *Curious George.* Boston: Houghton Mifflin.
Sendak, M. (1988). *Where the wild things are.* New York: Harper.
Seuling, B. (1975). *You can't eat peanuts in church and other little-known laws.* New York: Doubleday.
Seuss, D. (1989). *The 500 hats of Bartholomew Cubbins.* New York: Vanguard.
Sharmat, M. (1984). *Gregory the terrible eater.* New York: Four Winds.

Stevenson, R. L. (1989). *A child's garden of verses.* Chicago: Contemporary.
Stover, J. (1989). *If everybody did.* New York: David McKay.
Tudor, T. (1961). *Tasha Tudor's book of fairy tales.* New York: Putnam.
Viorst, J. (1972). *Alexander and the terrible, horrible, no good, very bad day.* New York: Atheneum.
Wood, A. (1984). *The napping house.* New York: Harcourt Brace Jovanovich.
Zemach, M. (1965). *The teeny tiny woman.* New York: Scholastic.

Intermediate Read-Aloud List

Aliki. (1976). *Corn is maize—The gift of the Indians.* New York: Crowell.
Asimov, I. (1977). *How did we find out about outer space?* New York: Walker.
Blume, J. (1972). *Tales of a fourth grade nothing.* New York: Dutton.
Brink, C. R. (1935, 1973). *Caddie Woodlawn.* New York: Macmillan.
Burnett, F. H. (1989). *The secret garden.* New York: Viking.
Burnford, S. (1977). *The incredible journey.* Boston: Little, Brown.
Cisneros, S. (1991). *House on Mango Street.* New York: Random House.
Collier, J. L., & Collier, C. (1987). *Jump ship to freedom.* New York: Dell.
Dahl, R. (1990). *James and the giant peach.* New York: Knopf.
Cleary, B. (1968). *Ramona the pest.* New York: Morrow.
Estes, E. (1944). *The hundred dresses.* New York: Harcourt Brace Jovanovich.
Farley, W. (1941). *The black stallion.* New York: Random House.
Fitzgerald, J. D. (1985). *The great brain.* New York: Dell.
Graham, A., & Graham, F. (1981). *The changing desert.* New York: Sierra Club/Scribner.
Hunt, I. (1987). *Across five Aprils.* Chicago: Follett.
L'Engle, M. (1962). *A wrinkle in time.* New York: Farrar, Straus & Giroux.
McCloskey, R. (1943). *Homer Price.* New York: Puffin.
Manes, S. (1987). *Be a perfect person in just three days!* New York: Bantam.
Montgomery, L. M. (1908). *Anne of Green Gables.* Cutchogue, NY: Buccaneer Books.
Newman, R. (1984). *The case of the Baker Street irregulars.* New York: Atheneum.
Norton, M. (1952). *The borrowers.* New York: Harcourt Brace Jovanovich.
Rockwell, T. (1973). *How to eat fried worms.* New York: Watts.
Silverstein, S. (1974). *Where the sidewalk ends.* New York: Harper.
Simon, S. (1980). *Strange mysteries from around the world.* New York: Four Winds.
Sobol, D. J. (1970). *Encyclopedia Brown saves the day.* Nashville, TN: Nelson.
Stevenson, R. L. (1947). *Treasure island.* New York: Grosset & Dunlap.
Wagner, J. (1971). *J.T.* New York: Dell.
White, E. B. (1952). *Charlotte's web.* New York: Harper & Row.
Wilder, L. I. (1975). *Little house on the prairie.* New York: Harper & Row.
Yolen, J. (1986). *Favorite folktales from around the world.* New York: Pantheon.

Secondary Read-Aloud List

Adams, R. (1974). *Watership down.* New York: Macmillan.
Allende, I. (1991). *Stories of Eva Luna.* New York: Macmillan.
Alvarez, J. (1991). *How the García girls lost their accents. New York: Algonquin.*
Angelou, M. (1972). *I know why the caged bird sings.* New York: Random House.

Armstrong, W. H. (1989). *Sounder*. New York: Harper & Row.
Asimov, I. (Ed.). (1978). *100 great science fiction short stories*. New York: Doubleday.
Auel, J. M. (1984). *The clan of the cave bear*. New York: Crown.
Blume, J. (1981). *Tiger eyes*. New York: Dell.
Bradbury, R. (1973). *When elephants last in the dooryard bloomed*. New York: Knopf.
Cerf, B. (Ed.). (1955). *Great modern short stories*. New York: Random House.
Cohen, D. (1990). *The ghosts of war*. New York: Putnam.
Du Maurier, D. (1948). *Rebecca*. New York: Doubleday.
Frank, A. (1967). *Anne Frank: The diary of a young girl*. New York: Doubleday.
Gaines, E. (1982). *Autobiography of Miss Jane Pittman*. New York: Dial.
Greene, B. (1973). *Summer of my German soldier*. New York: Bantam.
Hamilton, E. (1942). *Mythology*. Boston: Little, Brown.
Harris, R. (Ed.). (1982). *Best selling chapters*. Providence, RI: Jamestown.
Herriot, J. (1974). *All things bright and beautiful*. Boston: St. Martin's.
Hinton, S. E. (1968). *The Outsiders*. New York: Dell.
Hughes, L. (1990). *Selected poems of Langston Hughes*. New York: Random House.
Janeczko, P. B. (1990). *The place my words are looking for: What poets say about and through their work*. Scarsdale, NY: Bradbury.
Lee, H. (1988). *To kill a mockingbird*. New York: Warner.
O'Dell, S. (1990). *Island of the blue dolphins*. Boston: Houghton Mifflin.
Paterson, K. (1977). *Bridge to Terabithia*. New York: Crowell.
Peck, R. N. (1972). *A day no pigs would die*. New York: Knopf.
Rawls, W. (1974). *Where the red fern grows*. New York: Bantam.
Rooney, A. (1987). *A few minutes with Andy Rooney*. New York: Atheneum.
Tolkien, J. R. R. (1973). *The hobbit*. Boston: Houghton Mifflin.

Suggested Readings for Students

Published Lists

1. *Children's Choices*: Since 1975, *The Reading Teacher* (a journal of the International Reading Association) has published an annual listing of children's book choices in the October issue. Books that a sample of 10,000 students like best are presented as an annotated bibliography and are categorized as follows: all ages, younger readers, middle grades, older readers. Children's choices from 1989 to 1991 are now available in monograph form (International Reading Association/Children's Book Council, 1991). If you would like to distribute the annual listing to teachers, reprints are available from IRA in bulk:
   International Reading Association
   P.O. Box 8139
   Newark, DE 19714-8139

2. *Young Adult Choices*: Since 1987, the *Journal of Reading* (a journal of the International Reading Association) has published an annual listing of choices of middle school and high school readers in the November issue.

Young adults' choices from 1987 to 1992 are now available in monograph form (International Reading Association, 1992). As with Children's Choices, reprints of the annotated lists are also available from IRA.

3. Updates on Newbery and Caldecott Medal Books.

4. Updates on other awards (e.g., Coretta Scott King Award, Children's Book Council, American Institute of Graphic Arts):
   Children's Books: Awards and Prizes
   Children's Book Council
   67 Irving Place
   New York, NY 10003

5. Lists in book form:
   Webb, C. A. (1993). *Your reading—A booklist for junior high and middle school*, 9th ed.
   Wurth, S. (1992). *Books for you—A booklist for senior high students*, 11th ed.
   National Council of Teachers of English
   1111 West Kenyon Road
   Urbana, IL 61801

6. *Newspaper reviews*: The *New York Times* and the *Christian Science Monitor* both publish reviews of books for children and adolescents. *The Book Review Index* (Gale Research Company) also provides information about where a book has been reviewed.

7. *Magazine reviews*: Regular book reviews appear in the following professional journals:

   — *Booklist* (American Library Association, 50 East Huron, Chicago, IL 60611)
   — *The Horn Book* (14 Beacon Street, Boston, MA 02108)
   — *Language Arts* (National Council of Teachers of English, 1111 Kenyon Road, Urbana, IL 60801)
   — *The New Advocate* (Christopher-Gordon Publishers, 480 Washington Street, Norwood, MA 02062)
   — *The Reading Teacher* (International Reading Association, P.O. Box 8139, Newark, DE 19714-8139)
   — *Journal of Reading* (International Reading Association, P.O. Box 8139, Newark, DE 19714-8139)
   — *School Library Journal* (R. R. Bowker Company, 121 Chanlon Road, New Providence, NJ 07974)

See also:
Stoll, D. R. (Ed.). (1990). *Magazines for children*. Glassboro, NJ: Educational Press Association of America. Newark, DE: International Reading Association.

Readings for Less Proficient Senior High and Adult Readers

Readings to spark discussion and debate (Aaron, 1990):
"Why I Went to the Woods"—Henry David Thoreau
"Civil Disobedience"—Henry David Thoreau
"Self-Reliance"—Ralph Waldo Emerson
"I Have a Dream"—Martin Luther King
"The Drum Major Instinct"—Martin Luther King
"The American Crisis"—Thomas Paine
"Richard Cory"—Edwin Arlington Robinson
"The Gettysburg Address"—Abraham Lincoln
"The Declaration of Independence"—Thomas Jefferson
"For White Only"—Dick Gregory
Readings to study identity and success (Aaron, 1990):
"Who Am I"—Felice Holman
"I Am"—June Jordan
"Clothes Make the Man"—Henri Duvernois
"Fight"—Richard Wright
"The Confrontation"—Raymond Barrio
"Be Someone Who Knows What You Want in Life"—Albert Schweitzer
"Journey Towards Your Dream"—Robert Louis Stevenson
"You Can Succeed"—Marycarol B. Soistman
"Celebrate Life"—Collin McCarty
"Let Go of the Past"—Kathleen O'Brien
"Hold On"—Collin McCarty
"Believe in Yourself"—Sherrie Householder
Classic novels with quality adaptations/abridgements (Schierloh, 1992):
Bronte, C. (1987). *Jane Eyre.* Adapted and abridged by S. E. Paces. Belmont, CA: David S. Lake.
Dickens, C. (1987). *Great expectations.* Adapted and bridged by T. E. Bethancourt. Belmont, CA: David S. Lake.
Haggard, H. R. (1976). *King Solomon's mines.* Retold by J. Oxley. New York: Oxford.
King Arthur and his knights. (1988). Adapted by W. Kottmeyer, New York: Phoenix.
Stephenson, R. L. (1985). *Dr. Jeckyll and Mr. Hyde.* Adapted and abridged by T. E. Bethancourt. Belmont, CA: David S. Lake.
Stevenson, R. L. (1988). *Kidnapped.* Adapted and abridged by W. Kottmeyer. New York: Phoenix.
Stevenson, R. L. (1973). *Treasure Island.* Adapted and abridged by J. Gray. Belmont, CA: David S. Lake.
Wells, H. G. (1986). *The time machine.* Adapted and abridged by T. E. Bethancourt. Belmont, CA: David S. Lake.
Picture books (adapted from Danielson, 1992):

For dialect and character development
Aylesworth, J. (1988). *Hanna's hog.* New York: Atheneum. (Rural American)
Chapman, C. (1980). *The tale of Meshka the Kvetch.* New York: Dutton. (Yiddish dialect)

Kimmel, E. A. (1989). *Charlie drives the stage*. New York: Holiday House. (American Old West slang)

McKissack, P. (1988). *Mirandy and Brother Wind*. New York: Knopf. (American southern Black)

Purdy, C. (1985). *Iva Dunnit and the big wind*. New York: Dial. (American Old West slang)

For vocabulary

Baese, G. (1987). *Animalia*. New York: Abrams.

Gwynne, F. (1970a). *A chocolate moose for dinner*. Englewood Cliffs, NJ: Prentice-Hall.

Gwynne, F. (1970b). *The king who rained*. Englewood Cliffs, NJ: Prentice-Hall.

Parish, P. (1986). *Amelia Bedelia*. New York: Harper & Row.

For jargon and lingo

Day, A. (1988). *Frank and Ernest*. New York: Scholastic. (lunch counter lingo)

Day, A. (1990). *Frank and Ernest play ball*. New York: Scholastic. (baseball terminology)

For parts of speech

Heller, R. (1987). *A cache of jewels* and other collective nouns. New York: Grosset & Dunlap. (collective nouns in rhyme)

Heller, R. (1988). *Kites sail high*. New York: Grosset & Dunlap. (verbs in rhyme)

Heller, R. (1989). *Many luscious lollipops*. New York: Grosset & Dunlap. (adjectives)

Heller, R. (1990). *Merry-go-round*. New York: Grosset & Dunlap. (all kinds of nouns in rhyme)

Appendix E

Student Assistance

Strategy for Helping Students Find the "Right" Book

Have you been to a bookstore lately? Bookstores in the 1990s are lively, colorful, exciting places that offer thousands of choices of things to read. But many people still say, "I don't read because it's boring." It may well be that such people just haven't found the RIGHT BOOK!!!!

How do you find the RIGHT BOOK? We're not talking about the RIGHT BOOK for a book report or the RIGHT BOOK to please your teacher. We're talking about the RIGHT BOOK to please *you!*

Start with your interests. Are you interested in rock music, antique cars, hairstyles, skiing?

No RIGHT BOOK? Then move on to your current needs. Maybe you need to learn how to play golf, redecorate your room, learn more about Colorado for your upcoming family vacation.

No RIGHT BOOK yet? Then think about your favorite TV show or movie. Think about the type of TV show or movie you like. Do you like comedies? mysteries? horror shows? science fiction? history? biographies? fantasies? others? Try to find a book that has a similar focus to that of your favorite programs and shows.

No RIGHT BOOK yet? Then start with magazines. Find a magazine article you *really* like, and then ask the librarian if he or she knows of a book that is similar to the article you read.

Still no RIGHT BOOK? Then talk to your friends, an adult you respect or share common interests with, or even your librarian. They may have some leads.

Source: Used with permission of J. S. Schumm and M. C. Radencich, *School Power— Strategies for Succeeding in School* (Minneapolis, MN: Free Spirit Publishing, 1992).

Student Survival Resources

Cummings, R., & Fisher, G. (1991). *The school survival guide for kids with LD*. Minneapolis, MN: Free Spirit. (E/S)

Grant, J. E. (1991). *Young person's guide to becoming a writer*. Minneapolis, MN: Free Spirit. (S)

McCutcheon, R. (1985). *Get off my brain—A survival guide for lazy students*. Minneapolis, MN: Free Spirit. (S)

Schumm, J. S., & Radencich, M. C. (1992). *School power: Strategies for succeeding in school*. Minneapolis, MN: Free Spirit. (S) (magazine-style format)

Test-Taking Tips for Students

How to Get Ready for Standardized Tests

1. *Get real.* Standardized tests are important, but they are only one measure of your progress in school. It is important to do your best. But remember, your daily work and performance on class tests are much better indicators of your academic achievement.

2. *Get sleep.* A good night's rest is a must for top-notch performance.

3. *Get food.* You need a good breakfast to nourish yourself for the test-taking task.

4. *Get equipped.* Bring extra No. 2 pencils to school for the test. If you have a watch or small clock, bring it along so that you can budget your test-taking time. Wear comfortable clothes.

5. *Get to school.* If you come to school late on the day of the test, you may feel rushed and text anxiety can build rapidly.

How to Take Standardized Tests

1. *Take notice.* Pay particular attention to the oral directions that your teacher gives you. Also, notice the written directions in your test booklet. On standardized tests it is important to follow directions carefully.

2. *Take time.* Most standardized tests are timed tests. Plan your time by skimming through the whole test section.

3. *Take advantage.* Take advantage of what you know by doing all the easy items first. This will help you earn more points on a test than if you waste too much time on the hard items. After you do all the easy items, go back and spend more time on the items that are more difficult.

4. *Take a chance.* Unless there is a penalty for guessing, don't skip any questions. You will not do well on a standardized test if you simply fill in any blank throughout the whole test. But if you have really thought about a question and have eliminated the most obviously incorrect answers, take a chance, fill in the blank, and move on to the next item.

5. *Take care.* If your standardized test requires you to fill in "bubbles," be sure to fill in the bubbles fully. If you erase an answer, do so completely. From time to tome, check that the number in your test booklet matches the number on your answer sheet.

6. *Take a break.* If you feel panic coming, on, take a twenty- or thirty-second minibreak to relax and refocus on the test. Simply close your eyes, take a few deep breaths, and then start working again.

7. *Take a check.* Take some time at the end of the test to review your answers and check for careless mistakes.

Reprinted with permission of J.S. Schumm and M.C. Radencich, *School Power—Strategies for Succeeding in School,* 1992. Minneapolis, MN: Free Spirit Publishing.

Index